Maddalena Campiglia

FLORI, A PASTORAL DRAMA
A Bilingual Edition

Edited and with an Introduction and Notes
by Virginia Cox and Lisa Sampson
Translated by Virginia Cox

THE UNIVERSITY OF CHICAGO PRESS
Chicago & London

Maddalena Campiglia, 1553–95

Virginia Cox is professor of Italian at New York University. She is the author of *The Renaissance Dialogue: Literary Dialogue in its Social and Political Contexts, Castiglione to Galileo* (1992) and the editor and translator of Moderata Fonte's *The Worth of Women* (1997), the latter published by the University of Chicago Press.

Lisa Sampson is lecturer in Italian at the University of Reading. She has published on sixteenth-century Italian theater.

The University of Chicago Press, Chicago 60637
The University of Chicago Press, Ltd., London
© 2004 by The University of Chicago
All rights reserved. Published 2004
Printed in the United States of America

13 12 11 10 09 08 07 06 05 04   1 2 3 4 5
ISBN: 0-226-09222-4 (cloth)
ISBN: 0-226-09223-2 (paper)

Acknowledgments

Grateful acknowledgment is made to the British Academy for their generous support in the preparation of this volume, through the award (to Lisa Sampson) of a Postdoctoral Research Fellowship and a small research grant.

Library of Congress Cataloging-in-Publication Data

Campiglia, Maddalena, 1553–1595.
[Flori. English & Italian]
Flori, a pastoral drama / edited and with an introduction and notes by Virgina Cox and Lisa Sampson ; translated by Virginia Cox.—Bilingual ed.
p. cm. — (The other voice in early modern Europe)
English and Italian.
Includes bibliographical references and index.
ISBN 0-226-09222-4 (alk. paper) — ISBN 0-226-09223-2 (pbk. : alk. paper)
I. Cox, Virginia. II. Sampson, Lisa. III. Title. IV. Series.
PQ4617.C272F5613 2004
851'.4—dc22   2003027674

CONTENTS

THE OTHER VOICE IN EARLY MODERN EUROPE: INTRODUCTION TO THE SERIES

Margaret L. King and Albert Rabil Jr.

THE OLD VOICE AND THE OTHER VOICE

In western Europe and the United States, women are nearing equality in the professions, in business, and in politics. Most enjoy access to education, reproductive rights, and autonomy in financial affairs. Issues vital to women are on the public agenda: equal pay, child care, domestic abuse, breast cancer research, and curricular revision with an eye to the inclusion of women.

These recent achievements have their origins in things women (and some male supporters) said for the first time about six hundred years ago. Theirs is the "other voice," in contradistinction to the "first voice," the voice of the educated men who created Western culture. Coincident with a general reshaping of European culture in the period 1300–1700 (called the Renaissance or early modern period), questions of female equality and opportunity were raised that still resound and are still unresolved.

The other voice emerged against the backdrop of a three-thousand-year history of the derogation of women rooted in the civilizations related to Western culture: Hebrew, Greek, Roman, and Christian. Negative attitudes toward women inherited from these traditions pervaded the intellectual, medical, legal, religious, and social systems that developed during the European Middle Ages.

The following pages describe the traditional, overwhelmingly male views of women's nature inherited by early modern Europeans and the new tradition that the "other voice" called into being to begin to challenge reigning assumptions. This review should serve as a framework for understanding the texts published in the series the Other Voice in Early Modern Europe. Introductions specific to each text and author follow this essay in all the volumes of the series.

TRADITIONAL VIEWS OF WOMEN, 500 B.C.E.–1500 C.E.

Embedded in the philosophical and medical theories of the ancient Greeks were perceptions of the female as inferior to the male in both mind and body. Similarly, the structure of civil legislation inherited from the ancient Romans was biased against women, and the views on women developed by Christian thinkers out of the Hebrew Bible and the Christian New Testament were negative and disabling. Literary works composed in the vernacular of ordinary people, and widely recited or read, conveyed these negative assumptions. The social networks within which most women lived—those of the family and the institutions of the Roman Catholic Church—were shaped by this negative tradition and sharply limited the areas in which women might act in and upon the world.

GREEK PHILOSOPHY AND FEMALE NATURE. Greek biology assumed that women were inferior to men and defined them as merely childbearers and housekeepers. This view was authoritatively expressed in the works of the philosopher Aristotle.

Aristotle thought in dualities. He considered action superior to inaction, form (the inner design or structure of any object) superior to matter, completion to incompletion, possession to deprivation. In each of these dualities, he associated the male principle with the superior quality and the female with the inferior. "The male principle in nature," he argued, "is associated with active, formative and perfected characteristics, while the female is passive, material and deprived, desiring the male in order to become complete."[1] Men are always identified with virile qualities, such as judgment, courage, and stamina, and women with their opposites—irrationality, cowardice, and weakness.

The masculine principle was considered superior even in the womb. The man's semen, Aristotle believed, created the form of a new human creature, while the female body contributed only matter. (The existence of the ovum, and with it the other facts of human embryology, was not established until the seventeenth century.) Although the later Greek physician Galen believed there was a female component in generation, contributed by "female semen," the followers of both Aristotle and Galen saw the male role in human generation as more active and more important.

In the Aristotelian view, the male principle sought always to reproduce itself. The creation of a female was always a mistake, therefore, resulting from an imperfect act of generation. Every female born was considered a "defec-

---

1. Aristotle, *Physics* 1.9.192a20–24, in *The Complete Works of Aristotle*, ed. Jonathan Barnes, rev. Oxford trans., 2 vols. (Princeton, 1984), 1:328.

tive" or "mutilated" male (as Aristotle's terminology has variously been translated), a "monstrosity" of nature.[2]

For Greek theorists, the biology of males and females was the key to their psychology. The female was softer and more docile, more apt to be despondent, querulous, and deceitful. Being incomplete, moreover, she craved sexual fulfillment in intercourse with a male. The male was intellectual, active, and in control of his passions.

These psychological polarities derived from the theory that the universe consisted of four elements (earth, fire, air, and water), expressed in human bodies as four "humors" (black bile, yellow bile, blood, and phlegm) considered, respectively, dry, hot, damp, and cold and corresponding to mental states ("melancholic," "choleric," "sanguine," "phlegmatic"). In this scheme the male, sharing the principles of earth and fire, was dry and hot; the female, sharing the principles of air and water, was cold and damp.

Female psychology was further affected by her dominant organ, the uterus (womb), *hystera* in Greek. The passions generated by the womb made women lustful, deceitful, talkative, irrational, indeed—when these affects were in excess—"hysterical."

Aristotle's biology also had social and political consequences. If the male principle was superior and the female inferior, then in the household, as in the state, men should rule and women must be subordinate. That hierarchy did not rule out the companionship of husband and wife, whose cooperation was necessary for the welfare of children and the preservation of property. Such mutuality supported male preeminence.

Aristotle's teacher Plato suggested a different possibility: that men and women might possess the same virtues. The setting for this proposal is the imaginary and ideal Republic that Plato sketches in a dialogue of that name. Here, for a privileged elite capable of leading wisely, all distinctions of class and wealth dissolve, as, consequently, do those of gender. Without households or property, as Plato constructs his ideal society, there is no need for the subordination of women. Women may therefore be educated to the same level as men to assume leadership. Plato's Republic remained imaginary, however. In real societies, the subordination of women remained the norm and the prescription.

The views of women inherited from the Greek philosophical tradition became the basis for medieval thought. In the thirteenth century, the supreme Scholastic philosopher Thomas Aquinas, among others, still echoed Aris-

---

2. Aristotle, *Generation of Animals* 2.3.737a27–28, in *The Complete Works*, 1:1144.

totle's views of human reproduction, of male and female personalities, and of the preeminent male role in the social hierarchy.

ROMAN LAW AND THE FEMALE CONDITION. Roman law, like Greek philosophy, underlay medieval thought and shaped medieval society. The ancient belief that adult property-owning men should administer households and make decisions affecting the community at large is the very fulcrum of Roman law.

About 450 B.C.E., during Rome's republican era, the community's customary law was recorded (legendarily) on twelve tablets erected in the city's central forum. It was later elaborated by professional jurists whose activity increased in the imperial era, when much new legislation was passed, especially on issues affecting family and inheritance. This growing, changing body of laws was eventually codified in the *Corpus of Civil Law* under the direction of the emperor Justinian, generations after the empire ceased to be ruled from Rome. That *Corpus*, read and commented on by medieval scholars from the eleventh century on, inspired the legal systems of most of the cities and kingdoms of Europe.

Laws regarding dowries, divorce, and inheritance pertain primarily to women. Since those laws aimed to maintain and preserve property, the women concerned were those from the property-owning minority. Their subordination to male family members points to the even greater subordination of lower-class and slave women, about whom the laws speak little.

In the early republic, the *paterfamilias*, or "father of the family," possessed *patria potestas*, "paternal power." The term *pater*, "father," in both these cases does not necessarily mean biological father but denotes the head of a household. The father was the person who owned the household's property and, indeed, its human members. The *paterfamilias* had absolute power—including the power, rarely exercised, of life or death—over his wife, his children, and his slaves, as much as his cattle.

Male children could be "emancipated," an act that granted legal autonomy and the right to own property. Those over fourteen could be emancipated by a special grant from the father or automatically by their father's death. But females could never be emancipated; instead, they passed from the authority of their father to that of a husband or, if widowed or orphaned while still unmarried, to a guardian or tutor.

Marriage in its traditional form placed the woman under her husband's authority, or *manus*. He could divorce her on grounds of adultery, drinking wine, or stealing from the household, but she could not divorce him. She could neither possess property in her own right nor bequeath any to her children upon her death. When her husband died, the household property passed not to her but to his male heirs. And when her father died, she had no claim to any family inheritance, which was directed to her brothers or more remote male relatives. The effect of these laws was to exclude women from civil society, itself based on property ownership.

In the later republican and imperial periods, these rules were significantly modified. Women rarely married according to the traditional form. The practice of "free" marriage allowed a woman to remain under her father's authority, to possess property given her by her father (most frequently the "dowry," recoverable from the husband's household on his death), and to inherit from her father. She could also bequeath property to her own children and divorce her husband, just as he could divorce her.

Despite this greater freedom, women still suffered enormous disability under Roman law. Heirs could belong only to the father's side, never the mother's. Moreover, although she could bequeath her property to her children, she could not establish a line of succession in doing so. A woman was "the beginning and end of her own family," said the jurist Ulpian. Moreover, women could play no public role. They could not hold public office, represent anyone in a legal case, or even witness a will. Women had only a private existence and no public personality.

The dowry system, the guardian, women's limited ability to transmit wealth, and total political disability are all features of Roman law adopted by the medieval communities of western Europe, although modified according to local customary laws..

CHRISTIAN DOCTRINE AND WOMEN'S PLACE. The Hebrew Bible and the Christian New Testament authorized later writers to limit women to the realm of the family and to burden them with the guilt of original sin. The passages most fruitful for this purpose were the creation narratives in Genesis and sentences from the Epistles defining women's role within the Christian family and community.

Each of the first two chapters of Genesis contains a creation narrative. In the first "God created man in his own image, in the image of God he created him; male and female he created them" (Gn 1:27). In the second, God created Eve from Adam's rib (2:21–23). Christian theologians relied principally on Genesis 2 for their understanding of the relation between man and woman, interpreting the creation of Eve from Adam as proof of her subordination to him.

The creation story in Genesis 2 leads to that of the temptations in Genesis 3: of Eve by the wily serpent and of Adam by Eve. As read by Christian theologians from Tertullian to Thomas Aquinas, the narrative made Eve responsible for the Fall and its consequences. She instigated the act; she deceived her husband; she suffered the greater punishment. Her disobedience made it necessary for Jesus to be incarnated and to die on the cross. From the pulpit, moralists and preachers for centuries conveyed to women the guilt that they bore for original sin.

The Epistles offered advice to early Christians on building communities of the faithful. Among the matters to be regulated was the place of women. Paul offered views favorable to women in Galatians 3:28: "There is neither Jew nor Greek, there is neither slave nor free, there is neither male nor female; for you are all one in Christ Jesus." Paul also referred to women as his coworkers and placed them on a par with himself and his male coworkers (Phlm 4:2–3; Rom 16:1–3; 1 Cor 16:19). Elsewhere, Paul limited women's possibilities: "But I want you to understand that the head of every man is Christ, the head of a woman is her husband, and the head of Christ is God" (1 Cor 11:3).

Biblical passages by later writers (although attributed to Paul) enjoined women to forgo jewels, expensive clothes, and elaborate coiffures; and they forbade women to "teach or have authority over men," telling them to "learn in silence with all submissiveness" as is proper for one responsible for sin, consoling them, however, with the thought that they will be saved through childbearing (1 Tm 2:9–15). Other texts among the later Epistles defined women as the weaker sex and emphasized their subordination to their husbands (1 Pt 3:7; Col 3:18; Eph 5:22–23).

These passages from the New Testament became the arsenal employed by theologians of the early church to transmit negative attitudes toward women to medieval Christian culture—above all, Tertullian (*On the Apparel of Women*), Jerome (*Against Jovinian*), and Augustine (*The Literal Meaning of Genesis*).

THE IMAGE OF WOMEN IN MEDIEVAL LITERATURE. The philosophical, legal, and religious traditions born in antiquity formed the basis of the medieval intellectual synthesis wrought by trained thinkers, mostly clerics, writing in Latin and based largely in universities. The vernacular literary tradition that developed alongside the learned tradition also spoke about female nature and women's roles. Medieval stories, poems, and epics also portrayed women negatively—as lustful and deceitful—while praising good housekeepers and loyal wives as replicas of the Virgin Mary or the female saints and martyrs.

There is an exception in the movement of "courtly love" that evolved in southern France from the twelfth century. Courtly love was the erotic love between a nobleman and noblewoman, the latter usually superior in social rank. It was always adulterous. From the conventions of courtly love derive modern Western notions of romantic love. The tradition has had an impact disproportionate to its size, for it affected only a tiny elite, and very few women. The exaltation of the female lover probably does not reflect a higher evaluation of women or a step toward their sexual liberation. More likely it gives expression to the social and sexual tensions besetting the knightly class at a specific historical juncture.

The literary fashion of courtly love was on the wane by the thirteenth century, when the widely read *Romance of the Rose* was composed in French by two authors of significantly different dispositions. Guillaume de Lorris composed the initial four thousand verses about 1235, and Jean de Meun added about seventeen thousand verses—more than four times the original—about 1265.

The fragment composed by Guillaume de Lorris stands squarely in the tradition of courtly love. Here the poet, in a dream, is admitted into a walled garden where he finds a magic fountain in which a rosebush is reflected. He longs to pick one rose, but the thorns prevent his doing so, even as he is wounded by arrows from the god of love, whose commands he agrees to obey. The rest of this part of the poem recounts the poet's unsuccessful efforts to pluck the rose.

The longer part of the *Romance* by Jean de Meun also describes a dream. But here allegorical characters give long didactic speeches, providing a social satire on a variety of themes, some pertaining to women. Love is an anxious and tormented state, the poem explains: women are greedy and manipulative, marriage is miserable, beautiful women are lustful, ugly ones cease to please, and a chaste woman is as rare as a black swan.

Shortly after Jean de Meun completed *The Romance of the Rose*, Mathéolus penned his *Lamentations*, a long Latin diatribe against marriage translated into French about a century later. The *Lamentations* sum up medieval attitudes toward women and provoked the important response by Christine de Pizan in her *Book of the City of Ladies*.

In 1355, Giovanni Boccaccio wrote *Il Corbaccio*, another antifeminist manifesto, although ironically by an author whose other works pioneered new directions in Renaissance thought. The former husband of his lover appears to Boccaccio, condemning his unmoderated lust and detailing the defects of women. Boccaccio concedes at the end "how much men naturally surpass women in nobility" and is cured of his desires.[3]

3. Giovanni Boccaccio, *The Corbaccio, or The Labyrinth of Love*, trans. and ed. Anthony K. Cassell, rev. ed. (Binghamton, N.Y., 1993), 71.

WOMEN'S ROLES: THE FAMILY. The negative perceptions of women expressed in the intellectual tradition are also implicit in the actual roles that women played in European society. Assigned to subordinate positions in the household and the church, they were barred from significant participation in public life.

Medieval European households, like those in antiquity and in non-Western civilizations, were headed by males. It was the male serf (or peasant), feudal lord, town merchant, or citizen who was polled or taxed or succeeded to an inheritance or had any acknowledged public role, although his wife or widow could stand as a temporary surrogate. From about 1100, the position of property-holding males was further enhanced: inheritance was confined to the male, or agnate, line—with depressing consequences for women.

A wife never fully belonged to her husband's family, nor was she a daughter to her father's family. She left her father's house young to marry whomever her parents chose. Her dowry was managed by her husband, and at her death it normally passed to her children by him.

A married woman's life was occupied nearly constantly with cycles of pregnancy, childbearing, and lactation. Women bore children through all the years of their fertility, and many died in childbirth. They were also responsible for raising young children up to six or seven. In the propertied classes that responsibility was shared, since it was common for a wet nurse to take over breast-feeding and for servants to perform other chores.

Women trained their daughters in the household duties appropriate to their status, nearly always tasks associated with textiles: spinning, weaving, sewing, embroidering. Their sons were sent out of the house as apprentices or students, or their training was assumed by fathers in later childhood and adolescence. On the death of her husband, a woman's children became the responsibility of his family. She generally did not take "his" children with her to a new marriage or back to her father's house, except sometimes in the artisan classes.

Women also worked. Rural peasants performed farm chores, merchant wives often practiced their husbands' trades, the unmarried daughters of the urban poor worked as servants or prostitutes. All wives produced or embellished textiles and did the housekeeping, while wealthy ones managed servants. These labors were unpaid or poorly paid but often contributed substantially to family wealth.

WOMEN'S ROLES: THE CHURCH. Membership in a household, whether a father's or a husband's, meant for women a lifelong subordination to others.

In western Europe, the Roman Catholic Church offered an alternative to the career of wife and mother. A woman could enter a convent, parallel in function to the monasteries for men that evolved in the early Christian centuries.

In the convent, a woman pledged herself to a celibate life, lived according to strict community rules, and worshiped daily. Often the convent offered training in Latin, allowing some women to become considerable scholars and authors as well as scribes, artists, and musicians. For women who chose the conventual life, the benefits could be enormous, but for numerous others placed in convents by paternal choice, the life could be restrictive and burdensome.

The conventual life declined as an alternative for women as the modern age approached. Reformed monastic institutions resisted responsibility for related female orders. The church increasingly restricted female institutional life by insisting on closer male supervision.

Women often sought other options. Some joined the communities of laywomen that sprang up spontaneously in the thirteenth century in the urban zones of western Europe, especially in Flanders and Italy. Some joined the heretical movements that flourished in late medieval Christendom, whose anticlerical and often antifamily positions particularly appealed to women. In these communities, some women were acclaimed as "holy women" or "saints," whereas others often were condemned as frauds or heretics.

In all, although the options offered to women by the church were sometimes less than satisfactory, they were sometimes richly rewarding. After 1520, the convent remained an option only in Roman Catholic territories. Protestantism engendered an ideal of marriage as a heroic endeavor and appeared to place husband and wife on a more equal footing. Sermons and treatises, however, still called for female subordination and obedience.

THE OTHER VOICE, 1300–1700

When the modern era opened, European culture was so firmly structured by a framework of negative attitudes toward women that to dismantle it was a monumental labor. The process began as part of a larger cultural movement that entailed the critical reexamination of ideas inherited from the ancient and medieval past. The humanists launched that critical reexamination.

THE HUMANIST FOUNDATION. Originating in Italy in the fourteenth century, humanism quickly became the dominant intellectual movement in

Europe. Spreading in the sixteenth century from Italy to the rest of Europe, it fueled the literary, scientific, and philosophical movements of the era and laid the basis for the eighteenth-century Enlightenment.

Humanists regarded the Scholastic philosophy of medieval universities as out of touch with the realities of urban life. They found in the rhetorical discourse of classical Rome a language adapted to civic life and public speech. They learned to read, speak, and write classical Latin and, eventually, classical Greek. They founded schools to teach others to do so, establishing the pattern for elementary and secondary education for the next three hundred years.

In the service of complex government bureaucracies, humanists employed their skills to write eloquent letters, deliver public orations, and formulate public policy. They developed new scripts for copying manuscripts and used the new printing press to disseminate texts, for which they created methods of critical editing.

Humanism was a movement led by males who accepted the evaluation of women in ancient texts and generally shared the misogynist perceptions of their culture. (Female humanists, as we will see, did not.) Yet humanism also opened the door to a reevaluation of the nature and capacity of women. By calling authors, texts, and ideas into question, it made possible the fundamental rereading of the whole intellectual tradition that was required in order to free women from cultural prejudice and social subordination.

A DIFFERENT CITY. The other voice first appeared when, after so many centuries, the accumulation of misogynist concepts evoked a response from a capable female defender: Christine de Pizan (1365–1431). Introducing her *Book of the City of Ladies* (1405), she described how she was affected by reading Mathéolus's *Lamentations*: "Just the sight of this book . . . made me wonder how it happened that so many different men . . . are so inclined to express both in speaking and in their treatises and writings so many wicked insults about women and their behavior."[4] These statements impelled her to detest herself "and the entire feminine sex, as though we were monstrosities in nature."[5]

The rest of *The Book of the City of Ladies* presents a justification of the female sex and a vision of an ideal community of women. A pioneer, she has received the message of female inferiority and rejected it. From the fourteenth

---

4. Christine de Pizan, *The Book of the City of Ladies*, trans. Earl Jeffrey Richards, foreword by Marina Warner (New York, 1982), 1.1.1, pp. 3–4.

5. Ibid., 1.1.1–2, p. 5.

to the seventeenth century, a huge body of literature accumulated that responded to the dominant tradition.

The result was a literary explosion consisting of works by both men and women, in Latin and in the vernaculars: works enumerating the achievements of notable women; works rebutting the main accusations made against women; works arguing for the equal education of men and women; works defining and redefining women's proper role in the family, at court, in public; works describing women's lives and experiences. Recent monographs and articles have begun to hint at the great range of this movement, involving probably several thousand titles. The protofeminism of these "other voices" constitutes a significant fraction of the literary product of the early modern era.

THE CATALOGS. About 1365, the same Boccaccio whose *Corbaccio* rehearses the usual charges against female nature wrote another work, *Concerning Famous Women*. A humanist treatise drawing on classical texts, it praised 106 notable women: ninety-eight of them from pagan Greek and Roman antiquity, one (Eve) from the Bible, and seven from the medieval religious and cultural tradition; his book helped make all readers aware of a sex normally condemned or forgotten. Boccaccio's outlook nevertheless was unfriendly to women, for it singled out for praise those women who possessed the traditional virtues of chastity, silence, and obedience. Women who were active in the public realm—for example, rulers and warriors—were depicted as usually being lascivious and as suffering terrible punishments for entering the masculine sphere. Women were his subject, but Boccaccio's standard remained male.

Christine de Pizan's *Book of the City of Ladies* contains a second catalog, one responding specifically to Boccaccio's. Whereas Boccaccio portrays female virtue as exceptional, she depicts it as universal. Many women in history were leaders, or remained chaste despite the lascivious approaches of men, or were visionaries and brave martyrs.

The work of Boccaccio inspired a series of catalogs of illustrious women of the biblical, classical, Christian, and local pasts, among them Filippo da Bergamo's *Of Illustrious Women*, Pierre de Brantôme's *Lives of Illustrious Women*, Pierre Le Moyne's *Gallerie of Heroic Women*, and Pietro Paolo de Ribera's *Immortal Triumphs and Heroic Enterprises of 845 Women*. Whatever their embedded prejudices, these works drove home to the public the possibility of female excellence.

THE DEBATE. At the same time, many questions remained: Could a woman be virtuous? Could she perform noteworthy deeds? Was she even, strictly speaking, of the same human species as men? These questions were debated over four centuries, in French, German, Italian, Spanish, and English, by authors male and female, among Catholics, Protestants, and Jews, in ponderous volumes and breezy pamphlets. The whole literary genre has been called the *querelle des femmes*, the "woman question."

The opening volley of this battle occurred in the first years of the fifteenth century, in a literary debate sparked by Christine de Pizan. She exchanged letters critical of Jean de Meun's contribution to *The Romance of the Rose* with two French royal secretaries, Jean de Montreuil and Gontier Col. When the matter became public, Jean Gerson, one of Europe's leading theologians, supported de Pizan's arguments against de Meun, for the moment silencing the opposition.

The debate resurfaced repeatedly over the next two hundred years. *The Triumph of Women* (1438) by Juan Rodríguez de la Camara (or Juan Rodríguez del Padron) struck a new note by presenting arguments for the superiority of women to men. *The Champion of Women* (1440–42) by Martin Le Franc addresses once again the negative views of women presented in *The Romance of the Rose* and offers counterevidence of female virtue and achievement.

A cameo of the debate on women is included in *The Courtier,* one of the most widely read books of the era, published by the Italian Baldassare Castiglione in 1528 and immediately translated into other European vernaculars. *The Courtier* depicts a series of evenings at the court of the duke of Urbino in which many men and some women of the highest social stratum amuse themselves by discussing a range of literary and social issues. The "woman question" is a pervasive theme throughout, and the third of its four books is devoted entirely to that issue.

In a verbal duel, Gasparo Pallavicino and Giuliano de' Medici present the main claims of the two traditions. Gasparo argues the innate inferiority of women and their inclination to vice. Only in bearing children do they profit the world. Giuliano counters that women share the same spiritual and mental capacities as men and may excel in wisdom and action. Men and women are of the same essence: just as no stone can be more perfectly a stone than another, so no human being can be more perfectly human than others, whether male or female. It was an astonishing assertion, boldly made to an audience as large as all Europe.

THE TREATISES. Humanism provided the materials for a positive counterconcept to the misogyny embedded in Scholastic philosophy and law and inherited from the Greek, Roman, and Christian pasts. A series of humanist treatises on marriage and family, on education and deportment, and on the nature of women helped construct these new perspectives.

The works by Francesco Barbaro and Leon Battista Alberti—*On Marriage* (1415) and *On the Family* (1434–37)—far from defending female equality, reasserted women's responsibility for rearing children and managing the housekeeping while being obedient, chaste, and silent. Nevertheless, they served the cause of reexamining the issue of women's nature by placing domestic issues at the center of scholarly concern and reopening the pertinent classical texts. In addition, Barbaro emphasized the companionate nature of marriage and the importance of a wife's spiritual and mental qualities for the well-being of the family.

These themes reappear in later humanist works on marriage and the education of women by Juan Luis Vives and Erasmus. Both were moderately sympathetic to the condition of women without reaching beyond the usual masculine prescriptions for female behavior.

An outlook more favorable to women characterizes the nearly unknown work *In Praise of Women* (ca. 1487) by the Italian humanist Bartolommeo Goggio. In addition to providing a catalog of illustrious women, Goggio argued that male and female are the same in essence, but that women (reworking the Adam and Eve narrative from quite a new angle) are actually superior. In the same vein, the Italian humanist Mario Equicola asserted the spiritual equality of men and women in *On Women* (1501). In 1525, Galeazzo Flavio Capra (or Capella) published his work *On the Excellence and Dignity of Women*. This humanist tradition of treatises defending the worthiness of women culminates in the work of Henricus Cornelius Agrippa *On the Nobility and Preeminence of the Female Sex*. No work by a male humanist more succinctly or explicitly presents the case for female dignity.

THE WITCH BOOKS. While humanists grappled with the issues pertaining to women and family, other learned men turned their attention to what they perceived as a very great problem: witches. Witch-hunting manuals, explorations of the witch phenomenon, and even defenses of witches are not at first glance pertinent to the tradition of the other voice. But they do relate in this way: most accused witches were women. The hostility aroused by supposed witch activity is comparable to the hostility aroused by women. The evil deeds the victims of the hunt were charged with were exaggerations of the vices to which, many believed, all women were prone.

The connection between the witch accusation and the hatred of women is explicit in the notorious witch-hunting manual *The Hammer of Witches* (1486) by two Dominican inquisitors, Heinrich Krämer and Jacob Sprenger. Here the inconstancy, deceitfulness, and lustfulness traditionally associated with women are depicted in exaggerated form as the core features of witch behavior. These traits inclined women to make a bargain with the devil—sealed by sexual intercourse—by which they acquired unholy powers. Such bizarre claims, far from being rejected by rational men, were broadcast by intellectuals. The German Ulrich Molitur, the Frenchman Nicolas Rémy, and the Italian Stefano Guazzo all coolly informed the public of sinister orgies and midnight pacts with the devil. The celebrated French jurist, historian, and political philosopher Jean Bodin argued that because women were especially prone to diabolism, regular legal procedures could properly be suspended in order to try those accused of this "exceptional crime."

A few experts such as the physician Johann Weyer, a student of Agrippa's, raised their voices in protest. In 1563, he explained the witch phenomenon thus, without discarding belief in diabolism: the devil deluded foolish old women afflicted by melancholia, causing them to believe they had magical powers. Weyer's rational skepticism, which had good credibility in the community of the learned, worked to revise the conventional views of women and witchcraft.

WOMEN'S WORKS. To the many categories of works produced on the question of women's worth must be added nearly all works written by women. A woman writing was in herself a statement of women's claim to dignity.

Only a few women wrote anything before the dawn of the modern era, for three reasons. First, they rarely received the education that would enable them to write. Second, they were not admitted to the public roles—as administrator, bureaucrat, lawyer or notary, or university professor—in which they might gain knowledge of the kinds of things the literate public thought worth writing about. Third, the culture imposed silence on women, considering speaking out a form of unchastity. Given these conditions, it is remarkable that any women wrote. Those who did before the fourteenth century were almost always nuns or religious women whose isolation made their pronouncements more acceptable.

From the fourteenth century on, the volume of women's writings rose. Women continued to write devotional literature, although not always as cloistered nuns. They also wrote diaries, often intended as keepsakes for their children; books of advice to their sons and daughters; letters to family members and friends; and family memoirs, in a few cases elaborate enough to be considered histories.

A few women wrote works directly concerning the "woman question," and some of these, such as the humanists Isotta Nogarola, Cassandra Fedele, Laura Cereta, and Olympia Morata, were highly trained. A few were professional writers, living by the income of their pens; the very first among them was Christine de Pizan, noteworthy in this context as in so many others. In addition to *The Book of the City of Ladies* and her critiques of *The Romance of the Rose*, she wrote *The Treasure of the City of Ladies* (a guide to social decorum for women), an advice book for her son, much courtly verse, and a full-scale history of the reign of King Charles V of France.

WOMEN PATRONS. Women who did not themselves write but encouraged others to do so boosted the development of an alternative tradition. Highly placed women patrons supported authors, artists, musicians, poets, and learned men. Such patrons, drawn mostly from the Italian elites and the courts of northern Europe, figure disproportionately as the dedicatees of the important works of early feminism.

For a start, it might be noted that the catalogs of Boccaccio and Alvaro de Luna were dedicated to the Florentine noblewoman Andrea Acciaiuoli and to Doña María, first wife of King Juan II of Castile, while the French translation of Boccaccio's work was commissioned by Anne of Brittany, wife of King Charles VIII of France. The humanist treatises of Goggio, Equicola, Vives, and Agrippa were dedicated, respectively, to Eleanora of Aragon, wife of Ercole I d'Este, duke of Ferrara; to Margherita Cantelma of Mantua; to Catherine of Aragon, wife of King Henry VIII of England; and to Margaret, duchess of Austria and regent of the Netherlands. As late as 1696, Mary Astell's *Serious Proposal to the Ladies, for the Advancement of Their True and Greatest Interest* was dedicated to Princess Anne of Denmark.

These authors presumed that their efforts would be welcome to female patrons, or they may have written at the bidding of those patrons. Silent themselves, perhaps even unresponsive, these loftily placed women helped shape the tradition of the other voice.

THE ISSUES. The literary forms and patterns in which the tradition of the other voice presented itself have now been sketched. It remains to highlight the major issues around which this tradition crystallizes. In brief, there are four problems to which our authors return again and again, in plays and catalogs, in verse and letters, in treatises and dialogues, in every language: the problem of chastity, the problem of power, the problem of speech, and the problem of knowledge. Of these the greatest, preconditioning the others, is the problem of chastity.

THE PROBLEM OF CHASTITY. In traditional European culture, as in those of antiquity and others around the globe, chastity was perceived as woman's quintessential virtue—in contrast to courage, or generosity, or leadership, or rationality, seen as virtues characteristic of men. Opponents of women charged them with insatiable lust. Women themselves and their defenders—without disputing the validity of the standard—responded that women were capable of chastity.

The requirement of chastity kept women at home, silenced them, isolated them, left them in ignorance. It was the source of all other impediments. Why was it so important to the society of men, of whom chastity was not required, and who more often than not considered it their right to violate the chastity of any woman they encountered?

Female chastity ensured the continuity of the male-headed household. If a man's wife was not chaste, he could not be sure of the legitimacy of his offspring. If they were not his and they acquired his property, it was not his household, but some other man's, that had endured. If his daughter was not chaste, she could not be transferred to another man's household as his wife, and he was dishonored.

The whole system of the integrity of the household and the transmission of property was bound up in female chastity. Such a requirement pertained only to property-owning classes, of course. Poor women could not expect to maintain their chastity, least of all if they were in contact with high-status men to whom all women but those of their own household were prey.

In Catholic Europe, the requirement of chastity was further buttressed by moral and religious imperatives. Original sin was inextricably linked with the sexual act. Virginity was seen as heroic virtue, far more impressive than, say, the avoidance of idleness or greed. Monasticism, the cultural institution that dominated medieval Europe for centuries, was grounded in the renunciation of the flesh. The Catholic reform of the eleventh century imposed a similar standard on all the clergy and a heightened awareness of sexual requirements on all the laity. Although men were asked to be chaste, female unchastity was much worse: it led to the devil, as Eve had led mankind to sin.

To such requirements, women and their defenders protested their innocence. Furthermore, following the example of holy women who had escaped the requirements of family and sought the religious life, some women began to conceive of female communities as alternatives both to family and to the cloister. Christine de Pizan's city of ladies was such a community. Moderata Fonte and Mary Astell envisioned others. The luxurious salons of the French *précieuses* of the seventeenth century, or the comfortable English drawing rooms of the next, may have been born of the same impulse. Here women not only might escape, if briefly, the subordinate position that life in the family entailed but might also make claims to power, exercise their capacity for speech, and display their knowledge.

THE PROBLEM OF POWER. Women were excluded from power: the whole cultural tradition insisted on it. Only men were citizens, only men bore arms, only men could be chiefs or lords or kings. There were exceptions that did not disprove the rule, when wives or widows or mothers took the place of men, awaiting their return or the maturation of a male heir. A woman who attempted to rule in her own right was perceived as an anomaly, a monster, at once a deformed woman and an insufficient male, sexually confused and consequently unsafe.

The association of such images with women who held or sought power explains some otherwise odd features of early modern culture. Queen Elizabeth I of England, one of the few women to hold full regal authority in European history, played with such male/female images—positive ones, of course—in representing herself to her subjects. She was a prince, and manly, even though she was female. She was also (she claimed) virginal, a condition absolutely essential if she was to avoid the attacks of her opponents. Catherine de' Medici, who ruled France as widow and regent for her sons, also adopted such imagery in defining her position. She chose as one symbol the figure of Artemisia, an androgynous ancient warrior-heroine who combined a female persona with masculine powers.

Power in a woman, without such sexual imagery, seems to have been indigestible by the culture. A rare note was struck by the Englishman Sir Thomas Elyot in his *Defence of Good Women* (1540), justifying both women's participation in civic life and their prowess in arms. The old tune was sung by the Scots reformer John Knox in his *First Blast of the Trumpet against the Monstrous Regiment of Women* (1558); for him rule by women, defects in nature, was a hideous contradiction in terms.

The confused sexuality of the imagery of female potency was not reserved for rulers. Any woman who excelled was likely to be called an Amazon, recalling the self-mutilated warrior women of antiquity who repudiated all men, gave up their sons, and raised only their daughters. She was often said to have "exceeded her sex" or to have possessed "masculine virtue"—as the very fact of conspicuous excellence conferred masculinity even on the female subject. The catalogs of notable women often showed those female heroes dressed in armor, armed to the teeth, like men. Amazonian heroines romp through the epics of the age—Ariosto's *Orlando Furioso* (1532) and Spenser's *Faerie Queene* (1590–1609). Excellence in a woman was perceived as a claim for power, and power was reserved for the masculine realm. A woman who possessed either one was masculinized and lost title to her own female identity.

THE PROBLEM OF SPEECH. Just as power had a sexual dimension when it was claimed by women, so did speech. A good woman spoke little. Excessive speech was an indication of unchastity. By speech, women seduced men. Eve had lured Adam into sin by her speech. Accused witches were commonly accused of having spoken abusively, or irrationally, or simply too much. As enlightened a figure as Francesco Barbaro insisted on silence in a woman, which he linked to her perfect unanimity with her husband's will and her unblemished virtue (her chastity). Another Italian humanist, Leonardo Bruni, in advising a noblewoman on her studies, barred her not from speech but from public speaking. That was reserved for men.

Related to the problem of speech was that of costume—another, if silent, form of self-expression. Assigned the task of pleasing men as their primary occupation, elite women often tended toward elaborate costume, hairdressing, and the use of cosmetics. Clergy and secular moralists alike condemned these practices. The appropriate function of costume and adornment was to announce the status of a woman's husband or father. Any further indulgence in adornment was akin to unchastity.

THE PROBLEM OF KNOWLEDGE. When the Italian noblewoman Isotta Nogarola had begun to attain a reputation as a humanist, she was accused of incest—a telling instance of the association of learning in women with unchastity. That chilling association inclined any woman who was educated to deny that she was or to make exaggerated claims of heroic chastity.

If educated women were pursued with suspicions of sexual misconduct, women seeking an education faced an even more daunting obstacle: the assumption that women were by nature incapable of learning, that reasoning was a particularly masculine ability. Just as they proclaimed their chastity, women and their defenders insisted on their capacity for learning. The major work by a male writer on female education—that by Juan Luis Vives, *On the Education of a Christian Woman* (1523)—granted female capacity for intellection but still argued that a woman's whole education was to be shaped around the requirement of chastity and a future within the household. Female writers of the following generations—Marie de Gournay in France, Anna Maria van Schurman in Holland, and Mary Astell in England—began to envision other possibilities.

The pioneers of female education were the Italian women humanists who managed to attain a literacy in Latin and a knowledge of classical and Christian literature equivalent to that of prominent men. Their works implicitly and explicitly raise questions about women's social roles, defining problems that beset women attempting to break out of the cultural limits that had bound them. Like Christine de Pizan, who achieved an advanced education through her father's tutoring and her own devices, their bold questioning makes clear the importance of training. Only when women were educated to the same standard as male leaders would they be able to raise that other voice and insist on their dignity as human beings morally, intellectually, and legally equal to men.

THE OTHER VOICE. The other voice, a voice of protest, was mostly female, but it was also male. It spoke in the vernaculars and in Latin, in treatises and dialogues, in plays and poetry, in letters and diaries, and in pamphlets. It battered at the wall of prejudice that encircled women and raised a banner announcing its claims. The female was equal (or even superior) to the male in essential nature—moral, spiritual, and intellectual. Women were capable of higher education, of holding positions of power and influence in the public realm, and of speaking and writing persuasively. The last bastion of masculine supremacy, centered on the notions of a woman's primary domestic responsibility and the requirement of female chastity, was not as yet assaulted—although visions of productive female communities as alternatives to the family indicated an awareness of the problem.

During the period 1300–1700, the other voice remained only a voice, and one only dimly heard. It did not result—yet—in an alteration of social patterns. Indeed, to this day they have not entirely been altered. Yet the call for justice issued as long as six centuries ago by those writing in the tradition of the other voice must be recognized as the source and origin of the mature feminist tradition and of the realignment of social institutions accomplished in the modern age.

We thank the volume editors in this series, who responded with many suggestions to an earlier draft of this introduction, making it a collaborative enterprise. Many of their suggestions and criticisms have resulted in revisions of this introduction, although we remain responsible for the final product.

PROJECTED TITLES IN THE SERIES

Isabella Andreini, *Mirtilla*, edited and translated by Laura Stortoni

Tullia d'Aragona, *Complete Poems and Letters*, edited and translated by Julia Hairston

Tullia d'Aragona, *The Wretch, Otherwise Known as Guerrino*, edited and translated by Julia Hairston and John McLucas

Giuseppa Eleonora Barbapiccola and Diamante Medaglia Faini, *The Education of Women*, edited and translated by Rebecca Messbarger

Francesco Barbaro et al., *On Marriage and the Family*, edited and translated by Margaret L. King

Laura Battiferra, *Selected Poetry, Prose, and Letters*, edited and translated by Victoria Kirkham

Giulia Bigolina, *Urania* and *Giulia*, edited and translated by Valeria Finucci

Francesco Buoninsegni and Arcangela Tarabotti, *Menippean Satire: "Against Feminine Extravagance" and "Antisatire,"* edited and translated by Elissa Weaver

Rosalba Carriera, *Letters, Diaries, and Art*, edited and translated by Shearer West

Madame du Chatelet, *Selected Works*, edited by Judith Zinsser

Vittoria Colonna, *Sonnets for Michelangelo*, edited and translated by Abigail Brundin

Vittoria Colonna, Chiara Matraini, and Lucrezia Marinella, *Marian Writings*, edited and translated by Susan Haskins

Princess Elizabeth of Bohemia, *Correspondence with Descartes*, edited and translated by Lisa Shapiro

Isabella d'Este, *Selected Letters*, edited and translated by Deanna Shemek

Fairy-Tales by Seventeenth-Century French Women Writers, edited and translated by Lewis Seifert and Domna C. Stanton

Moderata Fonte, *Floridoro*, edited and translated by Valeria Finucci

Moderata Fonte and Lucrezia Marinella, *Religious Narratives*, edited and translated by Virginia Cox

Francisca de los Apostoles, *Visions on Trial: The Inquisitional Trial of Francisca de los Apostoles*, edited and translated by Gillian T. W. Ahlgren

Catharina Regina von Greiffenberg, *Meditations on the Life of Christ*, edited and translated by Lynne Tatlock

In Praise of Women: Italian Fifteenth-Century Defenses of Women, edited and translated by Daniel Bornstein

Louise Labé, *Complete Works*, edited and translated by Annie Finch and Deborah Baker

Madame de Maintenon, *Dialogues and Addresses*, edited and translated by John Conley, S.J.

Lucrezia Marinella, *L'Enrico, or Byzantium Conquered*, edited and translated by Virginia Cox

Lucrezia Marinella, *Happy Arcadia*, edited and translated by Susan Haskins and Letizia Panizza

Chiara Matraini, *Selected Poetry and Prose*, edited and translated by Elaine MacLachlan

Eleonora Petersen von Merlau, *Autobiography (1718)*, edited and translated by Barbara Becker-Cantarino

Alessandro Piccolomini, *Rethinking Marriage in Sixteenth-Century Italy*, edited and translated by Letizia Panizza

Christine de Pizan et al., *Debate over the "Romance of the Rose,"* edited and translated by Tom Conley with Elisabeth Hodges

Christine de Pizan, *Life of Charles V*, edited and translated by Charity Cannon Willard

Christine de Pizan, *The Long Road of Learning*, edited and translated by Andrea Tarnowski

Madeleine and Catherine des Roches, *Selected Letters, Dialogues, and Poems*, edited and translated by Anne Larsen

Oliva Sabuco, *The New Philosophy: True Medicine*, edited and translated by Gianna Pomata

Margherita Sarrocchi, *La Scanderbeide*, edited and translated by Rinaldina Russell

Justine Siegemund, *The Court Midwife of the Electorate of Brandenburg* (1690), edited and translated by Lynne Tatlock

Gabrielle Suchon, *"On Philosophy" and "On Morality,"* edited and translated by Domna Stanton with Rebecca Wilkin

Sara Copio Sullam, *Sara Copio Sullam: Jewish Poet and Intellectual in Early Seventeenth-Century Venice*, edited and translated by Don Harrán

Arcangela Tarabotti, *Convent Life as Inferno: A Report*, introduction and notes by Francesca Medioli, translated by Letizia Panizza

Laura Terracina, *Works*, edited and translated by Michael Sherberg

Katharina Schütz Zell, *Selected Writings*, edited and translated by Elsie McKee

Alessandro Maganza, *Portrait of Maddalena Campiglia* (late 1580s?). Inventory no. A.00228.
Reproduced by permission of the Museo Civico, Vicenza.

VOLUME EDITORS'
INTRODUCTION

THE OTHER VOICE

In a literary landscape, that of sixteenth-century Italy, whose rich tradition of women's writing has attracted much critical interest over the past two or three decades, the poet and dramatist Maddalena Campiglia (1553–1595) remains a relatively shadowy figure. Campiglia was born and spent her life in Vicenza, some fifty miles west of Venice and at this time under the rule of the Venetian republic; her work has, however, received far less attention than that of her Venetian compatriots and contemporaries Veronica Franco (1546–1591), Isabella Andreini (1562–1604), and Moderata Fonte (1555–1592), and her name is still generally unfamiliar even to specialists in early modern women's writing, especially in the English-speaking world. This neglect is unfortunate, since Campiglia is potentially a figure of great interest to present-day readers, on account of both her unconventional life and the originality and distinction of her writings, qualities especially evident in her most substantial literary work, the pastoral drama *Flori* (1588), presented here in its first modern edition.

By the time Campiglia came to write, a tradition of published writings by women was already well established in Italy, stimulated by the vast publishing success enjoyed by the poetry of Vittoria Colonna (1490–1547), which had first appeared in the late 1530s. Although it is sometimes maintained that this tradition faded in the latter decades of the sixteenth century as a result of the reactionary cultural policies of the Counter-Reformation, there is in fact little evidence that this was the case. Women continued to write and be published in this period, and to innovate within the tradition; indeed, it is around this time that we first see Italian women beginning to venture beyond the bounds of lyric and devotional verse, which had up to this point comprised the majority of their output, into a more varied production, including chivalric romance and epic, religious narrative, and pastoral drama.   *1*

It is within this expansive and experimental phase in the history of Italian women's writing that Campiglia's oeuvre must be located: indeed, along with Isabella Andreini's *Mirtilla*, which appeared in the same year, her *Flori* was one of the earliest works of secular drama by a female writer to be published anywhere in Europe. Of her other substantial works, her pastoral eclogue *Calisa* (1589) is similarly innovative in terms of genre, while her *Discourse on the Annunciation of the Blessed Virgin Mary* (1585) is also unusual for a woman writer in this period, as an extended work of devotional prose.

The originality of Campiglia's *Flori* does not reside in chronological priority alone. While in many ways adhering to the highly standardized poetic and dramatic conventions of pastoral drama, *Flori* significantly departs from them in other respects, not least in its striking portrayal of its central protagonist, the nymph Flori, whose transgressive passions for, in turn, her fellow-nymph Amaranta and the wandering shepherd Alessi form the nucleus of the main plot of the play. In her representation of Flori, Campiglia exploits the conventional pastoral type of the nymph vowed to chastity in the service of Diana to explore the dilemmas of a woman whose intellectual and affective impulses conflict with existing social values. In this respect, *Flori* offers a fascinating point of comparison with the better-known work of Moderata Fonte, whose *Floridoro* (1582) and *The Worth of Women* (1600) similarly exploit the resources of fantasy to explore issues of concrete social concern. Campiglia's nymphs and shepherds interact in a conventional Arcadia, and their stylized passions and laments may seem remote from any connection with contemporary realities. As has been widely recognized in criticism, however, despite its obvious escapist thrust, the pastoral mode in literature was often used as a vehicle for an implicit critique of the contemporary social order. This is undoubtedly true of *Flori*, but Campiglia takes this potential within the pastoral idiom in unexpected directions, exploring areas of women's psychological and emotional experience rarely examined in the literature of this time.

LIFE, WORKS, AND CONTEXT

Maddalena Campiglia's irregular life has to date attracted a greater degree of critical attention than her writings, and it may now be reconstructed with reasonable confidence, though some areas of uncertainty remain.[1] She was born,

---

1. The most comprehensive study of Campiglia's life and works remains Morsolin, *Maddalena Campiglia*, though important new biographical information is contained in Mantese, "Per un profilo storico della poetessa vicentina Maddalena Campiglia." See also De Marco, *Maddalena Cam-*

illegitimately, to Carlo Campiglia and Polissena Verlato, both members of established Vicentine noble families, and widowed at the time of their union; their relationship was regularized in 1565, when they married, legitimizing Maddalena and her two brothers.[2] Successive wills of Carlo Campiglia urge his sons to do their duty by settling their sister in marriage, and it seems, indeed, that Maddalena was married at the age of twenty-three, in 1576, to the Vicentine noble Dionisio Colzè, who was already connected with the family through the marriage of his elder brother to Maddalena's cousin, Elisabetta Campiglia.[3] Maddalena's marriage was clearly a failure, for a few years later, in the early 1580s, she appears to have left her husband to return to the residence of her father, now deceased.[4] The reasons for this marital separation are unclear, though some clue may be provided by a legal document drawn up in April 1576 hinting at concerns that the marriage might prove childless. That the split was not without acrimony is indicated by a document of 1583, suggestive of a dispute over property between the couple, and, more dramatically, by Campiglia's will of 1593, which expressly excludes any claim on her property by Colzè, whom she strikingly claims, "in the sight of God," had "never truly been her husband."[5] There is no evidence of any reconciliation, or of any formal dissolution of the marriage, and it appears that Campiglia spent the last decade or so of her life living separately from her estranged spouse.[6]

Given the anomalousness of her new position, as a woman of the social elite living outside either conventual vows or the accepted "estates" of marriage or widowhood, it might seem natural to suppose that social propriety would have compelled Campiglia to adopt a rigorously reclusive style of life. Her nineteenth-century biographer, Bernardo Morsolin, speaks of her as "disillusioned with the world" and as "retiring . . . into a secluded and solitary existence," and modern scholars still speculate that she may have attempted

---

piglia; and Perrone, *"So che donna ama donna": La* Calisa *di Maddalena Campiglia,* esp. 29–42. Briefer discussions of Campiglia and her works include Sartori, "Maddalena Campiglia"; Mutini, "Campiglia, Maddalena"; and Daniele, "Attività letteraria."

2. Mantese, "Profilo storico," 90–95.

3. Ibid., 99, 103, 105.

4. Ibid., 104–6. The documents cited by Mantese suggest that the separation took place between June 1581 and April 1583. By the time she drafted her will in 1593, Campiglia appears to have been living in the house of a cousin, Lavinia Gualdo (108–9).

5. Morsolin, *Maddalena Campiglia,* 71–72; cf. Mantese, "Profilo storico," 98, n. 23.

6. A passage of Campiglia's eclogue, *Calisa* (1589) that speaks of the poet's desire to see herself liberated at last from her "wretched long-borne yoke" ("antico giogo indegno") suggests that she had not given up hope at this stage that a formal dissolution of the marriage might be possible. See Campiglia, *Calisa,* 85 (lines 216–18), and, for an interpretation of the passage, see Mantese, "Profilo storico," 108.

to secure a more recognized social identity for herself by becoming a Dominican or Franciscan tertiary.[7]

Interestingly, however, there is no evidence for either of these assertions; indeed, the energy with which Campiglia threw herself into constructing her literary career, from the mid-1580s, and the eagerness with which she sought and fostered high-profile cultural relations suggest an attitude very different from the pious and shrinking asceticism attributed to her by Morsolin. In practice, far from suffering cultural isolation as a result of her socially equivocal position, Campiglia seems to have been well integrated in Vicentine literary society, in a manner attested by the barrage of commendatory sonnets that accompany her works. Nor was her circle of acquaintance circumscribed to her home city. Her literary connections elsewhere included the poets Angelo Grillo (1550–1629) and Orsatto Giustinian (1538–c.1603), respectively Genoese and Venetian in origin, as well as, most prestigiously, the peripatetic Torquato Tasso (1544–1595), the greatest poet of his day. Among her most strenuously cultivated aristocratic patrons, meanwhile, were the poet Curzio Gonzaga (?1530–1599), of a junior branch of the great Mantuan dynasty, and the dowager Marchioness of Soragna (near Parma), Isabella Pallavicino Lupi (c. 1550–1623).[8] Although these relationships were doubtless sustained largely by correspondence, Campiglia does also seem to have enjoyed a certain freedom of movement, if we are to judge from a passage of her dedicatory letter to Gonzaga's comedy, *Gli Inganni* (Tricks [1592]), where she alludes to conversations she enjoyed with the author during an extended visit to Venice the previous winter.[9] All in all, if we compare Campiglia's life with that of her contemporary Moderata Fonte, who lived the classically secluded lifestyle of the Venetian upper-class wife, what is most striking is the relative extensiveness of Campiglia's opportunities for social

7. Morsolin, *Maddalena Campiglia*, 16. For the hypothesis that Campiglia was a Franciscan or a Dominican tertiary, see, respectively, Daniele, "Attività letteraria," 57; and Perrone, *La Calisa di Maddalena Campiglia*, 31–34 (following Morsolin). Mantese, generally the most reliable of Campiglia's biographers, notes the lack of evidence for either hypothesis, though he regards the Franciscan possibility as more likely (Mantese, "Profilo storico," 112).

8. On Gonzaga, see Ridolfi, "Gonzaga, Curzio"; Grandi, "Di Curzio Gonzaga e delle sue opere," and Pignatti, *Un principe letterato*. Campiglia had a family connection to Gonzaga through her cousin Elena's marriage to the Marquis Guido Sforza Gonzaga (see Morsolin, *Maddalena Campiglia*, 25; and Mantese, "Profilo storico," 97). Insufficient work has been done to date on the interesting figure of Isabella Pallavicino Lupi, but see Andretta, *La venerabile superbia*, 56–57, which cites previous bibliography; see also Ossola, *Dal Cortegiano all' "Uomo di mondo,"* 113–20; and Ceruti Burgio, *Donne di Parma*, 2: 113–20.

9. "Buona parte del verno passato io lo dispensai in Venetia, ove esso sta anchora per stanza quasi tutto il tempo dell'anno" ("I spent a good part of last winter in Venice, where he [Gonzaga] is almost permanently domiciled"). Gonzaga, *Gli inganni*, dedicatory letter to Marfisa d'Este.

and cultural interaction. Though we should be wary of exaggeration, it is almost tempting to compare the quasi-single Campiglia with the vivid but fantastic exemplars of domestically unencumbered femininity that we find in Fonte's dialogue, *The Worth of Women*, of one of whom it is said that, having renounced marriage and devoted herself instead to intellectual pursuits, she is free to "share the treasures of her mind with every person of refinement she encountered."[10]

The difference between Fonte's and Campiglia's situations is largely due to the very different contexts in which they were living. A closer consideration of Campiglia's home environment in Vicenza will be useful at this point. By the late Cinquecento, Vicenza had for almost two centuries formed part of the mainland empire of the republic of Venice, and this political affiliation inevitably left its mark on the cultural life of the city. Like other major cities of the Veneto, however, Vicenza was far from being simply a cultural suburb of Venice; on the contrary, a distinctive and distinguished civic culture was fostered by the city's aristocratic elite.[11] The character of this elite was a major factor in determining Vicenza's cultural differences from Venice: Where the Venetian patriciate was urban and mercantile in its origins and republican in its values, the Vicentine aristocracy was feudal in origin and culturally closer in many respects to the ruling elites of the princely courts of mainland Italy than to that of its sovereign city. This had implications for the position of women. Consistent with republican tradition, elite women in Venice had conventionally maintained a relatively low cultural profile. It is striking, for example, how few of the two hundred or so published female writers recorded in Italy in this period came from Venetian patrician families.[12] The princely courts of Italy had, by contrast, traditionally offered an environment notably favorable to women's cultural agency, largely as a result of the powers of patronage enjoyed there by the women of the ruling dynasties. Soragna, men-

---

10. Fonte, *The Worth of Women*, 55. On the seclusion of Fonte's life and her relatively limited possibilities for cultural interaction, see 3–4.

11. On cultural activity in sixteenth-century Vicenza, see Daniele, "Attività letteraria"; Niccolini, "Le accademie." On Vicenza's political situation and relationship with Venice, see Grubb, *Firstborn of Venice*, 179–83 (focused on the fifteenth century, but relevant as well to the sixteenth). On the lifestyle and values of the aristocratic elite of Vicenza, see also Grubb, *Provincial Families of the Renaissance.*

12. The best-known sixteenth-century female writer from a Venetian patrician background is Olimpia Malipiero (d. c. 1559?); others—often represented by only one or two surviving poems—include Giannetta Tron, Adriana Trevisani Contarini, and the nun Laura Beatrice Cappello. The better-known Venetian female writers of the period either come from the "citizenry," the second tier in the Venetian social hierarchy (e.g., Moderata Fonte, Lucrezia Marinella), or from more socially equivocal backgrounds (e.g., the courtesan Veronica Franco).

tioned above, and its dowager Isabella Pallavicino Lupi, is a telling example of this. A distinguished patron of literature in general—it was at Parma, under her aegis, that one of the first editions of Tasso's *Jerusalem Delivered* was published—Pallavicino Lupi appears to have had a special interest in fostering women's cultural activity. Particularly interesting in relation to Campiglia is her connection with Barbara Torelli Benedetti of Parma (1546–post 1603), author of a pastoral drama, *Partenia* (c. 1587), which, though unpublished, was widely praised by contemporaries and may well have been Campiglia's inspiration in writing *Flori*.[13] In any case, Campiglia's choice of genre and patron is a good illustration of the courtly affiliations of Vicentine culture and of the advantages these connections could offer to a woman of literary ambition. While we do not know precisely by what means Campiglia first entered into contact with Isabella Pallavicino Lupi, possible channels of connection are not lacking among her circles in Vicenza. One of her closest literary associates in the city, the Brescian Benedictine Gregorio Ducchi (d. 1591), had dedicated a work to Pallavicino Lupi in 1586,[14] and another frequent visitor to Vicenza, the distinguished dramatist and critic Angelo Ingegneri (c. 1550–1613), had directed a production of his pastoral, *La danza di Venere* (The dance of Venus), in Soragna in 1583, in which Isabella's daughter, Camilla, had performed.[15]

Besides its connections with courtly networks beyond the city, Vicenza offered more immediate, local advantages as a cultural environment for a writer like Campiglia. Though it produced no writers of national distinction after Giangiorgio Trissino (1478–1550), Vicenza had a thriving literary and intellectual scene, centering around the celebrated Accademia Olimpica (Olympic Academy), which was especially noted in this period for its striking initiatives in the field of drama. Most noteworthy among the latter was the construction of the Teatro Olimpico (Olympic Theater), originally de-

---

13. The text of *Partenia* survives in a single manuscript at the Biblioteca Statale of Cremona (ms. AA.1.33). For a description, see Zonta, "La *Partenia* di Barbara Torelli-Benedetti"; and Sampson, "'Drammatica secreta': Barbara Torelli's *Partenia*." On evidence of plans for a staging of the play involving figures in Campiglia's circle, see Calore, "Muzio Manfredi tra polemiche teatrali e crisi del mecenatismo," 42–43; and Denarosi, "Il principe e il letterato," 158. More generally, on female writers of pastoral drama in Italy, see Cox, "Fiction, 1560–1650," 54–57.

14. Ducchi, *La Schacheide*. The work contains a passage in praise of Campiglia at canto 4, stanzas 34–35 (57r), and is accompanied by four sonnets of Campiglia's in praise of Pallavicino Lupi (reproduced in De Marco, *Maddalena Campiglia*, 73–76).

15. Ingegneri, *Della poesia rappresentativa e del modo di rappresentare le favole sceniche*, xxv–xxvi. Ingegneri spent an extended period in Vicenza (1583–85), and was closely involved with the theatrical scene in the city. He is mentioned in the *Flori* under the pastoral pseudonym Leucippo; see p. 183.

signed by the great architect Andrea Palladio, a native of the city, and launched as a dramatic venue in 1585 with a famous performance of Sophocles's *Oedipus Rex*, which is celebrated in a passage of *Flori*.[16] While it was not customary in this period for women to participate formally in academic gatherings, Campiglia was certainly acquainted with many individual members of the Accademia Olimpica and, we may assume, would have been informed about the discussions and readings that took place there, including those concerned with pastoral drama. Most notably, Paolo Chiappino (?1538– 1593), whom she credits in *Flori* with having provided her with critical feedback on the drama, was a prominent member of the *Olimpici* and their secretary from 1582.[17] In addition to the academy, an additional, more informal locus for literary encounters in Vicenza appears to have been the library established in the 1580s by the local publisher and bookseller Perin Libraro, who, along with his widow and successor, Anna Giovanni, was to publish Campiglia's *Discourse* and *Flori*.[18] The records that survive of this unusual initiative afford a vivid glimpse of the liveliness and domestic scale of Vicentine literary culture, both features that may be assumed to have served Campiglia well in her progress to cultural "visibility." This last is an important point. Recent studies of early modern women's cultural agency have, quite properly, emphasized the material conditions that facilitated or impeded women's access to the public literary sphere. Campiglia's case suggests that, in certain respects, provincial cities may have provided more supportive environments for female writers than larger and more prestigious cultural centers, precisely because of the more intimate scale of their literary circles and the institutions that sustained them.

Campiglia's first published work, the *Discourse on the Annunciation of the*

16. See below, p. 183 and n. 72. For a general account of the activities of the Academy in this period, see Niccolini, "Le accademie," 95–100; Maylender, *Storia della accademie d'Italia*, 4, 109–20. On its theatrical activities in particular, see Mazzoni, *L'Olimpico di Vicenza;* also, more generally, on drama in Vicenza in this period, see Mancini et al., *I teatri del Veneto*, 2: 175–247.

17. For Campiglia's mention of Chiappino, see p. 49. Other members of the Olympic Academy (Antonmaria Angiolello, Gerardo Bellinzona, Giovanni Battista Titoni, Paolo Volpe) are among those contributing commendatory verses to Campiglia's published works. On pastoral drama in Vicenza in this period, see Crovato, *La drammatica a Vicenza nel Cinquecento*, 129–42; Calore, "Muzio Manfredi," 39. On women's general exclusion from academic activities in late-sixteenth-century Italy, see Fahy, "Women and Italian Cinquecento Literary Academies."

18. Mantese, *I mille libri che si leggevano e vendevano a Vicenza alla fine del secolo XVI*, 7–16; Colla et al., "Tipografi, editori e librai," 125–26. Among the figures in Campiglia's circle who appear to have used the library are Vespasiano Giuliani and Angelo Ingegneri (Mantese, *I mille libri*, 161–68). For a further indication of the role that booksellers may have played in this period as centers for cultural exchange accessible to women as well as men, see Kolsky, "Moderata Fonte, Lucrezia Marinella, Giuseppe Passi: An Early Seventeenth-Century Feminist Controversy," 987.

Blessed Virgin Mary, appeared in 1585, probably some three or four years after
the effective termination of her marriage.[19] Regarded as the first essay into
print of a woman who found herself in a position of potential social vulnera-
bility, the *Discourse* is a remarkable testimony to Campiglia's dexterity in
handling her public image. For a woman in Campiglia's delicate situation,
there were obvious advantages in associating herself with the ultimate feminine ideal in Catholic culture, and no opportunity is missed in the *Discourse*
to reinforce the power and relevance of the Marian stereotype of humility,
chastity, and piety, nor to berate contemporary women for their failure to adhere to these ideals.[20] The moral zeal of the work is enthusiastically champi-
oned in the prefatory letter by Vespasiano Giuliani (Zugliano) and in the af-
terword by Gregorio Ducchi, which praises Campiglia as a "most ardent soul"
(*ardentissimo spirito*) and as a "lady more celestial than terrestrial" (*Donna più ce-
lestre che terrestre*), devoting herself equally to the contemplation of divine
truths and the edification of her fellow men and women. Ducchi's encomium
alludes discreetly to Campiglia's anomalous marital situation, noting that "to
the amazement of all," she "lives in a manner that is utterly unaccustomed
among women." The extraordinary character of her intellectual ambitions is
similarly noted: "[U]nique among her sex, she has set herself to follow in the
footsteps of erudite men."[21] If a degree of anxiety may be detected in Ducchi's
comments concerning Campiglia's "uniqueness," the impeccably pious *Discourse* seems well calculated to defuse the potential threat this anomalous figure might pose.

Where the *Discourse* sketches out one possible—and perhaps predict-
able—authorial strategy for a writer in Campiglia's position, her two later independent works represent a significant deviation from this line. Both are

---

19. Campiglia, *Discorso sopra l'Annonciatione della Beata Vergine, e la Incarnatione del S[ignor] N[ostro]
Giesu Christo*. The *Discourse* was a novelty at the time of its publication, as an extended piece of devotional prose writing by a secular woman. Its main precedent was Vittoria Colonna's *Pianto sopra la passione di Christo* (Lament on the passion of Christ [1556]), though two substantial lives of
the Virgin by Chiara Matraini (1590) and Lucrezia Marinella (1602) were shortly to follow. A
translation of selections from these writings is forthcoming in the present series, edited by Susan Haskins.

20. See, for example, Campiglia, *Discorso*, 46v–47r, for a vivid description of contemporary
women's concern with fashion and trivia, and their inattention at church. Aside from Campiglia's
reference to Mary's youthful studies, which rendered her "maestra d'alta filosofia," "an expert in
the loftiest philosophy" (27r), Campiglia's account of the Virgin's life contains little to parallel
the feminist revisionism a recent study has detected in Colonna's portrayal of the Virgin in her
Lament; see Brundin, "Vittoria Colonna and the Virgin Mary," 61–81.

21. "unica fra questo sesso, seg[ue] ella l'orme degli huomini dotti, vivendo al tutto diversa-
mente, con gran stupore altrui, dal costume donnesco" (Campiglia, *Discorso*, letter by Gregorio
Ducchi).

secular in character (a fact, as Campiglia acknowledged in the dedicatory letter to the *Flori*, that might occasion some criticism from her readers), and
both are couched in the pastoral idiom currently much in vogue in the Italian courts. The more substantial of the two works, *Flori*, published in 1588, is
a pastoral drama in five acts, chronicling the tortured, though ultimately fe-
licitous, amorous career of its eponymous heroine.[22] *Calisa*, which was published the following year, is a pastoral eclogue written to celebrate the marriage of Isabella Pallavicino Lupi's son Giampaolo to Beatrice degli Obizzi.[23]
It takes the form of a dramatized dialogue, in which a nymph, again named
Flori, speaks of her love for her companion Calisa, the pastoral personae here
transparently veiling the figures of, respectively, Campiglia and Pallavicino
Lupi.[24] Both works are discussed in greater detail below; here, it is sufficient
to note briefly the novelty they represent within Campiglia's literary career.
Both the *Flori* and *Calisa* are clearly oriented toward a less parochial audience
than the earlier *Discourse*, and represent a bid by Campiglia for a visibility extending beyond her home city of Vicenza. The authorial persona projected in
the two works is correspondingly more assertive and challenging, as well as
considerably more complex, given Campiglia's ambiguous self-identification
with the troubled nymph-protagonist of the *Flori*. While we should be wary
of mapping the traits of the character Flori onto those of her creator in too
simplistic a manner, Campiglia's use of the pseudonym Flori in the *Calisa* and
elsewhere seems to invite some kind of biographical reading.[25] Interpreted in
this light, the drama may be seen as encapsulating a highly original authorial *apologia pro vita sua*, which recasts Campiglia's marital travails in the heroic
light of Flori's principled rejection of marriage and boldly adumbrates an image of the independent, creative woman, dedicated to spirituality and art. As

---

22. Campiglia, *Flori, favola boschereccia*. For discussion, see Morsolin, *Maddalena Campiglia*, 37–47;
Crovato, *La drammatica a Vicenza*, 136–38; Carrara, *La poesia pastorale*, 355; Chiodo, "Tra l'*Aminta* e
il *Pastor fido*," 572–73; Perrone, *La Calisa di Maddalena Campiglia*, 43–46; Cox, "Fiction, 1560–
1650," 55–57; and Ultsch, "'Vedova delle cose mondane': Secular Celibacy in Maddalena
Campiglia's Pastoral Heterocosm."

23. Campiglia, *Calisa, ecloga*. The text is available in a modern edition, in Perrone, *La Calisa di
Maddalena Campiglia*; her discussion of the text is on pp. 46–59; see also Morsolin, *Maddalena
Campiglia*, 48–49.

24. Flori's interlocutor in the eclogue, Edreo, is similarly identifiable as Muzio Manfredi (see
below, n. 70). Campiglia is referred to as Flori in poems by a number of contemporaries; see
pp. 33–34, and compare p. 310.

25. The autobiographical substrate of the *Flori* is explored in a rather heavy-handed manner by
Morsolin, who identifies the spurned shepherd Androgeo, for example, with Campiglia's re-
jected husband Dionisio Colzè (*Maddalena Campiglia*, 38–44). For a more nuanced discussion, see
Perrone, *La Calisa di Maddalena Campiglia*, 38–39, 44.

well as through the texts of the *Flori* and *Calisa,* this image is articulated through Campiglia's personal emblem of a phoenix, symbolizing at the same time her "uniqueness" and her aspirations to spiritual and literary immortality.[26]

The three works discussed constitute the main body of Campiglia's published output, the remainder consisting principally of occasional poetry. Within this minor area of her literary production, one small corpus of works is especially worthy of interest. This is the group of four poems in rustic dialect, published in 1584 in an anthology assembled to commemorate the death of the celebrated Vicentine dialect poet, Agostino Rava ("Menon").[27] The unexpected character of these works, as dialect poems by a woman writer, deserves to be underlined. A tradition of dialect literature existed in many cities in Italy in this period, where it served as an expression of local civic identity and as an earthy counterpoint to the unrelenting gentility of the dominant, Tuscan poetic tradition. Precisely on account of its earthiness, however, this area of literary culture generally excluded female writers; the Rava anthology, which includes contributions by four female poets, all from the Veneto, is exceptional in this respect. Like the other women published in the volume, Campiglia upholds gender decorum by writing *in propria persona* rather than adopting a comic peasant identity, as was the custom of male dialect poets.[28] In its bantering tone, however, and its stylized rustic idiom, her dialect poetry is consistent with the norms of the genre and is thus strikingly different from her more elevated and conventional verse. Part of the interest of these poems, indeed, is the glimpse they offer of the flexibility of Campiglia's authorial persona, capable, evidently, of a wit and sprightliness not always apparent in her more "serious" writings. More generally, the presence of women in an anthology of this kind invites us to consider the distinctive character of the Venetian mainland as a cultural environment for female writers. As the preceding examination of Campiglia's context has suggested, this may prove a more fruitful area for study than has been hitherto supposed.[29]

26. See appendix B, "Maddalena Campiglia's Emblem and Portrait."

27. Milani, "Quattro donne fra i pavani," 393–95. A fifth dialect poem by Campiglia, addressed to Menon during his lifetime, was included in another anthology published in the same year (ibid., 388). On the tradition of dialect poetry in Vicenza in this period, see Bandini, "La letteratura in dialetto del Cinquecento al Settecento," 16–23; and Daniele, "Attività letteraria," 54–57.

28. Milani, "Quattro donne," 408–9.

29. Other female writers of note living and writing on the Venetian mainland in this period were Issicratea Monte of Rovigo (1564?–1585?), who wrote a number of orations and also contributed to the volume of dialect poetry mentioned in the text, and the Paduan Valeria Miani Negri, author of a pastoral drama (*Amorosa speranza,* 1604) and, most unusual for a female writer, a tragedy (*Celinda,* 1611). An important, though unpublished Paduan writer of the previous gen-

Besides a smattering of occasional poems and some editorial material in works by Curzio Gonzaga, Campiglia published nothing between the *Calisa*, in 1589, and her death six years later.[30] Although she appears to have been plagued in the early 1590s by an eye ailment that may have impeded her literary activities, she apparently continued to write; indeed, her will of 1593, which appoints Gonzaga and Orsatto Giustinian as her literary executors, makes explicit mention of a number of manuscripts she would hope to see published after her death.[31] Although these writings are lost, a clue to the character of one of them is offered by an undated sonnet by Angelo Grillo mentioning a work of Campiglia's on the martyrdom of St. Barbara.[32] It is unclear from the sonnet exactly what form the work took, but there are reasons for speculating that it may have been an early essay in the genre of the hagiographic verse epic later practiced by writers such as Lucrezia Marinella (?1571–1653). Certainly, there are grounds for thinking that Campiglia had plans for some such large-scale narrative work, given the hints to this effect both in her dedicatory letters to the *Flori* and *Calisa*, and in one of the commendatory sonnets by fellow poets that accompany the former work.[33] Had she achieved her end, Campiglia would have been characteristically in the forefront of developments in Italian women's writing; despite some prece-

---

eration was Giulia Bigolina (c. 1518/19–before 1569), whose prose romance *Urania* (1558) has recently been edited by Valeria Finucci (Rome: Bulzoni, 2002). Of these writers, Issicratea Monte, at least, was known to Campiglia; see Mantese and Nardello, *Due processi per eresia*, 21. For some interesting observations on the social position of aristocratic women in the Veneto in this period, see Smith, "Locating Power and Influence within the Provincial Elite of Verona," 439–48.

30. A selection of Campiglia's occasional poetry is collected in the appendix to De Marco, *Maddalena Campiglia*. The most interesting of her editorial interventions are the summaries (*argomenti*) in *ottava rima* that she contributed to the second edition (1591) of Curzio Gonzaga's chivalric epic, *Il Fidamante* (The faithful lover), a poem she appears to have held in particular reverence.

31. Morsolin, *Maddalena Campiglia*, 72; on Campiglia's poor health in her later years, see 53–54. See also Manfredi, *Lettere brevissime*, 285–86.

32. Grillo, *Poesie Sacre*, 263 (poem lxxv). The sonnet is reproduced in Morsolin, *Maddalena Campiglia*, 53. Grillo's description of the work in question as a "tragico . . . carme," "tragic song" (line 4), has led to its being conjecturally identified as a tragedy (Crovato, *La drammatica a Vicenza*, 79). The term *carme*, however, more readily implies a narrative than a dramatic form.

33. For Campiglia's own allusions to her plans, see 45 and 49 below, and Perrone, *La Calisa di Maddalena Campiglia*, 71–72. The sonnet referred to, by the Vicentine poet and dramatist Fabio Pace (1547–1614), augurs that Campiglia may cap her success with the *Flori* by going on to "speak in a higher style of ladies and knights, rage and war," "dir con stil maggior . . . / Le Donne e i Cavallier, gli sdegni e l'arme" (*Diversi componimenti in lode dell'opera*, in Campiglia, *Flori*, sig. i, fol. 6v). The term "higher style" here suggests an epic poem, while the description of the proposed subject matter pointedly echoes the opening line of Ariosto's chivalric romance *Orlando furioso* (1532).

dents, it is only really from the last decade of the sixteenth century and the first of the seventeenth that women began to find the confidence to attempt writing on this kind of "heroic" scale.[34]

FLORI AND PASTORAL DRAMA

In writing a pastoral play, Campiglia was engaging with a dramatic genre that had only acquired serious literary credentials relatively recently and whose critical status was still somewhat problematic.[35] While "regular" comedy and tragedy (in five acts and observing the neoclassical unities of time, place, and action) had been written since around the turn of the sixteenth century, the earliest examples of pastoral drama only date from 1554. These first experiments, variously known as *favola pastorale* or *boschereccia*, developed out of a great range of existing tragicomic forms (such as eclogues, mythological dramas, and pageants) and were written by a few humanistically trained intellectuals, mainly operating in Ferrara, but also in Mantua. While diverse in their structure and tone, these early dramas already demonstrated what would become some of the key features of the genre: an Arcadian setting deriving from classical pastoral poetry such as that of Theocritus and Virgil, complex love-plots drawing on the traditions of Roman and modern comedy, and a cast of characters roughly divided between the "noble" (elegant and refined shepherds and nymphs, venerable elders) and the "base" (goatherds, satyrs, and fauns).

The first example of this still undefined genre to reach a wider reading public was Torquato Tasso's highly acclaimed *Aminta*, originally performed in Ferrara in 1573. *Aminta* was first published in 1580 and went through no fewer than seventeen editions by the end of the century, rapidly establishing itself as a classic of the genre.[36] Though anomalous in some respects, Tasso's pastoral was vastly influential on the subsequent development of the genre in Italy; while later writers tended to prefer more complex, comic-style plots to the *Aminta*'s simple, linear structure, they strove stylistically to echo the play's

---

34. See Cox, "Fiction, 1560–1650," 57–62; also, on a similar trend within contemporary Italian musical culture, Bowers, "The Emergence of Women Composers in Italy, 1566–1700," 123, 134, 137–38.

35. On the development of pastoral drama as a genre in Italy, see Clubb, *Italian Drama in Shakespeare's Time*, 93–187; Pieri, *La scena boschereccia nel rinascimento italiano*; Henke, *Pastoral Transformations: Italian Tragicomedy and Shakespeare's Late Plays*; and Tylus, "Purloined Passages: Giraldi, Tasso, and the Pastoral Debates." On the related changes within tragicomedy, see Herrick, *Tragicomedy*, esp. 126–42. See also note 43 below.

36. Carpanè, "La fortuna editoriale tassiana del '500 ai giorni nostri," 546.

elegant, lyric style and endlessly recycled key scenes and plot devices.[37] The influence of the *Aminta* is clear in the *Flori,* especially in the prologue, but Campiglia was certainly no slavish imitator of a single "master text."[38] On the contrary, her writing reveals an awareness of the rich tradition of pastoral literature, which included not only drama, but also lyric verse dating back to antiquity (Virgil, Theocritus, Moschus, and Bion) and modern writings such as Iacopo Sannazaro's very influential prose romance, *Arcadia* (1504). Where pastoral drama is concerned, besides the *Aminta,* Campiglia's main influences are to be sought in plays composed in her own circles, whether in Vicenza or in the sphere of influence of Isabella Pallavicino Lupi in Soragna. The latter environment is particularly important. As we have already seen, Campiglia's only predecessor as a female writer of pastoral drama, Barbara Torelli, was associated with these circles, as was the dramatist and theorist Angelo Ingegneri, whose *Dance of Venus* was one of Campiglia's main inspirations in the *Flori.* The Marchioness of Soragna also commissioned the printing of Giovanni Donato Cucchetti's *La Pazzia* (Madness [first printed 1581; reprinted Parma, 1586]), which, like Ingegneri's play anticipates the *Flori* in its foregrounding of the theme of love-madness.[39]

Another important source for Campiglia was undoubtedly Battista Guarini's masterpiece, *Il Pastor fido,* which was, along with Tasso's *Aminta,* unquestionably the most influential Italian pastoral play of this period. Although not published until 1589, the *Pastor fido* was composed in the early 1580s and circulated in manuscript in numerous cultural centers of northern Italy, including Venice and the university city of Padua, some twenty miles from Vicenza. As early as 1583, Guarini discussed his pastoral at the small court of Ferrante Gonzaga in Guastalla before an audience that included Campiglia's close friend and the future dedicatee of the *Flori,* Curzio Gonzaga.[40] In the same year, Guarini became associated with the Accademia Olimpica of Vicenza, and the following year he presented *Il Pastor fido* at a meeting of the Academy.[41] Given these connections, we can be almost sure that Campiglia would have known of—and perhaps actually read—*Il Pastor fido,* while working on

37. On the *Aminta*'s influence, see Clubb, *Italian Drama in Shakespeare's Time,* 104; Chiodo, "Tra l'*Aminta* e il *Pastor fido*"; Di Benedetto, "L'*Aminta* e la pastorale cinquecentesca in Italia."

38. For the idea of master authors and texts in relation to imitative practices and literary theory, see Javitch, "The Emergence of Poetic Genre Theory in the Sixteenth Century," 157–60.

39. Ossola, *Dal Cortegiano all' "Uomo di mondo."* 113–14.

40. See Guarini, *Opere,* 107 (letter to Francesco Maria Vialardi of 22 July 1583).

41. *Atti dell'Accademia Olimpica,* Biblioteca Bertoliana, Vicenza, MSS, busta 2., fasc. 10 ("L"), 18 September 1584 (fol. 30v).

her own pastoral. *Flori* seems to draw particularly on the "tragic" aspects of Guarini's play and on its moralizing and sententious style. Another point of resemblance is the prominence Campiglia gives to the religious dimension of Arcadian society; her play is similarly structured around a ritual sacrifice conducted by a priest, and the outcome is predicted by an oracle.

If the text of *Flori* reveals Campiglia's keen attention to contemporary developments in pastoral drama, her dedicatory letter to Curzio Gonzaga displays an equal degree of alertness to theoretical discussions of the genre. Italian literary culture in the second half of the sixteenth century was characterized by a consuming interest in literary theory, largely inspired by the critical "rediscovery" of Aristotle's *Poetics* in the first half of the century. Aristotelian concerns with verisimilitude and unity of plot dominated literary debate in the period, as writers and theorists sought to apply Aristotle's precepts to ancient and also more recent flourishing, but "irregular," vernacular genres such as chivalric romance.[42] As a prime case of such a "modern" genre, pastoral drama became a particular target of neo-Aristotelian strictures, especially following the circulation in the 1580s of Guarini's *Il Pastor fido*, which sought to elevate what had traditionally been a relatively "lightweight" genre through the introduction of tragic devices and serious themes.[43] Campiglia's attitude to Aristotelian theory, as evinced in her letter to Gonzaga, is interestingly ambiguous. On the one hand, she is clearly eager to establish her credentials as a serious writer by showing herself to be familiar with current theoretical issues and aware of the potential weaknesses that Aristotelian critics might detect in her play. In particular, she attempts to fend off the damaging accusation that *Flori* transgresses against unity of plot, arguing that the play's subplots are correctly subordinated to, and integrated with, the main plot. At the same time, however, Campiglia claims a certain independence from theoretical jurisdiction, "freely confessing" that she has consulted her own tastes in the composition of her play rather than complying with the prescriptions of theorists. This freedom, she suggests, should be the more readily conceded to her in that she is writing as a "mere" woman, and should thus, by implication, not be subjected to the same exacting standards that apply to men. The claim is significant, even if it is couched in the language

---

42. See Javitch, "Emergence of Poetic Genre Theory," 163–66.

43. *Il Pastor fido* was attacked for its inappropriate mingling of comedy and tragedy by Giason Denores, of the University of Padua, in 1586, in a work that triggered fierce debate, especially in the area of the Veneto and Ferrara. For an outline of the quarrel (1586–1601) and its wider implications for poetry, see Weinberg, *A History of Literary Criticism in the Italian Renaissance*, 1: 26–31; 2: 1074–1105. For a discussion more sensitive to geographical issues, see Cavazzini, "Padova e Guarini."

of conventional feminine self-deprecation. We are being given a first hint here that, as the work of a woman, the *Flori* may not necessarily adhere to "male" rules.

On a structural level, the *Flori* follows the complex pattern of many dramatic and narrative works of this period by combining a main plot with several others, interspersed with episodic sections. As was customary, the individual plot-strands intertwine over the five acts, through a series of often convoluted love intrigues among the Arcadian cast of nymphs and shepherds. Through various encounters and frequent monologues these characters reveal their intrinsic nobility or baseness, as well as attitudes to marriage, death, authority (especially religious), and that most important of pastoral preoccupations, love. Like most pastoral dramas, *Flori* is tragicomic, submitting its protagonists to the experiences of bereavement, madness, and unrequited passion before allowing them solace in the form of the concluding sequence of family reunions and love-matches. Campiglia's play is, indeed, slightly unusual for the period in the weight it gives to this "tragic" dimension, while, correspondingly, the farcical scenes in which many writers of pastoral delighted are reduced to a marginal presence. *Flori*'s main originality is thematic, however, and resides in its treatment of its eponymous protagonist, whose love-madness, return to sanity, and subsequent new love form the principal action of the play. Though it has some roots in previous literary traditions, the Flori plot contains a number of striking departures from convention in the treatment of both her early, "mad" passion for Amaranta and her subsequent, "sane" love for Alessi.

To summarize the plot briefly, in the first three acts the chaste nymph Flori is mad with obsessive love for her dead female companion, Amaranta. She is released from this madness through a sacrifice organized by her concerned fellow Arcadians but, immediately afterwards, falls in love with an unknown shepherd, Alessi, who is passing through Arcadia at that time. On being reassured that Alessi returns her feelings (act 5), Flori astounds those around her by rejecting the option of marriage, resolving instead to establish a chaste union with her lover that will allow her to pursue her spiritual and intellectual aspirations. Meanwhile, in the principal subplot, Flori's faithful companion, Licori, is secretly in love with Androgeo, a shepherd driven mad by love for Flori. After he too is cured by the sacrifice, Flori intervenes to unite Licori in marriage with her beloved. From act 2, another minor love story develops between the emotionally fickle shepherd Serrano and a rather vain

and naïve nymph, Urania; this, however, does not prevent Serrano from attempting to pursue a doomed courtship of Flori, in which he guiltily indulges
despite his affection for his love-rival and adoptive brother, Androgeo. The
beginning of act 3 introduces us to the last, more comic-style subplot of the
young shepherd, Leggiadro, who has left his home and his rich elderly father,
Tirsi, to seek out the lovely Gelinda, Serrano's sister, disguising himself as a
servant in order to gain access to her house. Tirsi's unexpected appearance in
Arcadia, in act 4, leads to two Aristotelian recognitions and reversals, assisted
by Alessi. Not only is Leggiadro's irregular situation legitimized, enabling him
to marry Gelinda, but Androgeo—who, we learned earlier, was adopted by
Serrano's father, having been discovered as a foundling in infancy—is fortu-
itously recognized as Tirsi's tragically lost elder son.

The action of the play is structured around the centrally positioned sacrifice (3.4–5),[44] which is held annually in honor of the pagan pastoral deities,
Pales and Pan. During the first half of the play, the Arcadians prepare this
event with the hope of curing the madness of Flori and Androgeo. As in Ingegneri's *Dance of Venus*, which also features such a sacrifice, two choruses are
assembled for this purpose: one of nymphs led by Licori, and one of shepherds led by Fronimo, Flori's brother.[45] An altar is prepared over the tomb of
the dead nymph, Amaranta, and the event is marked by prayers, ritual pro-
cessions, and propitiatory gifts, recalling funeral rituals in Sannazaro's *Arcadia*.[46] Just before the ceremony itself, the mysterious foreign shepherd Alessi
appears, as the god of Love had promised in the prologue. From this point,
there is a distinct shift in tone. The predominantly melancholic mood, the
morbid insistence on death, and dramatic representations of madness are dis-
pelled and replaced by an atmosphere of hope and marvel, and by the promise of transcendence. Flori herself, too, is radically transformed after the sacrifice. Initially, a passive, confused character, reliant on the protection of
Licori and, on one occasion, that of her suitor Androgeo (during an attack by
a satyr and a "wild man," [1.6]), she assumes a central, active role in the second half of the play. She now determines how her reciprocated love for Alessi
is to be realized and arranges the marriage between Androgeo and Licori. In
contrast to her incoherent, mad rambling at the start of the play, her often
lengthy speeches reveal a striking linguistic and intellectual mastery, partic-

---

44. Such parenthetical citations are to act and scene of *Flori;* thus, (3.4–5) indicates act 3, scenes
4–5.

45. Ingegneri, *La danza di Venere,* 71–74 (act 3, scene 3).

46. See *Arcadia, Prosa* 5, Eclogue 5 (at the tomb of Androgeo), and *Prose* 10–11 (vigil and games
at the tomb of Massilia). The funeral games are modeled on those for Anchises in Virgil's *Aeneid,*
bk. 5, in turn imitating Homer's *Iliad,* bk. 23.

ularly of Neoplatonic thought on love. Even more provocatively, she chal-
lenges the institution of marriage, asserting the benefits of the single life as a
woman.

Unlike various earlier pastoral plays (such as Agostino Beccari's *Sacrificio*,
first printed 1555), where the sacrifice appears as little more than a decora-
tive frame, justifying sung, danced, and magical interludes, the religious values of the sacrifice permeate *Flori* at a deeper level, affecting the dramatic
structure, characterization, imagery, and linguistic style. As was traditional in
pastoral drama, the play is set in an ancient, pagan Arcadia, complete with its
associated deities (such as Pan, Diana, Venus, Pales) who are ritually worshiped. Through this means, writers could lend a religious dimension to their
work—beneath its ostensible paganism, the Renaissance Arcadia is imbued
with Christian values—while avoiding the possible dangers of representing
Christian rituals in a work of fiction intended for the stage. Like many other
Italian writers, after the Congregation of the Index was set up in 1571, Campiglia would have been careful not to attract any unwanted attention from inquisitors, who had been actively engaged in censoring print publication in
Vicenza since 1569.[47] Dramatic productions were also viewed with suspicion; since 1581, professional theater had largely been banned by the Venetian state on moral grounds.[48] The religious situation was generally a source
of tension in the 1560s–80s, in Vicenza as in other mainland cities of the
Veneto, as various high-profile members of the community were placed under investigation for Calvinist sympathies or suspected "heresy."[49] A trace of
this background—and conceivably of more personal experiences—is perhaps discernible in a strangely vehement minor episode in the *Flori*, concerning a malicious attempt by the evil shepherd Darello to denounce Flori
for blasphemy to the Priest (2.4).[50] His accusation having failed, the embit-
tered would-be denouncer attempts suicide by hanging (3.3), though we
later discover (5.5) that his victim, Flori, has magnanimously saved his life.

Despite its apparently peripheral status, the Darello episode has a degree of structural importance within the *Flori*, in that his accusation—

---

47. Colla et al., "Tipografi, editori e librai," 124, 126; also, more generally, Grendler, *The Roman Inquisition and the Venetian Press, 1540–1605*.

48. See Mancini, *I teatri del Veneto,* 1, pt. 1: xv–xviii; also, more generally, Andrews, *Scripts and Scenarios: The Performance of Comedy in Renaissance Italy,* esp. 220–26.

49. See Mantese and Nardello, *Due processi per eresia;* Puppi, *Cronaca di Fabio Monza [1548–1592],* 3; and Mantese, "La famiglia Thiene e la Riforma Protestante a Vicenza nella seconda metà del Sec. XVI."

50. Parenthetical citations refer to act and scene numbers in the English translation in this volume. Thus, for example, (2.4) refers to act 2, scene 4 of the English translation.

unconvincingly motivated by a seemingly innate and global misanthropy—
is intended to block the sacrifice on which the main action of the pastoral
turns. In this way, it serves as the "obstacle" that dramatic convention required to impede the resolution of the main plot, even if, ultimately, it fails to
alter the divinely ordained pattern of events and serves only to highlight
Flori's spiritual purity. Such an example of treachery is not unprecedented
within the tradition of pastoral drama; it recalls that practiced by lone characters in various other plays, especially Corisca in Guarini's *Il Pastor fido.* Yet
in *Flori* the expressions of hatred and the Christian associations of evil sur-
rounding the traitor are unusually strong, and his guilty isolation is highlighted at the end in contrast to the other shepherds' celebrations (5.5).
Darello is regarded by the Arcadians as being almost as loathsome as Death
itself (3.3); his attempted suicide by hanging suggests Judas, the traitor *par excellence;* and the description of his evil tongue, "more venomous and malign
than that of any serpent," (2.4) even seems to allude to the Genesis myth and
the serpent's temptation of Eve. Strikingly, then, evil is embodied by a *male*
character, while perfection finds its representation in the nymph Flori. This
is paralleled by the consistent moral superiority of female over male characters in Campiglia's play.

The allusions to sin and blasphemy in the episode just discussed are not
the only quasi-Christian elements that we find in the *Flori;* on the contrary,
the play's powerful religious concerns are embedded in the dramatic structure itself. By the end, the divine force of Providence, partly represented by
the god of Love, is observed to have been guiding events all along to a propitious conclusion, instilling a sense of wonder in the Arcadians at the "eternal mysteries of the heavens" (5.5). The priest Damone may acknowledge
that humans can consciously choose evil over good, following the Catholic
conception of Free Will (1.2), but the play generally presents little scope for
individual human agency, emphasizing rather a lack of confidence in the ability to perceive and act on the truth.[51] Male characters in particular (apart
from Alessi to some extent), demonstrate this tendency. Androgeo remains
passive even after his madness is cured, and both Serrano's plan to insure that
he alone will capture the attentions of Flori at the divinely ordained sacrifice
(2.3) and Darello's attempt to thwart it (2.4) ultimately fail. Darello later
laments, "Oh how we deceive ourselves when we think to escape our destiny!
I realize now that the heavens rarely or never reward evil thoughts." (3.3).

---

51. On the treatment of Providence in Italian pastoral drama, see Clubb, *Italian Drama in Shake-*
speare's Time, 13, 100–12. For a more "pagan" reading of the theme as fate, in the manner of classical tragedy, see Perella, "Fate, Blindness, and Illusion in *Il Pastor fido.*"

Even his attempt to commit suicide is prevented by Flori, "following the dictates of the gods" (5.5). By contrast, Flori's actions are successful, reflecting their conformity to divine dictates; for example, her intervention to arrange the marriage of Licori and Androgeo unwittingly realizes a union established since their childhood (5.5; cf. 1.2).

Besides this structurally informing concern with Providence and divine wisdom, Campiglia's religious and moral preoccupations also invest the texture of the play at a more superficial level. Moralizing *sententiae* are sprinkled liberally throughout the play, highlighted by the capitalization of the first word in the Italian edition. They are particularly associated, in the first half of the play, with the authoritative figures of Melampo (Licori's elderly father) and the priest, though also with Licori, while, in the second half, Alessi, who to some extent supercedes the priest as the moral anchor of the work, provides a more explicitly Christian model of charity and humility, encouraging prayer and fortitude in the face of adversity, and hope in divine mercy (4.5, pp. 217–19, 223; 4.6, p. 241). These exhortations to Christian virtue are reminiscent of passages from Campiglia's earlier *Discourse on the Annunciation,* as are the criticisms of contemporary avarice and worldliness that recur throughout the play. Although this moralizing tendency reflects a trend widely apparent in Italian literature in this period, and especially noticeable in pastoral drama after the publication of the *Pastor fido,*[52] the particular solemnity of tone of the *Flori* may reflect Campiglia's situation as a "respectable" woman tentatively experimenting with secular fiction. Certainly, a sharp difference may be registered in this respect between Campiglia's *Flori* and Isabella Andreini's *Mirtilla* (1588), which, as another early attempt at pastoral drama by a woman, makes an interesting point of comparison. As an actress, Andreini was less strictly bound by decorum than was a member of the civic elite like Campiglia, while, as a married woman in a supportive marriage, she had less to fear than Campiglia from malicious tongues. Perhaps partly in consequence, the *Mirtilla* is significantly less "grave" than the *Flori* and more sensual and carefree in tone.[53]

Whatever its motives, in any case, one purpose served by the *Flori's* pious and high-minded tone is likely to have been to render more digestible to its early readers aspects of the play that might otherwise have been perceived as problematic. Prime among these is the challenge the play offers to con-

---

52. Andrews, "Pastoral Drama," 297.

53. Cox, "Fiction, 1560–1650," 57. For Andreini's social status as an actress, see Andrews, "Isabella Andreini and Others: Women on Stage in the Late Cinquecento." *Mirtilla* is available in a modern critical edition (Andreini, *Mirtilla*) and an English translation by Julie Campbell (Andreini, *La Mirtilla: A pastoral*).

ventional conceptions of love as portrayed within pastoral drama. Love was a central concern of pastoral, typically debated in various forms by nymphs and shepherds in contrasting pairs (older/younger; pro-love/anti-love), and explored through Petrarchan-style lovers' laments, prayers to Venus or Diana, and even descriptions of dreams or visions, drawing on a long-established, especially courtly, tradition of lyric verse and dialogues on love.[54] Within the green, secluded setting of pastoral drama, such idealized discussions and out-pourings by the noble-minded Arcadians (in contrast to the typically sensual or violent peasants and satyrs) could offer more psychological and emotional examinations of love than the apparently "realistic" comedy and tragedy. Fur-thermore, by comparison with comedy, where "decent" female characters were often kept offstage or silent for reasons of decorum, appearing mainly as the objects of marital transactions by male characters, pastoral drama allowed more scope for subjective expression to its female characters.[55] Plots usually focus on the finely nuanced process of transformation of a beautiful young nymph from a state of proud but naïve indifference to one of greater matu-rity; the resolution depends on her choice to surrender her fiercely defended virginity to her lover. The heroine initially appears as a devoted member of the all-female entourage of the virgin goddess, Diana, interested only in hunt-ing, and cruelly rejecting her suffering shepherd-lover. Gradually, she is per-suaded through his desperate acts, the words of older nymphs (themselves converts to love), or even divine intervention, to pity and then to reciprocate the other's passion, finally agreeing to marriage. This entails the abandon-ment of a lifestyle that offers an unusually active model of feminine freedom, while conforming to contemporary Christian ideals of feminine chastity. The nymph is thereby "tamed," or socialized, and prepared for the vital institu-tion of marriage, pastoral plays being in consequence frequently staged for wedding festivities, in the manner of epithalamiums (nuptial verse).

Throughout her pastoral play, Campiglia tests the potential within the genre for an exploration of female autonomy, most strikingly in her polemi-cal rejection of marriage as a resolution to the main plot. Following tradition, the two main female protagonists, Flori and Licori, are nymphs vowed to the service of Diana. Both thus start the play ideologically committed to a life outside marriage, scorned by Flori as a "yoke" (2.5, p. 133; compare Licori at

---

54. On the theme of love in pastoral drama, see Clubb, *Italian Drama in Shakespeare's Time*, 14–15, 104–5, 161–62; Pieri, *La scena boschereccia nel rinascimento italiano*, 101–10; and Radcliff-Umstead, "Love in Tasso's *Aminta*: A Reflection of the Este Court."

55. See Andrews, "Pastoral Drama," 298; and, particularly, Andrews, "The Dilemma of Chastity and Sex." On the representation of women in Renaissance comedy, see Günsberg, *Gender and the Italian Stage*, 6–48.

1–2 [p. 75]) and as an impediment to the pursuit of the literary immortality for which she yearns (1.1, p. 65; 5.3, p. 269). Licori's attachment to the cult of virginity, however, cedes to her nascent love for Androgeo, and she becomes the spokeswoman within the play for the conventional ideal of a youthful attraction leading seamlessly to the joys of marriage and motherhood. Flori, too, seems destined for this path when, following her original, "deviant" passion for Amaranta, she is smitten at the sacrifice with a love for the eligible stranger-shepherd Alessi. To the amazement of all, however, instead of a full "conversion," she seeks a compromise between her old life and her new one, vowing herself to an eternal love for Alessi but only on condition that he join her as a votary of Diana, relinquishing the lower pleasures of a sexual love for a nobler, spiritual attachment (5.1). This he accepts without demur (5.2), binding himself to his new beloved in a union that fully realizes, in its novelty and strangeness, the initial prophecy of the god of Love that he will create in Flori and Alessi "a pair of lovers such as the world has never seen" (prologue, p. 55).

Cupid's initial boast and the wonderment with which the other characters in the play greet the news of Flori and Alessi's chaste union serve to underline the novelty of this plot resolution within the dramatic tradition in which Campiglia was writing. If unusual, it was not unheard of for nymphs in pastoral drama to persist in their attachment to chastity, and the figure of the "committed bachelor" shepherd is found, most notably, in Tasso's *Aminta*.[56] The ideal of a chaste, spiritual union as an alternative to sexual love was also, of course, anything but original. Already present in embryo in the Italian lyric tradition from the time of Dante and Petrarch, this ideal had become codified, in a classicizing, Neoplatonic form, in the theoretical love literature of the fifteenth and sixteenth centuries, where it performed a valuable role in reconciling the courtly cult of love with the ascetic traditions of Christianity. Pervasive as the discourse of Neoplatonic love was in sixteenth-century literary culture as a whole, however, it mostly remained remote from the "natural," pagan world of Arcadia, which traditionally appealed to Renaissance writers partly because it offered opportunities to portray an innocent sensuality, untrammeled by sexual guilt. Although Neoplatonic ideas had emerged to some degree in earlier pastoral works (especially by Sannazaro and Poliziano), Campiglia's importation into pastoral drama of the alien ideal of Neoplatonic love to such an extent was, in context, a significant novelty. Even

---

56. Nymphs resistant to a "conversion" to love appear, for example, in Alberto Lollio's *Aretusa* (1564) and in an unpublished and undated pastoral, *Cinthia*, by the Vicentine Livio Pagello (d. 1599). In both cases, though, the nymphs' motives ultimately appear more conventional than in Campiglia's *Flori*, since they result in the avoidance of incestuous matches.

more striking was that she used this discourse in a way for which we rarely find parallels within early modern literature in general—as the solution to the existential dilemma of a female protagonist concerned to maintain her creative freedom and psychological autonomy.[57] What is sought, and found, in Flori's spiritual union with Alessi is a male-female relationship of genuine equality, an equality underlined in their parallel declarations of servitude (he is her "king," she his "queen"; 5.3, p. 275). Whether or not we accept the tantalizing hints in the text that Alessi may be identified with Torquato Tasso, we may find it plausible to accept the suggestion of Carlachiara Perrone, in her recent edition of *Calisa*, that the supportive and mutually admiring union of souls that Flori attains with Alessi may be seen as an idealized staging of the intellectual relationships Campiglia sought with her male literary peers.[58] Certainly, Alessi is enthusiastic in championing Flori's aspirations to literary immortality (5.3, p. 269–71), and the two are portrayed as well matched in particular in their parallel devotion to their art (5.3, pp. 285–87).

Regarded in this light, as an attempt to envisage an alternative lifestyle enabling female creativity, Campiglia's *Flori* offers an intriguing point of comparison with Moderata Fonte's near-contemporary *The Worth of Women*. The two texts are comparable in their use of fiction to explore possibilities for women beyond marriage or the convent; specifically, appropriating the male humanistic topos of bachelorhood as the optimum condition for scholarship, both propose an ideal of uncloistered and freely chosen celibacy as the state most conducive to women's intellectual development. The coincidence of ideas here is striking, especially since no mutual influence is apparent, and it may well be that this consonance in thinking stems from contextual factors common to both writers. It has been argued that Fonte's championing of a secular, single life for women is partly a reflection of social and economic trends in Venice, which were tending to reduce the marriage possibilities for upper-class women, thus problematizing the previously unquestioned social convention that the daughters of the elite were destined to marriage or the convent.[59] This same social trend is also relevant to the case of Campiglia's Vicenza; indeed, it was here in the 1580s that the first order was founded of Dimesse, which was intended to provide a recognized social status for the otherwise vulnerable group of elite women living unmarried lives outside con-

---

57. On Isabella Andreini's exploration of neoplatonic love madness to construct an alternative, gendered self-image, see MacNeil, "The Divine Madness of Isabella Andreini," 206–8.

58. Perrone, *La Calisa di Maddalena Campiglia*, 44. On the possible identification of Alessi with Tasso, see note 92 to the English text in this volume.

59. Cox, "The Single Self"; Malpezzi Price, *Moderata Fonte*, 91–92 and 94–95.

ventual bounds.[60] Contextual factors may be equally important in explaining the differences between Fonte's and Campiglia's treatment of the theme of female celibacy. One immediately striking difference is that Fonte locates her vision of the celibate creative life for women within a circle of exclusively female relationships, while Campiglia envisages her celibate heroine within a supportive and equal relationship with a man. This might be seen as reflecting the difference between Fonte's and Campiglia's cultural context noted earlier, the quasi-courtly social environment of Campiglia's Vicenza offering more opportunities for cultural interaction between the sexes than the more sexually segregated society of Venice.

Despite the originality of Campiglia's treatment of the love story of Flori and Alessi, particularly within the context of the literary tradition in which she was working, what is more likely to strike the modern reader is the novelty of her representation of Flori's first love for her dead childhood friend, Amaranta. Explicit depictions of female-female desire were extremely rare in the Italian Renaissance, both in literature and in theoretical writings on love; indeed, lesbianism is infrequently mentioned even in scientific or legal writings or in religious manuals listing condemned sexual practices.[61] In pastoral drama, likewise, *Flori* is unprecedented in its narrative foregrounding of female-female desire, although some have argued that overtones of erotic self-sufficiency, as well as female empowerment, are inherent in the traditional representations of the cult of Diana and her nymphs.[62] Despite the play's insistence on the chaste character of Flori's love for Amaranta—consistent with its generally desexualized representation of the erotic—this exploration of same-sex desire between women undoubtedly constituted a challenge to the canonical, male perspective on love. Traces of unease are certainly present in a number of the commendatory poems that accompany the text in its published edition, jarring oddly with the blandly eulogistic rhetorical conventions that normally govern such pieces. Most explicit is a madrigal by Paolo Chiappino, which counterposes the "chaste" love Flori

---

60. Ibid., 548 and n. 90. For speculation concerning Campiglia's possible relationship with the Dimesse movement in Vicenza, see Ultsch, "Secular Celibacy."

61. Brown, "Lesbian Sexuality in Medieval and Early Modern Europe" 67–75. For a recent critical attempt to probe beyond this apparent "invisibility," see Simons, "Lesbian (In)visibility in Italian Renaissance Culture: Diana and Other Cases of *Donna con Donna.*"

62. Simons, "Lesbian (In)visibility in Italian Renaissance Culture," 94–109; see also Traub, *The Renaissance of Lesbianism in Early Modern England*, esp. 229–75; Berry, *Of Chastity and Power: Elizabethan Literature and the Unmarried Queen*, 8, 123–24. The titillating scenes featuring erotic games between nymphs occasionally found in male-authored Italian pastoral dramas of the period (on which see, for example, Traub, *Renaissance of Lesbianism*, 1–3) are not convincing precedents for Campiglia's treatment of this theme.

feels for Alessi with her previous "lascivious" desire for Amaranta, which he sternly assimilates to a series of "infamous" representatives of male and female homosexual love found in classical literature.[63] Two other poems, by Muzio Manfredi and Prospero Cattaneo, express disbelief or bafflement at Campiglia's depiction of same-sex love, with Cattaneo describing Flori's passion as a "strange, contrary, and unwonted effect of Nature," and Manfredi flatly stating that "you must know that no woman feels for a woman what Flori felt for Amaranta."[64] The only interpretation of the play that can make this plot motif acceptable for these readers, it appears, is a moralizing and didactic one, which regards Flori's passion for Amaranta as an expression of her madness. Her subsequent love for Alessi can thus be interpreted as a welcome return to sanity and reason, and Flori can come to serve as an ultimately "happy example"—in Manfredi's words—"of one who attempted to defy nature."[65]

The question of the degree to which such a moralizing and normalizing reading is legitimized by the text of the *Flori* itself is complex. Certainly, Flori's passion for Amaranta is portrayed as excessive and irrational, and a clear implication of Neoplatonic moral "progress" is inherent in her abandonment of a love rooted in the mortal and physical—symbolized by her morbid attachment to the urn holding her dead beloved's ashes—in favor of the more exalted form of spiritual love she feels for Alessi. Equally, the passage between these two loves explicitly coincides with the restoration of Flori's sanity through the sacrifice. The elements are certainly in place, therefore, to read *Flori* as depicting a process of ideological recuperation, with the mad nymph's initially errant and "unnatural" desire being redirected towards a more "acceptable" object through a social ritual—the sacrifice—conducted

---

63. *Diversi componimenti in lode dell'opera*, in Campiglia, *Flori, favola boschereccia*, sig. k, fol. 5v: "Oggi imparar ben denno / e le Ninfe e i Pastori / da la follia trar senno / far di lascivi onesti i loro amori / da te già pazza, or saggia e casta FLORI / a mal grado di quei, ch'infame fenno / i nomi loro, Crati e Coridone / Ciparisso, Atti, Saffo, e Amintone" ("Shepherds and nymphs should now learn to convert their folly into wisdom and their lascivious loves into honest ones, looking at your example, Flori; for you were once mad and have now returned to sanity and chastity, in defiance of those who brought infamy upon themselves, like Cratys and Corydon, Cyparissus, Atthis, Sappho, and Amynton"). The grouping of female names here (Sappho and her lovers Atthis and "Amynton"—the last a corrupt reading of the name Anactoria) suggest that Chiappino's source here is a passage in Sappho's love letter to Phaon in Ovid's *Heroides*, 15.15–20, which Renaissance commentators often glossed with prurient accounts of Sappho's lesbianism (Andreadis, "Sappho in Early Modern England," 107).

64. *Diversi componimenti*, in Campiglia, *Flori*, sig. k, fol. 7r, lines 10–11 ("O di Natura / Strano, contrario, inusitato effetto"); sig. k, fol. 4r, lines 7–8 ("Sai che Donna per Donna alfin non sente / Quel che sentì per Amaranta Flori").

65. *Diversi componimenti*, in Campiglia, *Flori*, sig. k, fol. 4r: "e però saggia ritornata, Alessi / ama, felice aventuroso essempio / Di chi contrasta a la Natura, amando" (the lines are addressed to Flori).

by a religious authority figure and attended by neatly gender-differentiated choruses of shepherds and nymphs. But such a reading would oversimplify what is in practice a more complex and ambiguous text. If Flori's "conversion" to the love of Alessi is portrayed as achieved through the agency of the societal gods Pan and Pales, the prologue complicates the issue by depicting it instead as the work of a characteristically mischievous Eros, who opens his speech by boasting of his ability to undermine social and gender hierarchies and overturn human rationality (prologue, p. 53–55). This double order of causality, never properly resolved, is reflected in the play's psychological ambiguities. On one level, Flori's "sane" love for Alessi is contrasted with her "mad" passion for Amaranta, yet Licori's first reaction on being apprised of her intentions towards her new beloved is to accuse Flori of a relapse into madness, and a recurrence of that "chasing the impossible" that had proved her downfall in her earlier life (5.1, p. 249).[66] Despite the tide of moral approval of Flori's choice in the closing scenes of the play, we should not discount Licori's response, especially if we take it in conjunction with her earlier conjecture that Flori's insanity might be a punishment from the gods for her refusal to accept her status as a woman and her aspirations to literary glory (1.1, 65). In these two passages, Licori identifies a line of continuity in Flori's behavior that undercuts the radical discontinuity suggested by her passage from madness into sanity. Flori's urge to exceptionalism, her yearning for the impossible, and her refusal, specifically, to accept the boundaries conventionally placed on feminine behavior are, it may be argued, traits that are as apparent in her later, "sane," persona as in her earlier, "errant" one. With regard to this "errancy," moreover, it is interesting to note that Flori does not unequivocally repudiate her past love for Amaranta when she recovers her sanity following the sacrifice. Rather, after an initial moment of wonderment ("Can it be true that I erred so long in folly for the sake of another woman, and a dead one?"; 3.5, p. 165), she honors the memory of Amaranta as "the most glorious nymph that ever followed Diana in the woods or meadows" and defends both the chastity of her feelings for the nymph and the purity and virtue of their object. We are left with the impression that, if Flori's love for Amaranta was aberrant, this was not primarily because Amaranta was a woman; rather, her folly was that she failed rationally to accept the reality of her beloved's death.

Two further considerations may be useful in understanding the signifi-

---

66. The phrase "chasing the impossible" echoes Flori's earlier description of her love for Amaranta as "pursuing the impossible" (3.5, 167; see also 1.1 [p. 63]). On the tradition of representing lesbianism as an *amor impossibilis*, see Traub, *Renaissance of Lesbianism*, 6.

cance of Campiglia's representation of Flori's love for Amaranta. One is that this portrayal of female-female desire is one instance of a more general tendency in the play to foreground relationships between women. This is especially apparent in Campiglia's strong depiction of the friendship between Flori and Licori, which had flourished, we learn, since their childhood, when, with Amaranta, they had been an inseparable threesome (1.2). Given the classical and Renaissance tradition of portraying the bond of friendship as essentially masculine, it is striking that Campiglia portrays the central female friendship in the play as purer and more disinterested than the parallel bond between Serrano and Androgeo, contrasting Licori's readiness to put Flori's interests before her own with Serrano's selfishness in a comparable situation (2.1; cf. 2.3).[67] Female-female relationships also feature significantly in the play's structure of authority, especially in the case of the fatherless Flori, whose proud autonomy is only mitigated by her obedience to the goddess Diana.[68] Also relevant is the connection made in the play between love and poetic inspiration: a connection deeply rooted within the Petrarchan lyric tradition, in which the beloved functions semi-explicitly as a symbol of the poet's literary creativity. Both Amaranta and Alessi are portrayed in the *Flori* as past or future inspirations for poetry. As Flori recalls, echoing a Petrarchan commonplace, it was her love for Amaranta that first ["spurred [her] to leave the vulgar crowd" in pursuit of literary immortality (3.5, p. 167).] Her subsequent passion for Alessi, it is implied, will inspire her to still greater poetic achievements, not least because the inspiration is in this case unusually mutual, since Alessi is a poet himself.[69]

At a metaliterary level, then, one important aspect of the "bisexuality" of *Flori's* nymph-protagonist is that it enables the depiction of a female poetic voice capable of addressing itself equally to women and men. The significance of this becomes apparent when we consider the autobiographical dimension of the figure of Flori, which, as has been noted, becomes explicit in

67. Campiglia's testament provides interesting evidence of the closeness of her own relationships with women: see Mantese, "Profilo storico," 108–9, 110–12, and particularly 113, on Campiglia's request that she be buried in the same tomb as Giulia Cisotta, abbess of the Franciscan convent of Santa Maria in Aracoeli.

68. Campiglia's choice to represent Flori as operating outside the jurisdiction of a male authority figure is striking, and contrasts sharply with her more conventional portrayal of Licori. This is especially obvious in the last act, where Licori's marriage to Androgeo is portrayed as depending on the consent of her father Melampo, while Flori's union with Alessi is decided between the protagonists, without reference to Flori's brother Fronimo.

69. The last appearance in the play of Flori and Alessi (5.3) prefigures their future poetic relationship by showing them mingling their talents to sing the praises of *Flori's* dedicatees.

Campiglia's subsequent pastoral eclogue, *Calisa,* written to celebrate the marriage of Isabella Pallavicino Lupi's son in 1589. One role that the language of love and courtship had conventionally performed within sixteenth-century literary culture was that of mediating the relationship between male writers and their aristocratic female addressees. In *Calisa,* casting herself in the role of Flori, Campiglia similarly uses the discourse of chaste erotic love to express her devotion to Pallavicino Lupi, depicted under the pastoral pseudonym of Calisa. Interestingly, the work takes the form of a dialogue between Flori-Campiglia and a shepherd ("Edreo") representing the poet and dramatist Muzio Manfredi (1535–1607/09), the same figure whose moral unease at the hints of lesbianism in the *Flori* was commented upon above.[70] Manfredi's stance in his sonnet accompanying the *Flori* finds an echo within the *Calisa* strong enough for us to suppose that one of the aims of the later poem is to address his critique of the play. The opening segment of *Calisa* depicts Edreo attempting to dissuade Flori of her love for an unknown nymph: a task, as he admits, that he has already attempted many times vainly in the past. As in his sonnet on the *Flori,* his aversion is based on a sense that it is contrary to nature ("O what folly! You are greatly in error to love a woman when you are a woman yourself" [lines 99–100]). Flori refuses to be persuaded, insisting that her passion goes too deep for reason. In the course of her self-defense, however, she reveals the identity of her beloved as Calisa, greatly reassuring Edreo, who henceforth resolves to dissolve his opposition and encourage her in this virtuous, if "peculiar," love (l.126).

In some respects, then, the *Calisa* might be seen as having something of the character of a palinode with regard to the *Flori's* provocative exploration of the theme of female-female love, desire for another woman being unthreateningly recast in the eclogue as a metaphor for devotion to a patron. It would be reductive, however, to regard the *Calisa* as purely defensive in this sense. As noted above, the treatment of Flori's passion for Amaranta in *Flori* cannot be separated from the play's treatment, more generally, of relationships between women, nor from its exploration of the connections between love and poetic inspiration. These same concerns are apparent in the treatment of Campiglia-Flori's relationship with Calisa in the eclogue. One fea-

---

70. The figure of Edreo is misidentified as Curzio Gonzaga in Morsolin, *Maddalena Campiglia,* 49, and Perrone, *La Calisa di Maddalena Campiglia,* 48. For the correct identification, see Pallantieri, *La Bucolica di Virgilio,* 2–3. On Manfredi, a key figure in Campiglia's literary acquaintance, with strong connections both to Vicenza and Parma/Soragna, see Calore, "Muzio Manfredi"; Denarosi, "Il principe e il letterato." 1997. On Manfredi's relations with Campiglia, see also pp. 24 and 33–34 below.

ture of the poem, indeed, is the manner in which it stages the relationship between a female poet and her female patron, underlining through the initial dialogue between Flori and Edreo the gendered character of this literary bond. The *Calisa's* recent editor regards the poem as consciously evoking the feminized poetic culture found in ancient Greece and embodied by Sappho, in which women could pursue poetic careers as speaking subjects, inspired by female objects and female literary authorities.[71] Although we should perhaps not exaggerate the extent of Campiglia's woman-identifiedness as a writer—the "bisexual" model of the *Flori* seems, in fact, closer to her practice—this element in her writing certainly deserves attention. Women's writing in Italy, as elsewhere in Europe, had grown up on the margins of a powerful and prestigious, male-authored literary culture and had initially negotiated itself a space in that culture by following its rules. Female writers typically established their authorial credentials by imitating the works of canonical male authors, especially Petrarch, and gained access to a public beyond their immediate circles through the mediation of male readers, editors, and publishers. While Campiglia is no exception to this general pattern, in her idealized portrayal of her relationship with her female patron in the *Calisa,* she does appear to be adumbrating the notion of a more autonomous and less dependent female-authored literature, in which the erotic self-sufficiency of a love discourse that places women in the roles of both subject and object figures the discursive self-sufficiency of a text both created by and addressed to a woman.[72] If this is the case, we should perhaps regard the unease provoked in certain of her male readers by her representation of female-female desire as prompted by impulses of literary protectionism as well as more obvious psycho-sexual motives. Although many men within the circles of the Italian courts supported the literary aspirations of women, it is not clear how far their sympathy could be guaranteed if those aspirations showed signs of extending beyond a position of grateful dependency to some form of "literature of their own."

71. Perrone, *La Calisa di Maddalena Campiglia,* 44–45.

72. An interesting precedent here is the love poetry written in the 1530s by the Sienese poet Laudomia Forteguerri to Margaret of Austria (1522–1586), the illegitimate daughter of Charles V and wife of Duke Alessandro de' Medici of Florence. The relationship between the two women was celebrated in a lecture by Alessandro Piccolomini in the Paduan Accademia degli Infiammati (Piccolomini, *Lettura del S. Alessandro Piccolomini*), and Agnolo Firenzuola mentions it as an example of a virtuous and chaste same-sex attraction between women, in contrast to the lascivious liaisons of Sappho (Firenzuola, *Celso: Dialogo delle bellezze delle donne,* 542). The possibility of a direct influence on Campiglia cannot be ruled out, especially given her contacts with the cultural sphere of Parma (Margaret of Austria was, in later life, Duchess of Parma through her second marriage to Ottavio Farnese).

FLORI: "CLOSET DRAMA" OR PERFORMANCE TEXT?

An obvious question that needs to be addressed when considering a dramatic text like Campiglia's *Flori* is that of its original performance context. In this case, however, we must be aware that, by the end of the sixteenth century, erudite drama was not necessarily meant for performance at all. While the professionals of the *commedia dell'arte* enjoyed enormous popularity in Italian cities and courts, more "academic" comedies and especially tragedies were frequently only read aloud, as "closet-drama." This situation had arisen for a variety of reasons.[73] Expense was clearly an issue, especially in the case of plays requiring elaborate stage scenery or special effects. Moral and religious reservations regarding the theater were also widespread, and may well have been effective, in particular, in deterring "respectable" women from writing for the stage. That said, however, a pastoral play was more likely to be performed than a comedy or tragedy, given the relatively undemanding staging requirements of pastorals, which might be performed even in informal outdoor settings.[74] In addition, there were some environments, particularly within the courts, in which high-born women might decorously participate in staged drama, both as playwrights and—perhaps more surprisingly—as actors. One such environment, of obvious relevance to Campiglia, was the circle of Isabella Pallavicino Lupi, whose own daughter, as has been noted, is recorded as having taken a leading role in Ingegneri's *Dance of Venus*.[75]

Given these considerations, it is possible that the *Flori* was written for performance. Internal textual evidence suggests, however, that the play was intended for literary fruition. The play does include various performative features, the most obvious being the central ritual sacrifice, choreographed with a priest and choruses of shepherds and nymphs.[76] There is also an attempted

73. Barish, "The Problem of Closet Drama in the Italian Renaissance"; Andrews, *Scripts and Scenarios*, 204–26.

74. Ingegneri notes that "were it not for pastoral dramas, one might say that the custom of staging plays was virtually obsolete" (*Della poesia rappresentativa*, 6); on the reasons for the popular preference for pastorals over comedy or tragedy, see pp. 6–7.

75. See above, p. 6. Besides Barbara Torelli's *Partenia* (mentioned above), which was at least prepared for performance, three pastoral ballets written by Laura Guidiccioni Lucchesini are known to have been staged in the court of Florence in the 1590s; see Cox, "Fiction, 1560–1650," 55. On noblewomen's participation as actors in private court spectacles, see further Andrews, "Isabella Andreini and Others," 317–18. For comparative material on the contemporary English context, see Findlay, Williams, and Hodgson-Wright, "'The Play Is Ready to Be Acted': Women and Dramatic Production, 1570–1670"; Cerasano and Wynne-Davis, *Readings in Renaissance Women's Drama*.

76. Rituals directed to pastoral gods in pastoral plays preceding *Flori* mostly remain off-stage. An exception is found in act 4, scene 1 of Alvise Pasqualigo's *Gli Intricati* (The entangled lovers),

abduction of two nymphs by a satyr and Silvano (1.6), some scenes of madness (which were becoming extremely popular set-pieces in professional theater),[77] and a dramatic recognition scene (4.6). Given Campiglia's experience as a writer of madrigal texts, which she set to music, it is not surprising to find two songs in the play: one in the form of a prayer (3.3), the other in praise of the play's dedicatees (5.3).[78] Both have irregular rhyme schemes, rather than being examples of strophic verse, so it is unclear whether they were meant for musical setting. Many other popular ingredients of pastorals are lacking in *Flori*: there are no instrumental or sung interludes (such as the female singing competition in Andreini's *Mirtilla* [3.5]), and no dances (as in Ingegneri's and Guarini's pastorals), though Flori is said to be dancing with the nymphs after the sacrifice (4.2). The echo episode is very short (3.6) and, most striking, there are no choruses or inter-act spectacles (*intermedi*), which had become almost commonplace in pastoral drama since Tasso's *Aminta*. Besides these omissions, moreover, the text as it stands suggests certain practical difficulties in staging. In contravention of Ingegneri's later advice on effective dramatic writing, the monologues are often extremely long (as Campiglia herself notes), some of the characters remain on stage too long in silence, and the device of the soliloquy, often overheard by other hidden characters, is overused.[79] The effect of thunder and lightning that the priest alludes to at the end of the sacrifice (3.5), if added to a performance, would also have required technical devices more elaborate than the rest of the play demands. Finally, the linguistic style is not well suited for a dramatic performance, since the Italian is grammatically complex and dense with conceits, and there are few fast-paced dialogues of the type that we find in a more obviously performance-oriented text such as Isabella Andreini's *Mirtilla*. A fea-

---

c. 1569, dedicated to the Olympic Academy, 1581. With the staged, all-male sacrifice in Guarini's *Il Pastor fido* (4.3–4) this practice became more common, probably drawing on tragedy (see Mazzoni, *L'Olimpico di Vicenza*, 140); but see the criticism of Ingegneri, *Della poesia rappresentativa*, 16–17.

77. On the popularity and typically comic ingredients of the "mad-scene" in this period, see Fabbri, "On the Origins of an Operatic Topos: The Mad-Scene," 158–76.

78. In a letter of 1588, Campiglia mentions that she intends to have five of her madrigals printed with music, though she has not played "viols, lutes and harpsichords" for three years (letter to Francesco Melchiori, 23 February 1588, cited in Morsolin, *Maddalena Campiglia*, 61–62). For the influence of Guarini's madrigal compositions on his *Il Pastor fido*, see Durante and Martellotti, "Il Cavalier Guarini e il Concerto delle Dame."

79. See Ingegneri, *Della poesia rappresentativa*, 13–15, 18. Serrano, for example, remains hidden behind a tree throughout act 2, scene 4, only reappearing halfway through the next scene. However, the device of "overhearing" a soliloquy is used more effectively for comic purposes in act 4, scene 3. For scenes which include the "mad" characters appearing on stage mostly without speaking, see, for example, 1.2; 1.4; 1.5.

ture such as the acrostic embedded in the second song in act 5, scene 3 is also clearly something intended for the eye rather than the ear.

To conclude, while it is conceivable that the printed play presents a revised and "polished" literary version of a previous acting script, in accordance with contemporary practice—and it is certainly attractive to imagine a performance featuring ladies from Isabella Pallavicino Lupi's circles—it seems most likely that Campiglia conceived *Flori* as a work of closet drama, as practiced by many of the members of the Accademia Olimpica in Vicenza.

THE FORTUNES OF CAMPIGLIA'S *FLORI*

Unsurprisingly, perhaps, the novelties Campiglia introduced into the tradition of pastoral drama in the *Flori* did not inspire imitators, male or female. Later published pastorals by women writers, of which several exist, are all more conventional in character. Despite the provocative aspects of its treatment of gender, however, it would be misleading to represent the *Flori* as a work too radical or transgressive to be appreciated by contemporaries. Certainly, its relatively local and small-scale publishing history contrasts sharply with the wide popular diffusion enjoyed by Isabella Andreini's less venturesome *Mirtilla*, but the comparison is hardly fair, given Andreini's diva-like status within the *Commedia dell'arte*.[80] In fact, notwithstanding the moral reservations it occasioned in some early readers, Campiglia's pastoral does seem to have achieved a large measure of critical approbation among her contemporaries, consolidating and extending the reputation she had already won locally with her *Discourse on the Annunciation*.

Interesting evidence of this is supplied in a series of commendatory poems that is attached to some copies of the published *Flori* as an appendix.[81] These "Various Compositions in Praise of the Work" (*Diversi componimenti in lode dell'opera*) include verses by no fewer than twenty-seven poets, many Vicentine (of whom a substantial subgroup are members of the Olympic Academy), but others from elsewhere in the Veneto or from circles associated with the courts and the aristocratic elite of Mantua and Parma. As a whole, the collection offers an impressive illustration of the expansion of Campiglia's reputation since the publication of the *Discourse*, which was accompanied by

---

80. Andreini's pastoral went through nine editions between 1588 and 1616, in publishing centers ranging from Verona and Ferrara to Venice and Milan (Andreini 1995, 23–29). This reflects the actress's strategic exploitation of the press to enhance her fame (Andrews, "Isabella Andreini and Others," 324–25).

81. See pp. 305–6.

contributions from around half this number of poets and was notably more "Vicentine" in character.[82] Though not, as has been noted, without hints of moral reserve where the play's treatment of lesbian desire is concerned, the "Various Compositions" voice an enthusiastic chorus of praise in the hyperbolic mode favored in this genre of verse. Campiglia has not only outshone "any nymph who has previously sung," but she is compared favorably to Tasso, Petrarch, Sophocles, and the classical canon of pastoral literature; she is the honor of her sex, the glory of her age, and the pride of her native city and native land.

Besides this immediate garland of tributes, external plaudits contributed to the enhancement of Campiglia's reputation. Most prestigiously, in 1589, she secured the accolade of a mention by the greatest poet of the day, Torquato Tasso, who politely speaks in a brief note to her of his paradoxical delight in seeing his own *Aminta* outshone by her *Flori*.[83] At around the same time, a happy geographical coincidence insured her a place in one of the popular "general knowledge" miscellanies that were such a feature of Italian print culture in this period, Luigi Contarini's *Vago e dilettevole giardino* (The beautiful and delightful garden), the first of whose numerous editions was printed in Vicenza by Campiglia's publishers in the same year as *Flori*, 1588. Campiglia is listed in Contarini's miscellany among his "diverse marvelous examples of women," where he singles out *Flori* in particular as "full of rare conceits, and composed with such ornament that it is read and admired with amazement by *literati* and connoisseurs."[84] The description is repeated verbatim in Cristoforo Bronzini *Della dignità e nobiltà delle donne* (On the nobility and dignity of women [1624]), illustrating the role played by Contarini's mention in perpetuating Campiglia's name after her death.[85] During her lifetime, Campiglia's growing literary reputation is indicated by the frequency with which, in the late 1580s and early 90s, her verse was requested for inclusion in collections by friends, or to frame other works. One or more sonnets by Campiglia appear, for example, in Bernardino Baldi's *La Corona dell'Anno* (The crown of the year [Vicenza, 1589]), Cesare Calderari's *Il Trofeo della Croce* (The triumph of the cross [Vicenza, 1588], Angelo Grillo's *Rime* (Collected verse [Bergamo, 1590]), and Curzio Gonzaga's revised version of his *Rime* (Venice,

---

82. The same tendency is apparent in the smaller group of poems accompanying the *Calisa,* which includes sonnets by the prestigious figures of Angelo Grillo and Curzio Gonzaga.

83. Letter of 12 August 1589, in Tasso, *Lettere,* ed. Guasti (see p. 38), 4: 234, no. 1160.

84. "piena di rari concetti, e così ornatamente composta, che con maraviglia de' letterati, ed intendenti è letta, e ammirata" (Contarini, *Il vago e dilettevole giardino,* 416; see also 481).

85. Bronzini, *Della dignità e nobiltà delle donne,* Day 2 [sic], 36–37.

1591).[86] Less conventionally, a sonnet of Campiglia's included among the verse accompanying Muzio Manfredi's tragedy *Semiramis* (originally published in Parma in 1593) takes her friend to task for abandoning his usual theme of the celebration of women's virtue to write on an ancient queen legendary for her depravity and vice.[87]

Perhaps the most vivid testimony to the acclaim Campiglia enjoyed during her lifetime comes from the volume of verse that her literary acquaintance Gregorio Ducchi put together for the marriage of Giampaolo Lupi and Beatrice degli Obizzi in 1589. Campiglia features here not only as one of the contributing authors (with the *Calisa*), but also as a substantial stakeholder in the celebratory honors of the work, along with the happy couple and the groom's mother, Isabella Pallavicino Lupi. Many of the lyrics collected in the volume praise Campiglia along with her aristocratic patrons; a sonnet by Angelo Grillo, for example, identifies as Pallavicino Lupi's most assiduous celebrants "the illustrious Campiglia" and the noble circle of 'lofty spirits' gathered round her.[88] The centrality accorded to Campiglia in this sonnet is borne out by her role in the longer poems in the collection, two of which, besides Campiglia's own *Calisa*, include Flori as one of their speakers and filter their praises of the marrying couple through the voice of this "celestial Muse."[89] Of these, the first, by Bernardino Baldi, is blandly eulogistic in its mention of Campiglia, praising her as a rival to Orpheus and a born poet who has "drunk the nectar of the Muses along with her mother's milk."[90] Characteristically more equivocal is Muzio Manfredi's *Arde la saggia e gloriosa Flori* (The wise and glorious Flori burns with ardor), which balances lavish praises of Campiglia's poetic talents with censure for her sexual deviance in devoting her love to other nymphs. Manfredi's eclogue opens, like Campiglia's own, with a dialogue between Flori and Edreo, the latter similarly intent on

---

86. Baldi, *La Corona dell'Anno*, A3v; Calderari, *Il Trofeo;* Gonzaga, *Rime*, 246, 247; and Grillo, *Rime*, 90. Campiglia's sonnets for Calderari and Baldi are reproduced in the appendix to De Marco, *Maddalena Campiglia*, 77–78, 86.

87. Manfredi, *La Semiramis, tragedia*, 130. It is interesting that, of the four other women who contributed sonnets to this volume (Barbara Torelli, Veronica Franco, Adriana Trevisani Contarini, and an anonymous poet), three express similar reservations; only Franco contributes a "straight" piece of commendatory verse.

88. "In tanto voi, Campiglia illustre e i chiari / spiriti ch'a voi fan nobil cerchio intorno / E in Parnaso a Febo aurea corona / Applaudate a l'augurio" (Ducchi, *Rime diversi di molti illustri compositori*, 2).

89. Ibid., 3–9, 61–71. The phrase "celestial Muse" is taken from the opening line of a sonnet of Angelo Grillo's at ibid., 2 (also published in the *Calisa*) which describes Campiglia as a "musa celeste sotto umano velo" ("celestial Muse in human guise").

90. "Flori, / Che col latte materno insieme ebbe / Il Nettar de le Muse, e può col canto / Quel, che potea con la sonora cetra / L'antico Trace" (Ducchi, *Rime diversi*, 5; cf. Baldi, *Ecloghe miste*, 191).

dissuading Flori from her "perverse" love for Calisa. Unlike Campiglia's Edreo, however, Manfredi's speaker seems unmoved by the identity of Flori's love-object, Calisa. Despite its honorable object, the love of nymph for nymph can only be conceived as a travesty of nature.[91] Flori-Campiglia also figures as a speaker in a later work of Manfredi's, his pastoral drama *Il Contrasto amoroso* (The amorous contest), only published in 1602 but probably written around a decade before. In a passage of particular interest, Flori is portrayed in this work in conversation with the nymph "Talia" (Barbara Torelli), celebrating the achievements of women *virtuose*—musicians and writers—and discussing the problems they face.[92]

Despite the optimistic predictions of some of Campiglia's admirers that her works would defy the depredations of mortality, the reputation she enjoyed in her lifetime was not to survive her death. This is not to say that her name was entirely forgotten. Her status as a correspondent of Tasso's insured her at least a toehold in literary history, and her name is duly registered in all the standard eighteenth-century monuments to Italian literary-historical erudition, such as Quadrio, Fontanini, and Tiraboschi.[93] She also appeared, represented by a handful of sonnets and a madrigal, in the remarkable anthology of Italian women's poetry assembled in the 1720s by Luisa Bergalli (1703–1779),[94] while the distinguished literary critic and biographer of Tasso, Pietro Antonio Serassi (1721–1791) paid *Flori* the unexpected honor of singling it out as one of only half a dozen or so Italian pastoral dramas that he considered "truly fine and worthy of praise."[95] Serassi's mention appeared to have been instrumental in stimulating an interest in Campiglia on the part of the

---

91. See particularly the opening monologue by Edreo in Ducchi, *Rime diversi*, 61, where he exclaims that "this is all that was lacking within your realm, O Cupid, that a nymph should burn for another nymph" ("Questo al tuo Regno sol mancava, Amore, / Ch'arda Ninfa per Ninfa"); also his conversation with Flori (67), where he accuses her of "abandoning reason" and "following Love along strange and twisting paths" ("Tal merito ha chi da ragion si parte / et segue Amor per vie distorte e strane"). The first line of Manfredi's eclogue (cited in main text) echoes the opening of Virgil's second eclogue, which similarly explores the themes of same-sex love and madness. A third poem in the collection, by Felice Passero, contains a passage in which a shepherd named Alessi complains of the obdurate chastity of his nymph "Fioretta" (18). Again, it seems plausible to read this as a response to Campiglia's portrayal of love in the *Flori*.

92. Manfredi, *Il Contrasto amoroso*, 39.

93. Fontanini, *Della eloquenza italiana*, 451; Crescimbeni, *L'istoria della volgar poesia*, vol. 4, pt. 2: 125; Quadrio, *Della storia e ragione d'ogni poesia*, 2: 612–78 and 5: 402; Tiraboschi, *Storia della letteratura italiana*, vol. 7, pt. 3: 152. A more detailed discussion, and a first attempt to reconstruct Campiglia's biography, may be found in the local literary history of Calvi, *Biblioteca e storia*, 5: 224–29.

94. Bergalli, *Componimenti poetici*, 2: 37–39.

95. Serassi's comment appears in the introduction to Torquato Tasso, *L'Aminta e Rime Scelte* (Florence, 1862), quoted in Morsolin, *Maddalena Campiglia*, 5.

Vicentine erudite, Bernardo Morsolin, who wrote a monograph on her, published in 1882, incorporating much new archival research.[96] While not devoid of sensitivity to the literary interest of her writings, Morsolin is primarily concerned by the details of Campiglia's life and, in the manner of his age, shows himself inclined to read her literary works through a biographical lens. The biographical narrative reconstructed by Morsolin was authoritatively revised in a 1967 journal article by the historian Giovanni Mantese, which establishes with more clarity the details of Campiglia's early life and the failure of her marriage. A third Vicentine contribution, Giuseppe De Marco's 1988 monograph, is more literary in its focus and emphasizes the religious inspiration of Campiglia's writing. His work contains a useful appendix assembling a selection of Campiglia's spiritual sonnets and occasional verse.

Where modern literary-critical studies are concerned, Campiglia was notably ill-served until the mid-1990s, when Carlachiara Perrone, of the University of Lecce, published a substantial article on the *Calisa*,[97] followed by a critical edition of the text. The critical pickings outside Italy are still more meager. In particular, despite her relative "accessibility" as a writer (she has an entry, for example, in the *Dizionario biografico degli italiani*), Campiglia has not to date been embraced by the tradition of Anglo-American feminist-inspired scholarship that has contributed so much in recent years to the understanding and appreciation of Italian women's writing of this period.[98] We hope that the present edition may remedy this situation by making her most substantial work available in English translation. As the preceding discussion affirms, the work of this challenging and original writer contains much that speaks directly to the critical preoccupations of our time.

96. References to this and other modern works mentioned subsequently in the text are given in note 1 above.

97. Perrone, "'So che donna ama donna': La *Calisa* di Maddalena Campiglia."

98. Although now see Ultsch, "Secular Celibacy."

VOLUME EDITORS'
BIBLIOGRAPHY

PRIMARY SOURCES

Andreini, Isabella. *Mirtilla.* Ed. Maria Luisa Doglio. Lucca: Pacini Fazzi, 1995.

————. *La Mirtilla: A pastoral.* Translated with an introduction and notes by Julie D. Campbell. Tempe, AZ: Arizona Center for Medieval and Renaissance Studies, 2002.

Baldi, Bernardino. *La Corona dell'Anno.* Vicenza: Appresso Agostino dalla Noce, 1589.

————. *Ecloghe miste.* Turin: Edizioni Res, 1992.

Beccari, Agostino. *Il Sacrificio, favola pastorale.* Ferrara: Francesco di Rossi da Valenza, 1555. 2d ed. Ferrara: Alfonso Caraffa, 1587.

Bergalli, Luisa, ed. *Componimenti poetici delle più illustri rimatrici d'ogni secolo, raccolti da Luisa Bergalli.* 2 vols. Venice: Antonio Mora, 1726.

Bigolina, Giulia. *Urania.* Ed. Valeria Finucci. Rome: Bulzoni, 2002.

Bronzini, Cristoforo. *Della dignità e nobiltà delle donne, dialogo . . . diviso in quattro settimane e ciascheduna di esse in sei giornate. Settimana prima e giornata prima.* Florence: Zanobi Pignoni, 1624.

Calderari, Cesare. *Il Trofeo della Croce di N[ostro] S[ignore] Giesù Christo.* Vicenza: Agostino dalla Noce, 1588.

Camilli, Camillo. *Imprese illustri di diversi.* Venice: Francesco Ziletti, 1586.

Campiglia, Maddalena. *Discorso sopra l'Annonciatione della Beata Vergine, e la Incarnatione del S[ignor] N[ostro] Giesu Christo.* Vicenza: Perin Libraro and Giorgio Greco, 1585.

————. *Flori, favola boscareccia.* Vicenza: Heirs of Perin Libraro and Tommaso Brunello, 1588.

————. *Calisa, ecloga.* Vicenza: Giorgio Greco, 1589.

————. *Calisa.* In *"So che donna ama donna": La Calisa di Maddalena Campiglia,* by Carlachiara Perrone, 71–88. Galatina: Congedo, 1996.

Contarini, Luigi. *Il vago e dilettevole giardino.* 2d ed. Vicenza: Heirs of Perin Libraro, 1589.

Cucchetti, Giovanni Donato. *La Pazzia: Favola pastorale.* Ferrara: Vittorio Baldini, 1581.

Diversi componimenti in lode dell'opra. In certain copies of *Flori, favola boscareccia,* by Maddalena Campiglia, sig. i, 1r–sig. k, 8v. (See appendix A, 306.)

Ducchi, Gregorio. *La Schacheide.* Vicenza: Perin Libraro and Giorgio Greco, 1586.

————, ed. *Rime diversi di molti illustri compositori per le nozze degli Illustrissimi Signori Gio[vanni] Paolo Lupi Marchese di Soragna e Beatrice Obici, raccolte da Gregorio Ducchi, gentil'huomo Bresciano.* Piacenza: Gio[vanni] Bazachi, 1589.

Firenzuola, Agnolo. *Celso: Dialogo delle bellezze delle donne.* In *Opere,* ed. Adriano Seroni, 519–96. 3d ed. Florence: Sansoni, 1993.

Fonte, Moderata. *The Worth of Women.* Trans. and ed. Virginia Cox. Chicago: University of Chicago Press, 1997.

Gonzaga, Curzio. *Rime.* 2d ed. Venice: Al segno del Leone, 1591.

————. *Gli inganni.* Venice: Giovanni Antonio Rampazetti, 1592.

Grillo, Angelo. *Rime.* Bergamo: Comin Ventura, 1590.

————. *Poesie sacre.* Venice: Bernardo Giunti, Giovanni Battista Ciotti, 1608.

Guarini, Battista. *Il Pastor fido, tragicommedia pastorale . . . di curiose, & dotte annotationi arricchito.* Venice: Giovanni Battista Ciotti, 1602.

————. *Opere.* Ed. Marziano Guglielminetti. Turin: UTET, 1971.

————. *Le Lettere di Torquato Tasso, disposte per ordine di tempo.* Ed. Cesare Guasti. 5 vols. Naples: Gabrielle Rondinella, 1857.

Ingegneri, Angelo. *La danza di Venere.* Vicenza: Stamperia Nova, 1584.

————. *Della poesia rappresentativa e del modo di rappresentare le favole sceniche.* Ed. Maria Luisa Doglio. Ferrara: Istituto di Studi Rinascimentali and Modena: Panini, 1989.

Lollio, Alberto. *Aretusa, comedia pastorale.* Ferrara: Valente Panizza, 1564.

Manfredi, Muzio. *La Semiramis, tragedia.* 2d ed. Pavia: Heirs of Girolamo Bartoli, 1598.

————. *Il Contrasto amoroso.* Venice: Giacomo Anton[io] Somascho, 1602.

————. *Lettere brevissime.* Venice: Roberto Megietti, 1606.

Ongaro, Antonio. *Alceo, favola piscatoria.* Venice: Francesco Ziletti, 1582.

Pallantieri, Girolamo. *La Bucolica di Virgilio, tradotta verso per verso.* Parma: Fratelli Borsi, 1760.

Piccolomini, Alessandro. *Lettura del S. Alessandro Piccolomini fatta nell'Accademia degli Infiammati.* Bologna: Bartholomeo Bonardo and Marc'Antonio da Carpi, 1541.

Sannazaro, Jacopo. *Arcadia.* 1504. Ed. Francesco Erspamer, Milan: Mursia, 1990.

Tasso, Torquato. *Aminta, favola boscareccia.* 1580/81. In *La tragedia del Cinquecento,* ed. Marco Ariani, 2: 649–721. 2 vols., part 2. Il teatro italiano, Turin: Einaudi, 1977.

————. *Le Lettere di Torquato Tasso, disposte per ordine di tempo.* Ed. Cesare Guasti. 5 vols. Naples: Gabriele Rondinella, 1857.

Torelli Benedetti, Barbara. *Partenia, favola boschereccia.* Biblioteca Statale di Cremona, Deposito Libreria Civica, ms. AA.1.33,1587?

SECONDARY SOURCES

Andreadis, Hariette. "Sappho in Early Modern England: A Study in Sexual Reception." In *Re-reading Sappho: Reception and Transmission,* ed. Ellen Greene, 105–21. Berkeley and Los Angeles: University of California Press, 1996.

Andretta, Stefano. *La venerabile superbia: Ortodossia e trasgressione nella vita di Suor Francesca Farnese (1593–1651).* Turin: Rosenberg & Sellier, 1994.

Andrews, Richard. *Scripts and Scenarios: The Performance of Comedy in Renaissance Italy.* Cambridge: Cambridge University Press, 1993.

————. "Pastoral Drama." In *The Cambridge History of Italian Literature*, ed. Peter Brand and Lino Pertile, 292–98. Cambridge: Cambridge University Press, 1996.

————. "The Dilemma of Chastity and Sex." Unpublished paper given at a symposium in University College, London, 1997.

————. "Isabella Andreini and Others: Women on Stage in the Late Cinquecento." In *Women in Italian Renaissance Culture and Society*, ed. Letizia Panizza, 316–33. Oxford: European Humanities Research Centre, 2000.

Ballarin, A., and G. Barioli. *Il gusto e la moda nel Cinquecento vicentino e veneto. Mostra a Palazzo Chiericati, Vicenza, 30 maggio–15 dicembre, 1973.* Vicenza: Direzione Musei Civici, 1973.

Bandini, Fernando. "La letteratura in dialetto del Cinquecento al Settecento." In *L'età della repubblica Veneta, 1404–1797*, ed. Franco Barbieri and Paolo Preto, 3, pt. 2: 15–26. Vol. 3 of *Storia di Vicenza*, ed. Alberto Broglio and Lellia Crucco Ruggini. Vicenza: Neri Pozza, 1990.

Barish, Jonas. "The Problem of Closet Drama in the Italian Renaissance." *Italica* 71 (1994): 4–31.

Berry, Philippa. *Of Chastity and Power: Elizabethan Literature and the Unmarried Queen.* New York and London: Routledge, 1989.

Bowers, Jane. "The Emergence of Women Composers in Italy, 1566–1700." In *Women Making Music: The Western Art Tradition, 1150–1950*, ed. Jane Bowers and Judith Tick, 116–67. Urbana: University of Illinois Press, 1986.

Brown, Judith C. "Lesbian Sexuality in Medieval and Early Modern Europe." In *Hidden from History: Reclaiming the Gay and Lesbian Past*, ed. Martin Duberman, Martha Vicinus, and George Chauncey, 67–75. New York: Dover, 1989.

Brundin, Abigail. "Vittoria Colonna and the Virgin Mary." *Modern Language Review* 96 (2001): 61–81.

Calore, Marina. "Muzio Manfredi tra polemiche teatrali e crisi del mecenatismo." *Studi Romagnoli* 36 (1985): 27–54.

Calvi, Paolo Antonio. *Biblioteca e storia di quegli scrittori così della città come del territorio di Vicenza che pervennero fin'ad ora a notizia del P. F. Angiolgabriello di Santa Maria Carmelitano Scalzo Vicentino.* 6 vols. Vicenza: Giovanni Battista Vendramini Mosca, 1779.

Carpanè, Lorenzo. "La fortuna editoriale tassiana dal '500 ai giorni nostri." *Italianistica* 24 (1995): 541–57.

Carrara, Enrico. *La poesia pastorale.* Milan: Francesco Vallardi, 1909.

Cavazzini, Giancarlo. "Padova e Guarini: La *Poetica* di Aristotele nella teoria drammaturgica prebarocca." In *Il diletto della scena e dell'armonia: Teatro e musica nelle Venezie dal Cinquecento al Settecento*, AA.VV., 137–88. Padua: Centro Arti Grafiche, 1990.

Cerasano, S. P., and Marion Wynne-Davis, eds. *Readings in Renaissance Women's Drama: Criticism, History, and Performance, 1594–1998.* London: Routledge, 1998.

Ceruti Burgio, Anna. *Donne di Parma.* 2 vols. Parma: PPS Editrice, 1994–98.

Chiappini di Sorio, Ileana. "Un letterato di Vicenza: Paolo Chiappino." In *Studi in onore di Antonio Bardella*, ed. Marcella Bardella, 37–84. Vicenza: Tipografia Istituto San Gaetano, 1964.

Chiodo, Domenico. "Tra l'*Aminta* e il *Pastor fido*." *Italianistica* 24 (1995): 559–75.

Cian, Vittorio. "Ancora di Giovanni Muzzarelli, la 'Fabula di Narciso' e le 'Canzoni e Sestine amorose.'" *Giornale storico della letteratura italiana* 38 (1901): 78–96.

Clubb, Louise George. *Italian Drama in Shakespeare's Time.* New Haven, CT: Yale University Press, 1989.

Colla, Angelo, et al. "Tipografi, editori e librai." In *L'età della repubblica Veneta, 1404–1797,* ed. Franco Barbieri and Paolo Preto, 3, pt. 2: 109–62. Vol. 3 of *Storia di Vicenza,* ed. Alberto Broglio and Lellia Crucco Ruggini. Vicenza: Neri Pozza, 1990.

Costabile, Patrizia. "Forme di collaborazione: Ri-edizioni, coedizioni, società." In *Il libro italiano del Cinquecento: Produzione e commercio,* 127–54. Rome: Istituto poligrafico e Zecca dello Stato, 1989.

Cox, Virginia. "The Single Self: Feminist Thought and the Marriage Market in Early Modern Venice." *Renaissance Quarterly* 48 (1995): 513–81.

———. "Fiction, 1560–1650." In *A History of Women's Writing in Italy,* ed. Letizia Panizza and Sharon Wood, 52–64. Cambridge: Cambridge University Press, 2000.

Crescimbeni, Giovanni Maria. *L'istoria della volgar poesia.* 3d ed. 6 vols. Venice: Lorenzo Basagio, 1731.

Crovato, Giambattista. *La drammatica a Vicenza nel Cinquecento.* 2d ed. Bologna: Arnaldo Forni, 1975.

Daniele, Antonio. 1990. "Attività letteraria." In *L'età della repubblica Veneta, 1404–1797,* ed. Franco Barbieri and Paolo Preto, 3, pt. 2: 39–68. Vol. 3 of *Storia di Vicenza,* ed. Alberto Broglio and Lellia Crucco Ruggini. Vicenza: Neri Pozza, 1990.

De Marco, Giuseppe. *Maddalena Campiglia: La figura e l'opera.* Vicenza: Editrice Vicentina, 1988.

Denarosi, Laura. "Il principe e il letterato: Due carteggi inediti di Muzio Manfredi." *Studi italiani* 9, no. 1 (1997): 151–76.

Di Benedetto, Arnaldo. "L'*Aminta* e la pastorale cinquecentesca in Italia." *Giornale storico della letteratura italiana* 173 (1996): 481–514.

Durante, Elio, and Anna Martellotti. "Il Cavalier Guarini e il Concerto delle Dame." In *Guarini, la musica, i musicisti,* ed. Angelo Pompilio, 91–137. Lucca: Libreria musicale italiana editrice, 1997.

Fabbri, Paolo. "On the Origins of an Operatic Topos: The Mad-Scene." Trans. Tim Carter. In *"Con che soavità": Studies in Italian Opera, Song, and Dance, 1580–1740,* ed. Iain Fenlon and Tim Carter, 157–95. Oxford: Clarendon Press, 1995.

Fahy, Conor. "Women and Italian Cinquecento Literary Academies." In *Women in Italian Renaissance Culture and Society,* ed. Letizia Panizza, 438–52. Oxford: European Humanities Research Centre, 2000.

Fenlon, Iain. *Music and Patronage in Sixteenth-Century Mantua.* 2 vols. Cambridge: Cambridge University Press, 1980.

Findlay, Alison, Gweno Williams, and Stephanie J. Hodgson-Wright. "'The Play Is Ready to Be Acted': Women and Dramatic Production, 1570–1670." *Women's Writing* 6, no. 1 (1999): 129–48.

Fontanini, Giusto. *Della eloquenza italiana.* Venice: Cristoforo Zane, 1737.

Garraffo, Ornella. "Il satiro nella pastorale ferrarese del Cinquecento." *Italianistica* 14 (1985): 185–201.

Grandi, Oler. "Di Curzio Gonzaga e delle sue opere." In *Per Cesare Bozzetti: Studi di letteratura e filologia italiana,* ed. Simone Alberico et al., 535–46. Milan: Mondadori, 1996.

Grendler, Paul F. *The Roman Inquisition and the Venetian Press, 1540–1605.* Princeton, NJ: Princeton University Press, 1977.

Grubb, James S. *Firstborn of Venice: Vicenza in the Early Renaissance State.* Baltimore, MD, and London: Johns Hopkins University Press, 1988.

―――. *Provincial Families of the Renaissance: Private and Public Life in the Veneto.* Baltimore, MD: Johns Hopkins University Press, 1996.

Günsberg, Maggie. *Gender and the Italian Stage: From the Renaissance to the Present Day.* Cambridge: Cambridge University Press, 1997.

Henke, Robert. *Pastoral Transformations: Italian Tragicomedy and Shakespeare's Late Plays.* London: Associated University Presses, 1991.

Herrick, Marvin T. *Tragicomedy: Its Origins and Development in Italy, France, and England.* Urbana: University of Illinois Press, 1962.

Husband, Timothy. *The Wildman: Medieval Myth and Symbolism.* New York: Metropolitan Musem of Art, 1980.

Imbriani, Vittorio. "L'Eco responsiva nelle pastorali italiane." *Giornale napoletano di filosofia e lettere* 2, no. 11 (1872): 279–314.

Ivaldi, Armando Fabio. *Le nozze Pio-Farnese e gli apparati teatrali di Sassuolo del 1587: Studio su una rappresentazione del primo dramma pastorale italiano, con intermezzi di G. B. Guarini.* Genoa: Erga, 1974.

Javitch, Daniel. "The Emergence of Poetic Genre Theory in the Sixteenth Century." *Modern Language Quarterly* 59, no. 2 (1998): 139–69.

Kolsky, Stephen. 2001. "Moderata Fonte, Lucrezia Marinella, Giuseppe Passi: An Early Seventeenth-Century Feminist Controversy." *Modern Language Review* 96 (2001): 973–89.

MacNeil, Anne E. "The Divine Madness of Isabella Andreini." *Journal of the Royal Musical Association* 120 (1995): 193–215.

Malpezzi Price, Paola. *Moderata Fonte: Women and Life in Sixteenth-Century Venice.* Madison and Teaneck: Fairleigh Dickinson University Press and London: Associated University Presses, 2003.

Mancini, Franco, et al. *I teatri del Veneto.* 5 vols. Vol. 1, pt. 1. *Venezia, teatri effimeri e nobili imprenditori* (1995). Vol. 2. *Verona, Vicenza, Belluno, e il loro territorio* (1985). Venice: Corbo e Fiore, 1985–95.

Mantese, Giovanni. "Per un profilo storico della poetessa vicentina Maddalena Campiglia: Aggiunte e rettifiche." *Archivio veneto* 81 (1967): 89–123.

―――. *I mille libri che si leggevano e vendevano a Vicenza alla fine del secolo XVI.* Vicenza: Accademia Olimpica, 1968.

―――. "La famiglia Thiene e la Riforma Protestante a Vicenza nella seconda metà del Sec. XVI." *Odeo Olimpico* 8 (1969–70): 81–186.

Mantese, Giovanni, and Mariano Nardello. *Due processi per eresia: La vicenda religiosa di Luigi Groto, il "Cieco d'Adria," e della nobile vicentina Angelica Piovene-Pigafetta.* Vicenza: Officine Graphiche, 1974.

Maylender, Michele. *Storia delle accademie d'Italia.* 5 vols. Bologna: L. Capelli, 1926–30.

Mazzoni, Stefano. *L'Olimpico di Vicenza: Un teatro e la sua "perpetua memoria."* Florence: Le Lettere, 1998.

Milani, Marisa. "Quattro donne fra i pavani." *Museum Patavinum* 1 (1983): 387–412.

Molinari, Cesare. "Scenografia e spettacolo nelle poetiche del '500." *Il Veltro. Rivista della civiltà italiana* 8 (1964): 885–902.

Morsolin, Bernardo. *Maddalena Campiglia, poetessa vicentina del secolo XVI: Episodio biografico.* Vicenza: Paroni, 1882.

Museo ritrovato: Restauri, acquisti, acquisizioni, 1984–1986. Catalogo della mostra a Vicenza, Basilica Palladiana, 1986. Milan: Electa, 1986.

Mutini, Claudio. "Campiglia, Maddalena." In *Dizionario biografico degli italiani,* 17: 541–42. Rome: Istituto dell'Enciclopedia Italiana, 1974.

Niccolini, Enrico. "Le accademie." In *L'età della repubblica Veneta, 1404–1797,* ed. Franco Barbieri and Paolo Preto, 3, pt. 2: 89–108. Vol. 3 of *Storia di Vicenza,* ed. Alberto Broglio and Lellia Crucco Ruggini. Vicenza: Neri Pozza, 1990.

Nolan, P. "Free Will." In *New Catholic Encyclopedia,* 6: 89–93. Washington: Catholic University of America, 1967.

Ossola, Carlo. *Dal Cortegiano all' "Uomo di mondo": Storia di un libro e di un modello sociale.* Turin: Einaudi, 1987.

Perella, Nicolas. "Fate, Blindness, and Illusion in the *Pastor fido.*" *Romanic Review* 49 (1958): 4, 252–68.

Perrone, Carlachiara. "'So che donna ama donna': La *Calisa* di Maddalena Campiglia." In *Les femmes écrivains en Italie au moyen âge et à la Renaissance,* ed. Centre Aixois de Recherches Italiennes, 293–313. Aix-en-Provence: Publications de l'Université de Provence, 1994.

———. *"So che donna ama donna": La* Calisa *di Maddalena Campiglia.* Galatina: Congedo, 1996.

Pieri, Marzia. *La scena boschereccia nel rinascimento italiano.* Padua: Liviana, 1983.

Pignatti, Gino. *Un principe letterato del secolo XVI. La vita e gli scritti di Curzio Gonzaga.* Milan, Palermo and Naples: Remo Sandron, 1921.

Puppi, Lionello, ed. *Cronaca di Fabio Monza [1548–1592].* Vicenza: La Tipo-Grafica, 1988.

Quadrio, Francesco Saverio. *Della storia e ragione d'ogni poesia.* Bologna: Ferdinando Pisarri, 1739.

Radcliff-Umstead, Douglas. "Love in Tasso's *Aminta:* A Reflection of the Este Court." In *Il teatro italiano del rinascimento,* ed. Maristella de Panizza Lorch, 75–84. Milan: Edizione di Comunità, 1980.

Ridolfi, Roberta Monica. "Gonzaga, Curzio." In *Dizionario biografico degli italiani,* 57: 704–6. Rome: Istituto dell'Enciclopedia Italiana, 2001.

Sampson, Lisa. "'Drammatica secreta': Barbara Torelli's *Partenia* (c. 1587) and Women in Late-Sixteenth-Century Theatre." In *Theatre, Opera, and Performance in Italy from the Fifteenth Century to the Present: Essays in Honour of Richard Andrews.* Ed. Brian Richardson. Leeds: Society for Italian Studies, forthcoming.

Sartori, Diana. "Maddalena Campiglia." In *Le stanze ritrovate: Antologia di scrittrici venete dal Quattrocento al Novecento,* ed. Antonia Arslan, Adriana Chemello, and Gilberto Pizzamiglio, 57–68. Mirano-Venice: Eidos, 1991.

Simons, Patricia. "Lesbian (In)visibility in Italian Renaissance Culture: Diana and Other Cases of *Donna con Donna.*" *Journal of Homosexuality* 27 (1994): 81–122.

Smith, Alison A. "Locating Power and Influence within the Provincial Elite of Verona: Aristocratic Wives and Widows." *Renaissance Studies* 8, no. 4 (1994): 439–48.

Tiraboschi, Girolamo. *Storia della letteratura italiana.* 11 vols. Modena: Società Tipografica, 1772–95.

Traub, Valerie. *The Renaissance of Lesbianism in Early Modern England.* Cambridge: Cambridge University Press, 2002.

Tylus, Jane. "Purloined Passages: Giraldi, Tasso, and the Pastoral Debates." *Modern Language Notes* 99, no. 1 (1984): 101–24.

———. "Colonizing Peasants: The Rape of the Sabines and Renaissance Pastoral." *Renaissance Drama*, n. s., 23 (1992): 113–38.

Ultsch, Lori J. "'Vedova delle cose mondane': Secular Celibacy in Maddalena Campiglia's Pastoral Heterocosm." Forthcoming.

Vaccaro, Emerenziana. *Le marche dei tipografi ed editori italiani del secolo XVI nella Biblioteca Angelica di Roma*. Florence: Olschki, 1983.

Weinberg, Bernard. *A History of Literary Criticism in the Italian Renaissance*. 2 vols. Chicago: University of Chicago Press, 1961.

Zappella, Giuseppina. *Le marche dei tipografi e degli editori italiani del Cinquecento: Repertorio di figure, simboli, e soggetti e dei relativi motti*. 2 vols. Milan: Editrice Bibliografica, 1986.

Zironda, Renato. "Giorgio Angelieri." In *Dizionario dei tipografi e degli editori italiani: Il Cinquecento*, ed. Marco Menato, Ennio Sandal, and Giuseppina Zappella. Milan: Editrice Bibliografica, 1997.

Zonta, Giuseppe. "La *Partenia* di Barbara Torelli-Benedetti." *Rassegna bibliografica della letteratura italiana* 14 (1906): 206–10.

FLORI, FAVOLA BOSCARECCIA

[†2r] ALLA ILLUSTRISSIMA SIGNORA DONNA ISABELLA
PALLAVICINA LUPI MARCHESANA DI SORAGNA,
MADDALENA CAMPIGLIA

Non s'è fermato il desiderio che nacque in me d'onorar Vostra Signoria Illustrissima, da che per fama la conobbi, fin tanto che non le ho dedicato questa mia opera pastorale, cosa da me debita sì per adempir la promessa fattale dal Signor Du-/[†2v] cchi[1] (le virtù del quale osservo grandemente), sì per sodisfar in parte all'obligo mio dei favori fattimi da lei più volte, e finalmente per non mostrarmi senza giudizio, avendo saputo scegler donna eccellentissima a' tempi nostri, non solo per nobiltà di sangue, e per grandezza di stato, ma per magnanimità, e per valore. E questo fermarmi non è già perché l'animo mio debba esser appagato di sì debole dimostrazion dell'affetto, e della riverenza ch'io debbo al singolar merito suo; ma è più tosto un respiro, un breve riposo per pigliar maggior forza a più degna impresa, onde (se concesso mi fia) Vostra Signoria Illustrissima ne resti da me molto più onorata e riverita. Perciò che la im-/[†3r] perfezione di questo mio poema è tale che per aventura ha più bisogno del favore de la sua protezione per farlo rispettare dai maldicenti, che che possa recare a lei alcuno accrescimento di gloria. Sono tuttavia sicurissima che, sendo ella tanto virile nei pensieri e nelle operazioni quanto donna nel bellissimo sembiante e negli onestissimi portamenti, aggradirà questo mio rozzo parto, e la viva candidezza del cuore con che lo accompagno. Sogliono tutte le madri d'oggidì, dovendo far comparir fuori le loro figlie, comporle nella più leggiadra maniera che si sanno imaginare, ricercando a questo effetto i più riposti e astrusi cantoni dell'arte; il/[†3v] che a me non giova di fare, procurando più tosto d'allontanarmi dall'ordinario costume donnesco. Miri ella dunque non con l'occhio della serena sua fronte in questa mia figlia estrinseca pompa di vanità volgare (che es-

FLORI, A PASTORAL DRAMA

TO THE MOST ILLUSTRIOUS LADY ISABELLA
PALLAVICINO LUPI,¹ MARCHIONESS OF SORAGNA,
FROM MADDALENA CAMPIGLIA

Most Illustrious Lady, ever since I first came to hear of you, I have desired to pay you homage, and it is in fulfillment of this desire that I now dedicate to you this pastoral work of mine. In doing so, I am observing the promise made to you by Signor Ducchi, a gentleman for whom I have the greatest respect, while, at the same time, I hope to repay in part the debt I have incurred with you for the many favors you have shown me. Finally, in choosing you as dedicatee, I have the opportunity to show myself to be someone not lacking in judgment, having selected a lady outstanding in our day not merely for the nobility of her blood and the pomp of her state, but also for her magnanimity and valor. And pray do not think that I am satisfied with this feeblest of demonstrations of the affection I bear you and the reverence that is due to your remarkable virtues. Rather, consider this only a moment of respite: a brief rest to allow me to gather force for greater and worthier enterprises, which—if it is permitted to me to complete them—will be a finer and fitter homage for Your Excellency than this that I am currently offering you. For, certainly, the imperfection of this poem is such that it is rather in need of your protection to shield it from its detractors, than capable of offering you any enhancement of your glory. But I am quite sure that you will be gracious enough to be pleased with this poor offspring of mine and with the keen and heartfelt affection that accompanies it, for I know you to be as virile in your thoughts and deeds as you are feminine in your beauty and the honesty of your manners. Mothers today, when they are sending their daughters out into the world, always dress them in the finest way possible, drawing on all the most recondite and abstruse artifices at their disposal. But this is not my way; on the contrary, I seek to depart from the normal habits of women. When this daughter of mine comes before you, then, let your serene eyes not seek in her the gaudy vanities of extrinsic appearance, for she was born in the

sendo nata fra' boschi ha dalla madre imparato a sdegnar i politici addobbamenti) ma, col lume del suo nobilissimo intelletto, la candida lealtà di che ella viene sì riccamante vestita; e con la prontezza della sua grazia gradisca il vivo affetto con che la guido all'onoratissima presenza di Vostra Signoria Illustrissima, alla quale, pregando ogni compiuta felicità, bacio le mani.

[†4r] ALL'ILLUSTRISSIMO SIGNOR CURZIO GONZAGA,
MADDALENA CAMPIGLIA

Non mi pareva d'aver per aventura sodisfatto al debito del desiderio mio se, mandando in luce questa mia favola boscareccia sotto il celebre nome della Signora Marchesa Isabella Pallavicina Lupi, non la raccomandav'anco a Vostra Signoria Illustrissima, il cui valore è solo celato ai poco stimatori della virtù. Mi furono donate le sue bellissime rime dal Signor Angelo Ingegneri, il quale molto mi commendò il suo poema eroico *Fido Amante*. L'ho più volte letto, e dalla vaghezza sua e dal leggiadro stile del verso m'ho sentita colmar di desiderio tale, che sono stata/ [†4v] costretta a farle dono di questo mio parto; parendomi assai convenevole che l'autore del più fido amante che celebrato in alcun tempo fosse, debba esser prenciple protettore di fedelissima ninfa. Al che s'aggiungeva l'osservanza mia verso la Serenissima Casa Gonzaga, sendovi maritata la Illustrissima Signora Elena Campiglia, mia cugina, ora moglie dell'Illustrissimo Signor Guido, da me amata e onorata non solo per la ragione del sangue, ma particolarmente per la bontà, e per la bellezza sua, le quali doti fino da' teneri anni le fecero annonziar sempre signorile, più tosto che privato, congiungimento. Ma sopra tutto la gentilezza del cortesissimo animo di Vostra Signoria Illustrissimo m'ha dato sicurezza, nonché speranza, ch'ella sia per difender questo mio poema pastorale da tutti quelli del sesso virile, i quali se ne scopriranno detrattori, o per ma-/ [†5r] ligna disposizione o per abuso di sinistro giudizio contra i componimenti poetici delle donne. So che le opposizioni saranno molte; ma di questa sola far dovrei stima, che fatto avessi meglio spendere il tempo in scritti spirituali, sì come avea cominciato, sviando la mente da qualunque vano pensiero; se da Sant'Agostino data non me ne fosse licenza con affermar che ogni sorte di virtù allontana l'uomo dai vizî. Confesso parimente che la favola sia più secondo

wild woods and learned from her mother to disdain all such vain, politick trappings. Rather, let the light of your most noble intellect search out the candor and devotion with which she is so richly adorned; and may the keen affection with which I guide her into your most honored presence win her the bounty of your grace. In that hope, and with the most sincere wishes for your perfect felicity, I take my leave, humbly kissing your hand.

TO THE MOST ILLUSTRIOUS LORD CURZIO GONZAGA, FROM MADDALENA CAMPIGLIA[2]

Your Excellency, I felt that I should not have satisfied the obligation of my desire if I had sent this pastoral play of mine out into the world under the famous name of the Marchioness Isabella Pallavicino Lupi without at the same time entrusting it to your Lordship, whose valor is known to all those who prize virtue. I was given your exquisite verses by Signor Angelo Ingegneri, who also warmly recommended to me your epic poem *The Faithful Lover.*[3] I have since read this several times, and so admired its beauty and stylistic refinement that I was possessed with a keen desire to dedicate to you this offspring of my intellect, for it seemed most fitting to me that the creator of the most faithful lover who has ever walked the earth should be the principal protector of so faithful a nymph. A further motive was the great respect I bear the most serene house of Gonzaga, with which I am connected through marriage, for the Most Illustrious Lord Guido of that dynasty has wedded my cousin, the Most Illustrious Lady Elena Gonzaga: a lady I have always loved and honored, not simply because of our family tie, but more particularly on account of her goodness and beauty, which always seemed, from her earliest years, to destine her for a marriage to one of princely rather than private estate.[4] But, above all, the choice to dedicate this pastoral poem of mine to you was inspired by Your Excellency's matchless graciousness and courtesy, which emboldens me to hope that you will be willing to defend it against all those of the male sex who will set themselves to attack it, either because of their innate ill disposition or because of that prejudice that leads some men automatically to condemn any poetic work by a woman. I know the poem will attract criticisms for all kinds of motives, but the only one I am prepared to take seriously is this: that it would have been better for me to devote my time to writing religious works, as I have done in the past,[5] and to turn my attention away from all worldly considerations. I feel myself absolved on this score, however, by none other than St. Augustine, who maintained that all forms of virtuous activity serve to preserve us from vice.[6] For the rest, I confess freely that I have composed the plot of this play more in accordance with

l'intenzion mia che le regole di coloro che hanno insegnato l'arte di questi poemi, perché gli episodi che ci sono inseriti superano di lunghezza l'azion prencipale. Ma tuttavia, avendo procurato che tutto ciò ch'in loro si tratta dipenda dal sacrificio, fatto per salute delli due pazzi, i quali son il soggetto; ed essendone state composte da persone di qualche nome altre ancora, senza la piena osser-/ [†5v] vazione dei precetti d'Aristotele e degli avvertimenti datici dai commentatori della sua poetica, io crederò che questa, fatta da donna, e da donna forse poco atta a simile impresa, debba esser letta se non con lode, almeno con sopportazione. Temo finalmente che la prolissità dei ragionamenti sia per aventura inescusabile appresso coloro che negli altrui scritti desiderano ogni perfezione. E di ciò sono stata specialmente avvertita dal Signor Paolo Chiappino, candidissimo osservatore della buona lingua, e giudiciosissimo scrittore, sì come fanno fede le sue lodate composizioni, per le quali non solo è figlio, ma degno figlio della famosa Academia Olimpica. Tuttavia, spero che questa azione, originata da due personaggi, e aggrandita dagli accidenti congiunti, e ornata d'insperati successi, e riconoscimenti— a guisa di moderna veste riempita in al-/ [†6r] cune parti da ben accorto artefice (perché un corpo quantunque robusto paia ancor vie più solido e più formato)—non abbia a riuscire affatto spiacevole se sia discretamente considerata. Accresca dunque Vostra Signoria Illustrissima il primo obligo che le tengo, avendomi la lettura del suo rarissimo poema spronata ad una tanta impresa, con questo secondo, degnandosi gradire il mio picciolo dono, se non corrispondente al merito suo, almeno conforme al poter mio. Poiché non le posso dar cosa più cara di questa mia figlia, vera figlia, e naturale, di che prencipalmente mi godo. Perciò che se io la vedrò benignamente accolta da lei, m'andrò preparando per porgerle maggior segno della divozione ch'io serbo al suo chiarissimo valore. Fra tanto, in grazia di Vostra Signoria Illustrissima riverentemente mi raccomando.

my own tastes than with the prescriptions of those who have written theoretically on the genre of pastoral, for the various digressive episodes that
have been introduced in fact occupy more space in the play than the principal action.[7] But I have been careful to ensure that the events of these
episodes are dependent on the sacrifice performed to cure the mad nymph
and shepherd who are the central protagonists. In any case, I am not the first
to compose such a play without following to the letter the precepts of Aristotle and the recommendations of his commentators; indeed, there are writers of some renown who are guilty of this same transgression. In view of this,
it seems to me that a play written by a mere woman (and a woman, perhaps,
ill-fitted for such an enterprise) deserves to be received, if not with generosity, at least with tolerance. A final area in which I anticipate some criticism is
that of the prolixity of the speeches in the play, which may be considered excessive by those who delight in minutely scrutinizing the imperfections of
others' writings.[8] I was warned of this by Signor Paolo Chiappino, that most
respected expert on all matters relating to language and style, and a refined
author himself, as is witnessed by his own praiseworthy works, which have
deservedly won him a place as a son of the famous Accademia Olimpica.[9] But,
despite all these supposed defects, I hope that this play, with its action initiated by two characters but then enriched by successive events and adorned
by unexpected happenings and sudden recognitions, will not be entirely distasteful to its readers, if they approach it in the right spirit. They might regard it as rather like some modern garments which have been cunningly
adorned with well-judged padding in places, and which are capable of making a body already robust in itself seem even more sturdy and well-formed.

To conclude, my debt to Your Excellency is already considerable, in that
I was inspired to undertake this enterprise by reading your remarkable poem,
but I hope, nonetheless, that you will grant me the further favor of accepting
this little gift, which, even if it is not equal to Your Excellency's merits, is the
finest offering that lies within my poor powers. For I have nothing to give
that is dearer to me than this daughter of mine: this true and natural daughter, the apple of my eye. If Your Excellency will be so gracious as to welcome
her benignly, I shall labor to produce for the future some greater sign of the
devotion I bear toward your splendid virtues. Meanwhile, I remain Your Excellency's most humble and devoted servant.

[†6v] PERSONAGGI DELLA FAVOLA

Flori	*Ninfa pazza*
Licori	*Ninfa, compagna di Flori*
Damone	*Sacerdote*
Serrano	*Fratello stimato d'Androgeo*
Androgeo	*Pastor pazzo*
Melampo	*Pastor vecchio, padre di Licori*
Satiro	
Silvano	
Urania	*Ninfa*
Darello	*Pastor maligno*
Fronimo	*Fratello di Flori*
Leggiadro	*Famiglio di Serrano*
Coro di pastori	
Alessi	*Pastore straniero*
Coro di ninfe	
Tirsi	*Pastore vecchio, padre d'Androgeo e Leggiadro*

La Scena si finge in Arcadia

CAST

Flori	*Mad nymph*
Licori	*Nymph and companion of Flori*
Damone	*Priest*
Serrano	*Supposed brother of Androgeo*
Androgeo	*Mad shepherd*
Melampo	*Elderly shepherd and father of Licori*
Satyr	
Wild man	
Urania	*Nymph*
Darello	*Malevolent shepherd*
Fronimo	*Brother to Flori*
Leggiadro	*Servant to Serrano*
Chorus of shepherds	
Alessi	*Unknown shepherd*
Chorus of nymphs	
Tirsi	*Elderly shepherd and father to Androgeo and Leggiadro*

The action takes place in Arcadia

PROLOGO

AMORE

Dalle città partito, e da' più ricchi	1
E pomposi palagi, ove tra mille,	
E mille vezzi accolto, e lieto stommi	
Son quà venuto; e non già perch'io pensi	
Che in questi folti boschi, e in queste piagge	5
Solinghe, ed ermi colli, ed antri opachi	
Anco non vi sia Amor, ché in cielo, in terra,	
E ne l'inferno il mio valor discopro.	
Dicalo Giove, su nel ciel monarca	
Degli altri Dei, s'anch'egli ben sovente	10
Del mio licor fatt'ebro in mille guise	
Errò quinci mortal fra' miei seguaci;	
E Pluto ancor, del cieco regno duce,	
D'ogni pietà spogliato, s'entro al petto	
Sentì sì la mia fiamma che cangiate	15
Le crude voglie sue si fè soggetto	
Ad un sol guardo di fanciulla diva.	
Alcide, poi Achille, e'l gran maestro	
De' più saggi, che più? Mill'altri, e mille	
Qui tra mortali a le mie forze resi,	20
Che non fero essi? Altri l'abietta, e molle	
Canocchia al fianco tenne, orrendi mostri/[†7v]	
Dianzi avezzo domar; chi da le tende	
Vide cader i suoi, nè per la rapta	
Donzella (irato) l'arme al maggior uopo	25
Mosse del gran Re Argivo, e altri pazzo	
(Già di natura interprete divino)	

PROLOGUE

LOVE

So, leaving behind the cities, and the rich and splendid mansions in which I make my usual pampered abode, I am come to this place. Not that I doubt that in these dense woods and these solitary clearings and bleak hilltops and dark caves, Love also has his rightful dwelling, for my power is felt in the heavens, on the earth, and in the reaches of hell.[10] Let Jove be my witness to this—monarch in the skies to all the gods—if he too has often strayed here on earth in a thousand guises as a mortal among my votaries, intoxicated by my sweet nectars.[11] And Pluto, also, pitiless ruler of the dark world below, felt the force of my flame so strongly when I entered his breast, that, laying aside all tyrannous urges, he fell subject to the glance of a divine girl.[12] And Hercules, and Achilles, and the great master of the wise . . .[13] What need to continue? There is no end to the number of mortals who have succumbed to my rule. And to what extremities were these heroes reduced! The first, once the tamer of fearsome monsters, now clasped the weak and abject distaff to his side, while the second watched from his tent as his companions fell, disdaining—so angry was he over the damsel who had been rapt from him—to put his hand to his sword in the service of the Greek king even at the hour of his direst need. The third, meanwhile, once godlike in his divining of nature,

Scordò se stesso, in animal converso,
Per seguir di mia turba l'orme impresse.
Ma che? So ben che in ogni loco i' tengo   30
Senz'altro sommo impero e son qua sceso
Per far a punto oggi palese al mondo,
Se con ragion d'ogni bell'alma ho'l freno.
In fatal acque due saete aurate
D'insolito valor temprai pur dianzi,   35
E perché so che qua passar dovea
Degno pastor da molte miglia giunto,
Per morte altrui d'eterna piaga offeso,
Ch'oggi trovarsi al sacrificio deve
D'altri invitato, una pensai di queste   40
Avventar al suo petto, e così a punto
Mi venne² fatto qui presso ad un fonte
Non molto lunge, ov'ei posava a l'ombra.
Quest'altra voglio che trapassi il seno
A Flori, del mio regno empia rubella,   45
E fia del primo assai maggiore il colpo;
Ma ferirolla a tempo, e sarà quando
Dal sacrificio offerto al sacro altare
La vegga a dietro ritirar fra l'altre,
Le crude luci sue guidando allora   50
Nel ferito pastor d'altre contrade.
Per costei (già per morte anch'ella pazza)
Oggi farassi il sacrificio, e anco/[†8r]
Per risanar Androgeo per lei pazzo.
Invisibil tra lor vo' star tutt'oggi   55
Aspirando a lor voti, sì perch'aggia
Felice effetto il miserabil caso
Del meschino pastor, ch'errando pazzo
Va per costei che lo disprezza, e folle
Se 'n va per altro amor estinto e vano,   60
Sì perché coppia tale unqua veduta
Anco non sia, qual scoprirassi (spero)
Questi da me feriti Alessi, e Flori.
Saran le piaghe lor d'Amore, e Amore
Avralle fatte a punto lor mal grado;   65
E ciò sarà per dimostrar che poco
Vale il proposto altrui se me gli oppongo.

now in his madness forgot himself and descended to the nature of a beast to join the throng of my followers.

But enough of this! I know full well that I reign unchallenged in all places, and indeed am come here today to reveal to the world with what good reason I hold all noble souls in my grasp. In preparation, I tempered in fatal waters two golden arrows of unwonted power.[14] And, since I happened to know that today there was destined to pass through this place a worthy shepherd come wandering from far-distant lands, stricken to the heart by the death of someone he loved, I thought it a good opportunity to shoot one of these arrows into his breast, especially since I knew that he would be tarrying here to attend the sacrifice on others' invitation.[15] And this I have done, having found him here resting in the shade by a spring. The other arrow I destine for Flori[16]—that hardened rebel to my rule!—and hers shall pierce far more deeply than the first. But I shall choose my time well, and the moment shall be when I see her retire with the other maidens from the sacrifice offered on the high altar, and her cruel eyes shall turn to meet the eyes of the wounded shepherd who comes from afar. It is for her sake today that the sacrifice is to be performed, for she too has lost her wits through another's death—for her sake, and to heal the shepherd Androgeo,[17] who has been in turn driven mad by love for her. And as it takes place, I shall be there, invisible, in their midst, mingling my influence in their vows. Thus shall be happily resolved the sad tale of that poor shepherd who goes madly wandering out of love for her, while she disdains him, herself consumed by folly for another love, now lost and vain. And, beyond this, I shall have created (as I hope) in Alessi[18] and Flori, by piercing them with my arrows, a pair of lovers such as the world has never seen. Their wounds shall be Love's, and Love will have smitten them against their wills. Let this be a sign that no vow may be kept when I choose to oppose it!

Vanamente piangendo ella dispose
Dopo la morte d'Amaranta, ninfa
Sua cara sì, di non amar più mai.   70
Al mio colpo fia vano il suo disegno
De l'ardir suo d'aver Amor sprezzato.
Gli averrà questo, che l'aurato strale
Con che ferirla intendo, e già ferito
Ho 'l pastor che sì altero anch'ei giurava   75
Di non amar più mai, virtute ha tale
Ch'eterna fa la piaga, e non mortale.
Ameranno, arderan, ma il fine ond'altri
Ogni lor brama appaga, non fie mai
Da lor pensato pur, non che bramato.   80
Virtute occulta inusitata, e nova
In somma avran gli dardi, che ferita
Faran profonda, ma sì onesta e santa,/ [†8v]
Che meraviglia altrui porran nel core
Spesso lor voglie, ardenti sì ma caste.   85
Tal vo' che sia l'emenda del lor fallo
Che s'amin sì, sì ch'ardano, ma'l fine
De' fidi Amanti, vero pregio mai
Non aggian, quando pur chiamar si voglia
Emenda grazia a nullo ancor concessa.   90
Ecco di novo arroto l'aureo dardo.
Misera Flori, e chi fia mai che salva
Ti possa far dal fiero colpo ond'ora
Movo a tuo danno il mio divin potere?
Ecco che vien, vo differir il colpo   95
Insino al far del sacrificio. Intanto
Qui invisibile intorno andrommi errando,
Ne le lingue, nei cori, e ne le menti
De' semplici pastori e ninfe il mio
Valor oprando sì, ch'altri gli udranno   100
In stil diverso oggi parlare insieme
Dal proprio lor, ch'io detarole il tutto.

Il fine del prologo

Vainly, Flori resolved, weeping, after the death of the nymph Amaranta,[19] who was so dear to her, never to love again; at my blow, all her designs will be shattered. Her punishment for having challenged the power of Love will be this: the golden arrow I have destined to wound her, and with which I have already pierced that shepherd who, like her, haughtily swore he would never love again, is such in its workings that its wounds will be eternal, but not fatal. Flori and Alessi will love, they will burn, but that end to which other lovers' burning desires are directed, and which can alone assuage their pain, will be by this pair not even contemplated, still less desired. Rather, my arrows will have a strange and unwonted hidden virtue, which will make their wounds deep, yes, but so honest and pure that others will marvel to see their desires, at once ardent and chaste.[20] In this way I will have them make amends for their offense against my power, that, though loving with true ardor, they will never attain that end and true prize sought by faithful lovers[21]—if it is right to speak of making amends when a grace is being granted that no other mortal has received.

So now, I once more flex my golden dart, wretched Flori! And who shall now preserve you from the fierce blow my divine power now prepares to wield against you? Ah, here she comes! But I shall delay my blow until the sacrifice is prepared. And, meanwhile, I shall go wandering around here, invisible to human eyes, and my power shall be infused so within the tongues and hearts and minds of the simple shepherds and nymphs that they shall be heard to speak today in a style quite other than their usual; for I shall be dictating all.[22]

End of the prologue

[1r] ATTO PRIMO

SCENA PRIMA

Flori, Licori

Flori

Deh, se dunque tu m'ami, non ti spiaccia   1
Del mio piacer, cara Licori, e'l core
Che tutt'altro aborrisce, lassa alquanto,
Che si consoli in dolce vista, e amara.

Licori

Amara sì, ma verace amico   5
Stimar sempre commune il bene e 'l male
Deve del caro amico: a me, che t'amo
Di me stessa non meno, come mai
Soffrirà di condurti a tanto strazio?
Torna, deh torna, Flori che se'l pianto   10
Avvivar lei potesse che tu piangi,
Io teco piangerei, sì che di Bibli
Il duro caso rinovar vorrei.

Flori

Ecco (lassa) chi cela il mio tesoro?
Deh come di natura incontro a l'uso   15
Entro al cenere freddo amor conservi
Le vivaci mie fiamme ogn'or più ardenti?
Oimè, morte, che fai?

ACT ONE

SCENE ONE

Flori, Licori

Flori

If you love me, ah! dearest Licori, do not disdain my wishes. Let my heart, which abhors all other objects, seek solace where it may—in a sight, for me, as sweet as it is bitter.

Licori

Bitter indeed! But if it is the lot of a true friend always to share in the good and ill fortune of the one he loves, then how shall I bear to conduct you to such misery, loving you, as I do, as dearly as myself? Turn back, Flori! Ah, turn back! If your weeping could restore to life the nymph for whom you weep, then I should gladly weep alongside you—weep like another Byblis, whose cruel fate I would happily embrace.[23]

Flori

Alas! Who is it that conceals my dearest treasure? And how is it that the bright flames of my love burn so fiercely still in these cold ashes, defying Nature's laws? Death, what is this that you are doing?[24]

Licori

    Orsù, qui veggio
Ch'abbiamo da star buon pezzo, ragionando
Vanamente co' morti, poiché tosto   20
Che mira il sasso ella di senno è fuore./[1v]
Misera or qui ti posa.

Flori

     Ah tu non vuoi,
Dolce cara, ch'io viva teco pure?
Vivo, e son morta, e tu non mori, io moro!

Licori

  O duro caso, e più d'ogn'altro degno   25
Di pietate. O follia ben sola al mondo!

Flori

  Oimè, Morte, non vieni? Io vengo pure,
Lassa, e tutt'altre cure
Quivi ripongo e poso.
O mio dolce riposo!   30
Cielo, chi mi nasconde
Colà tra quelle fronde
Il mio ben dolce e caro?
Invido marmo avaro?
Ah! che pur vedo lei,   35
Di tutti i pensier miei
Solo e gradito obietto.

Licori

  Odi come talora
Saggiamente ragiona
E come forsennata poi vaneggia.   40

Flori

  Non più vezzi, ch'io vengo.
Ah perché fuggi? Aspetta!
Non fuggir, cara ninfa; o Morte arresta!
Forse che a l'alma bella
Non spiacerà s'in terra   45

Licori

Well! I see we are to remain here some time, speaking vainly with the dead. When once she sees the tomb, she quite loses her wits! *[To Flori]* Poor creature, come rest here awhile.

Flori

So, my beloved, you will not even have me live alongside you? I live and yet am dead. You do not die. I die!

Licori

O cruellest of fates, and most pitiful! O rarest of follies[25]

Flori

Alas! Death, where are you? I am here, and, miserable as I am, put all other things aside. Ah, my sweet solace! But heavens, what is hiding my own sweet one among these fronds? O hated, jealous tomb! Still I see her before me. Still she is my heart's dearest object.[26]

Licori

Hark how she will now speak with reason, now rave like a mad creature!

Flori

No more of your teasing! Here I am! But, oh, why do you still flee? Wait! Do not flee, dearest nymph! Death, halt your steps! Perchance her lovely soul will be pleased that I loved her so well on this earth

Tanto l'amai ch'in cielo anco la segua.
Ma qual orrido speco è quel ch'io miro?
Non vo' venirci! Io vengo (lassa) io vengo.

Licori

Questa meschina ninfa,
Che vanamente a l'impossibil dietro/[2r]   50
Si strugge e si consuma,
Quanta mi fa pietate! Temo, temo
Che sia Fronimo tardo a darle aita.
Ne le mie forze almen l'aitarla stesse,
Ch'oggi non coprirebbe sotto l'onde   55
Febo l'aurato carro, ch'io vorrei
De l'oracolo santo le veraci
Note adempir, che sogliono apportare
Ne l'esseguirle un fin lieto e felice.
Non fu sì lunga quella notte, in cui   60
L'invitto Alcide glorioso nacque:
Quant'ha sembrato, a me questa passata.
Quivi sapendo ch'oggi far si deve
Il sacrificio per sanar a un tempo
E di Flori e d'Androgeo la pazzia.   65
Levai per tempo, poiché qui mi disse
Fronimo che verrebbe a darmi l'ora
Prefissa del dover poi ritrovarmi
Con l'altre ninfe al sacrificio insieme.

Flori

Di questa vita l'alma vera, o Morte   70
Crudel, dov'è? Ahi che per te lontana
Ella da me s'è fatto; io ben ti veggio.
Vieni, e sottraggi al duol questa mia spoglia!
Ecco Morte, ecco lei; ah dove andate?
Vi fuggite crudeli, e ambe paghe   75
Del mio duol vi ridete?
Contra lor tu per me guerreggia, o cielo,
E poi vinte le uccidi, che farai
Del fiero strazio mio degna vendetta.
Ogni fera t'arride, ecco ogni pianta,/[2v]   80
A che tardi? Deh Morte; ahi ninfa, o cielo!

that I now wish to follow her even into the heavens. But what is this hor-
rid cave I see? I shall not come there! I shall! Alas! I shall!

Licori

Ah, this wretched nymph, consuming herself in a vain yearning after the
impossible—what pity she awakens in me! Alas, I fear that Fronimo will
be too late to assist her. Would that it were within my power to help her!
If it were, Phoebus's chariot would not sink beneath the waves[27] this day
before I had carried out to the letter the righteous commandments of our
sacred oracle, which are wont to bring a happy outcome to those who
obey them.[28] The night that watched over the peerless Alcides's glorious
birth was not so long as this last has seemed to me![29] I woke early, knowing that the sacrifice that is to heal the madness of both Flori and Androgeo is planned for today. Fronimo told me he would meet me here to let
me know the hour appointed for that rite, for I am expected there with
my fellow nymphs.[30]

Flori

Cruel Death, where is she—she who was my heart and soul? Alas, far
from me now, by your doing. I see you, Death! Come! Wrest this poor
mortal shell of mine from its pain! Death, I see you! And she! Together—
oh, where are you bound? You are fleeing from me, in your cruelty, and
laughing at my pain. Heavens, take my part against this cruel pair! Take
arms against them, slay them—such would be a worthy vengeance for the
agonies I have suffered. Every beast smiles on you! And, see, every plant!
Oh, death, come to me! Why do you tarry? O nymph! Oh heavens!

Licori

    Flori, infelice, a che spietato scempio
    T'ave ridotta l'altrui colpa forse?
    Che saresti venuta indegna preda
    Ben mille volte di rapaci fere   85
    O d'immodesti satiri e silvani
    S'allungata mi fossi pur brev'ora
    Da te, che ogn'or qua torni e non val prego.
    Lassa, deh ciel, fia mai
    Che tu sanata, io lieta, di Diana   90
    L'orme seguiamo ancor, da lei qual dianzi
    Favorite più d'altre? e rapportiamo
    In perigliose caccie, eterne lodi?
    E ch'innanzi a Montan, pastor sì saggio,
    Con mille ninfe a prova ancor cantando,   95
    N'abbiamo il ricco pregio e un chiaro nome?
    Ahi cara amica, Flori, cara, cara
    Compagna, come semiviva stai
    Fra tanto duolo avolta vaneggiando?
    Forse è del ciel castigo, che per donna   100
    Tu vada errando folle; poiché sempre
    Le volevi sprezzar, dicendo "quale
    Di questo nome donna è più vil nome?"5
    O quante volte ella dicea, "Licori,
    Tenta meco poggiar per quel sentiero   105
    Ove donna immortal sola sen gìo
    VITTORIOSA e DIVA tra mai quante
    Del sesso nostro fur chiare e illustri.
    Ben sallo il Mincio e'l Tebro,
    Ch'arrestaro il lor corso al dolce canto/ [3r]   110
    Di lei, che vinse a prova
    I più degni pastor di quell'etate."

Flori

    O Cielo, o Morte ingrati!
    Ch'or mi tien? che mi tolse
    La mia cara Amaranta?   115
    O Morte, o cara ninfa,
    Ove ti fuggi, e mi abbandoni? Torna
    Morte, non mi lasciar; ma qual rimiro

Licori

O wretched Flori! To what a pitiful state you have been reduced, perhaps through others' fault more than your own. You would have fallen prey a thousand times to scavenging beasts or shameless satyrs and wild wood-gods if I had strayed but one brief hour from you. Always you are drawn back to this place; no one can stop you. Alas! O heavens! Will it ever come to pass that, you cured, I happy, we will once more follow in the footsteps of Diana, once again favored by her above all other nymphs?[31] And shall we again one day win eternal praise through our prowess in the perilous hunt? And vying with a thousand other nymphs in our songs before the wise shepherd Montano, shall we carry off the richest trophies and highest fame? Ah, sweetest friend, my Flori, sweetest, sweetest companion! How can it be that you are left thus wandering, half-dead and shrouded in such pain! Perhaps it is a punishment from the heavens that for the sake of a woman you are led to this raving, for you would always despise your sex, saying "What name is more contemptible than this of *woman*?" And how often would she beg me, "Licori! Come, let us set ourselves to tread that lonely path where one immortal woman alone has ventured, the most VICTORIOUS and DIVINE among all those of our sex who have won fame!"[32] The Mincio well knows it, and the Tiber, which arrested their course at the sweet singing of her who far outventured the worthiest shepherds of her age.

Flori

O heavens! O death! O cruel ones! Who now holds me in his clutches? Who snatched from me my darling Amaranta? O death! O sweet nymph! Where do you flee and abandon me? O death, return! Do not leave me!

L'aspetto già si vago? E come oscuro
È il loco oimè? Più non ti veggio. Ah bene   120
Or di novo ti scorgo.
Lassa, e chi mi t'invola?
Morte pietosa, vieni!
Vien perché lei giungiamo; ah ch'è fuggita.

Licori

Meschina, come parla e par che veggia,   125
E non vede e non parla, che vaneggia.
Mille larve di duol l'ingombran l'alma.
Misera ninfa, qui tra l'erbe pure
Amaramente fuor di senno sfoga
Questo tuo van dolor, che teco assisa   130
Qui mi starò fin tanto, che ne giunga
Fronimo. Or ecco il sacerdote a punto.

SCENA SECONDA

Sacerdote, Licori, Flori

Sacerdote

Sei tu forse Licori, o ninfa? E questa   1
Già l'impazzita tua compagna Flori?

Licori

Benvenuto Damone. Oimè, che quelle/[3v]
Siamo a punto che dici, ed ecco Flori
Languente stare al duro marmo a canto,   5
Il cui misero caso senso porge
Per risentirsi (penso) insino ai sassi.

Damone Sacerdote

Quanta pietà costei mi desta al core.
Ahi de' pazzi mortali
Presumer vano, or ecco   10
In qual'esser t'induce
Misero stato uman brevissim'ora?
A un ventilar repente
D'Euro maligno; e tu pur gonfio affidi

But what is now become of that image once so fair? And how dark the place! Alas! You have vanished. But now I see you once more. Who wrests you from me? Come, merciful Death—come, let us catch her! Ah, she is flown!

Licori

Poor creature, how she speaks, and seems to see. Yet she does not see, nor yet speak; she is raving. A thousand specters of grief are haunting her heart. Wretched nymph! Come, here among these fronds bitterly give vent to your vain sorrow, and I shall remain with you until Fronimo comes. Ah, indeed, here is the priest come already.

SCENE TWO

Priest, Flori, Licori

Priest

Are you perchance Licori, O nymph? And might this be your stricken companion Flori?

Licori

Welcome, Damone![33] Alas! We are indeed those two. There you see Flori, languishing beside the hard marble slab, her wretched plight fit to awaken pity even in the stones themselves.

Damone, the Priest

Ah, what pity I feel for her! O foolish mortals! What vain presumption is yours! Now see to what a pitiful state the briefest hour can reduce you, the merest change of wind! And yet, swollen with pride, you still stub-

Ne la stoltizia tua (che di sapere   15
Ha finta faccia) i tuoi desiri arditi?
Giovane sfortunata, troppo, troppo
Di terrena beltà ti compiacesti.

Licori
Deh, cortese Damon, s'unqua pietate
Ti mosse a oprar per infelice caso,   20
Or di costei ti caglia;
In suo favor t'accingi, e la risana,
Che più degn'opra ancor fatta non hai.

Damone Sacerdote
Per questo a punto oggi adoprarmi spero,
E Fronimo ricerco per narrargli   25
Certa risposta di prodigio avuta
Da l'oracolo in fin de la dimanda,
Ch'io per Flori le feci; da la quale
Scorgo per lei gran bene, e un nuovo male.

Licori
Oimè, qual s'apparecchia   30
Dolcissima sorella,
A le miserie tue nova sciagura?

Damone Sacerdote
Non ti doler ninfa gentil cotanto,/[4r]
Che s'io ben miro anco di pregio eterno
Le fia poco martir ch'è già vicino.   35

Licori
Qual fia questo martir? Deh me lo scopri.

Damone Sacerdote
"Sana verrà: ma di repente sguardo
Viril fia ch'arda onestamente, e in terra
Abbia perpetuo la sua fede il giorno."
Tal de l'oracol santo la risposta   40
Ultima fu, dov'io
Se ben rimiro dei celesti detti

bornly entrust your most deeply held desires to your folly, believing it to be wisdom. Poor maid, poor maid! Too keenly did you revel in earthly beauty!

Licori

Courteous Damone, if ever pity moved you to come to the aid of some poor unfortunate, now bend your heart to this wretched nymph. Exert yourself for her, cure her! You will have done no finer deed.

Damone

I intend to devote myself today to this very task, and am even now searching for Fronimo to tell him of a true augury of a forthcoming miracle that I have just received from the oracle. For when I consulted it on the fate of Flori, its reply foretold for her great good fortune—though not detached from new ills.

Licori

Alas! Sweetest sister, what new evil can add itself to your sufferings?

Damone

Do not grieve so, gentle Nymph, for if I see aright, the briefest of torments, already imminent, will win her eternal rewards.

Licori

What torment do you speak of? Tell me, pray.

Damone

"She will be cured, but will then be set afire by a man's sudden gaze. In honesty will she burn, and on earth perpetual will remain the faith of this day." This was the last response that I had from the sacred oracle, which I take to mean (if I rightly discern the true sense of these divine words)

A dentro il vero senso,
Trovo che nova fiamma le sovrasta,
Ma sì gentil, sì casta,   45
Che ben bastar devran de la sua fede
L'eccelse lodi a ricambiar di lei
Un qualche lieve affanno.
Non sarà mal ch'ancor scoperto l'abbia
A te, poiché in te posa   50
Dei pensieri di Fronimo gran parte.

Licori

Sian gli Dei benedetti, e tu lodato!
Purché costei si sani, il tutto segua.
So che Fronimo tiene
Le sue maggior speranze   55
Nel grand amor ch'a la sorella porto;
E ben è grande, s'ho lasciato il padre,
La casa, e ogn'altra cosa, allor venendo
Per consolar il suo dolor che intesi
La morte d'Amaranta, la cui nova   60
Non meno il mio che'l cor di lei trafisse.

Damone Sacerdote

Ahi di degna pietà ben pietos'opra:
O verace amicizia quanto puoi!

[4v] Licori

In fin dal latte, fanciullette insieme,
Tutte tre ci allevammo, i padri nostri   65
Vicini avendo i lor poderi e i greggi:
Finché'l padre di Flori, quel Carino
Sì ricco, e vago di piaceri, venne
Ad abitar questa più bella parte
D'Arcadia, e seco poco dopo Nico,   70
D'Amaranta gentile il genitore,
I quai piegar non poter le voglie
Di Melampo, mio padre, al lor disio
Che vi venisse anch'egli.

that a new flame will engulf her, but one so noble and chaste that the high praise she will win for this new love will handsomely recompense her for whatever slight pain she must endure. It is well that I should have told you of this, for I know that Fronimo's hopes rest in great part on you.

Licori

May the gods be thanked and you praised! Let what will follow, if only she is cured. I well know that Fronimo's best hopes are reposed in the great love I bear his sister. And great indeed is this love, if I left my father, my home, and all else to come and console her when I heard of Amaranta's death, which pierced my heart with grief as keenly as it did hers.

Damone

Ah, true pity, for so pitiful a case! How great is the power of true friendship!

Licori

From the time that we were babes in arms, we three grew up together, for our fathers' lands were neighboring, and their flocks grazed side by side. But then Flori's father, the rich Carino, ever eager for new pleasures, came to live instead in these fairer reaches of Arcadia, and Nico, sire to the gentle Amaranta, was not slow in following his friend. But for all their pleas, my own father, Melampo, could not be moved to join them.

Sacerdote

Da qual pensiero,

O da qual fera opinione indotto   75

Fu il tuo padre a negar dimanda onesta?

Licori

Di questo sol (come n'intesi poi)

Fu la cagion, ch'avendo già contratto

Con Tirsi il padre mio lunga amicizia,

Là dov'inonda il Tebro (ancor che stesse   80

L'un da l'altro lontan per molte miglia)

Aveva intenzion (come poi disse)

Di darmi in matrimonio ad'un suo figlio

Dianzi pur nato allora

Quanda a l'età fossimo stati giunti   85

Ch'atti ci rende al marital legame.

Ma non molto dopo questo pastore,

Tirsi, quel dì solenne che nel tempio

Colà sopra del monte Pan s'onora,

Trovò il mio padre, e lagrimando forte   90

Così gli disse: "il ciel, Melampo, (lasso)

Troppo crudel mi è stato, il caro figlio/[5r]

Di tutte le mie dolci, alte speranze

Sola e cara cagione (ahi rimembranze)

D'altro duol m'ha lasciato eterna preda."   95

Più volea dir, ma da singhiozzi tronche

E interrotte le voci, qui si tacque.

Né potè il padre mio cercar più inanti

Questo fatto, ch'a pena per risposta

E per saluto in un "mi duole," e "a dio,"   100

Le potè dir, che i sacerdoti allora

Le lor preci moveano a' sacri altari,

E umile (intenti a sacrificî) ogn'uno

Tacito intanto, e riverente stava.

E fra la turba de' pastori al fine   105

Sì di vista smarillo, che per quanto

Ei lo cercasse, più trovar nol seppe.

Né in molto tempo ancor novella alcuna

N'ha avuta mai, che da disturbi oppresso,

E or da gli anni, a' Baccanali giochi   110

Damone

What doubt or trepidation could have led him to refuse so honest a proposal?

Licori

This alone (as I later learned) was the reason. My father had long before this time contracted a friendship with Tirsi, when both dwelled by the flowing Tiber, although many miles now separated them. And to honor this friendship, he had resolved to give me in marriage to a son of that shepherd's, who was born just before me, when once we had reached a marriageable age. But not long afterwards, on that solemn day when the rites of Pan are celebrated there in the temple that stands on the mount,[34] Tirsi sought out my father and, weeping bitterly, addressed this speech to him: "Alas! The heavens, Melampo, have dealt too cruelly with me. For my son, sole and sweet object of all my dearest hopes—how cruel the remembrance!—has left me eternal prey to deep sorrow." He would have spoken on, but that his voice was choked by sobs, and he fell silent. Nor could my father discover more of the event; indeed, he could barely even reply to Tirsi's words more than to say "It grieves me" and "God be with you," as the priests were already turning to address their prayers to the sacred altars, and all stood in silent reverence and humility, intent on the ritual at hand. And then, amidst the throng of shepherds, Tirsi was lost to his sight, and he could no longer find him, search for him as he might. And at no point since has he been able to learn anything of the fate of his lost friend, for his troubles and now his advancing years have prevented him from frequenting, as he once did, the games of Bacchus

Più non si trova o 'l dì solenne al tempio,
Qual già solea, fra gli altri.
Ché ne la molta turba de' pastori
Che si trovano insieme, a l'ora forse
Stato sarebbe alcun da quelle parti   115
Ch'avrebbe il caso a lui riferto a pieno.
Ma pur di tal successo il ciel lodato!
Non avrà il padre mio cagion di dire
D'amorevole padre ingrata figlia,
Sì come senza dubbio avuto avrebbe   120
Allor ch'al figlio de l'amico Tirsi
Voluto avesse in matrimonio unirmi.

[5v] *Damone Sacerdote*

Succederà di te ciò che disposto
In cielo avran gli Dei, s'empio volere
Non s'oppone al già ordito   125
Tuo nodo su ne la divina mente.

Licori

Forza dunque mortal può contra il cielo?

Damone Sacerdote

Sì, mentre ch'altri irrita
Con le sue colpe la bontate eterna,
E ella allor sospende   130
Sua giusta mano a l'uomo sopra, e'l lascia
Nel libero voler suo gir rotando
Tra precipizî avolto.

Licori

Altro non vo saperne.
Nacqui d'Amor nemica, e ne' primi anni   135
Più teneri con Flori e Amaranta
Sacrai miei giorni a la gelata Dea.
Tal d'Imeneo l'aspro legame io fuggo.

Flori

Oimè, qual miro nel mio danno intento
Lungo giro d'affanni. Ahi cara Morte!   140

and the feast-days at the temple, where, among the great crowds of shepherds who attend, he might have encountered some man from those parts who could have told him what had chanced.

But yet may the heavens be praised that this mysterious event occurred! For in this way my father will have no cause to call himself the loving father of an ingrate daughter—as he would have, for sure, had he attempted to unite me in marriage to the son of his friend Tirsi.

Damone

Your fate will be that which the gods in heaven have ordained for you, unless it be that the knot that has been tied for you in the divine mind is loosed by some malign will.

Licori

Can then mortal will prevail against the heavens?[35]

Damone

Yes, when divine goodness is goaded by men's sins. For then the just hand He wields over us is suspended, and we are left to career between the chasms that surround us, propelled by our free will.

Licori

Tell me no more. I was born an enemy to love, and in my earliest years with Flori and Amaranta I pledged my days to the icy goddess; thus I flee the harsh bonds of Hymen.[36]

Flori

Alas! What great horde of troubles is this, all conspiring to my doom? Ah, sweetest death!

Damone Sacerdote

Meschina, odi, vaneggia. Vo' affrettarmi
Per risanarla. A dio Licori.

Licori

                      A dio.

Non so qual vada intorno
Serpendo al cor buon pezzo fa, d'ardore
Novello incendio, in ùn dolce e amaro.   145
Sarà (sì com'io spero)
Prodigio lieto forse
Del sacrificio ch'oggi far si deve?
Mira come mi balza il sovra ciglio
De l'occhio destro. Di Montano soviemmi,   150
Che non suol ragionar indarno mai,
Che m'ha detto più volte/[6r]
Che tal segno rapporta o bone nove
O cara vista di persona amata.
Segua che piace al ciel. Qui vo' posarmi.   155
In oriente fiammegiando sorge
Pur or vezzosa e lieta la bell'Alba.

SCENA TERZA

Serrano, Androgeo

Serrano

Dal tuo grave dolore, Androgeo, impetra   1
Omai poco di pace, e qui tra l'erbe
L'infelici tue membra posa alquanto.
Forse dal lungo pianto afflitti gli occhi
Preda del sonno al sibilar faranti   5
Di queste lievi frondi, e al susurro
Di zefiro soave che contende
Con l'armonia di mille dolci augelli.
Anch'io starommi teco. La bell'Alba
Sparge a pena del sol l'aurata soglia   10
Di matutine rose, verrà intanto
Fronimo o 'l sacerdote, e a qual'ora
Si faccia il sacrificio intenderemo.

Damone

> Poor wretch! Do you hear? She is raving. I must hasten to cure her. Licori, farewell!

Licori

> Farewell! What can this be that has been creeping into my heart as we spoke—some new ardor, sweet, at once, and bitter? Can it be (as I hope, indeed) a happy presage of today's sacrifice? Strange! I feel some twitching in my right brow. I remember Montano, whose words are never idle, telling me that this sign betokens either good news or the welcome sight of a loved one. But let the heavens decree what they will. I must rest, for in the east the sprightly dawn is rising, trailing clouds of fire.

SCENE THREE

Serrano, Androgeo

Serrano

> Androgeo, seek now some brief solace from your great woe, and here in this glade rest your unhappy limbs. Perhaps your eyes, weary with long weeping, will here fall prey to sleep, bidden by the rustling of these light leaves and the whispering of spring breezes, which vie with the harmonies of the sweet birds' song. I will stay with you. For lovely dawn has yet but barely sprinkled with her morning roses the Sun's golden threshold; soon Fronimo will be here, or the priest, and we will learn at what time to expect the sacrifice.

Androgeo

    Son privo d'alma, senza cor, né ho vita.
    O Morte, o ninfa, o cielo!   15
    Selve correte, campi non vedete
    Voi chi m'uccide? Ah ninfa,
    O cielo piglia l'arme!

Serrano

    O quanto è grande la tua forza, Amore!
    Come l'esperienza a me dimostra/[6v]   20
    Nel miserabil caso di costui.
    Che quanto ei privo de la dolce vista
    De la sua ninfa resta, anco de l'alma
    Privo resta e di senno, né di bocca
    Altro mai se le cava, se non "Flori,   25
    Son privo d'alma," e mille altre sciochezze.
    A l'amata presenza poi ritorna
    Quel ch'era pria, sì saggio e grazioso
    Ch'al suono, al canto, a' suoi consigli trasse
    Molte miglia lontan pastori e ninfe   30
    Per udirlo e vederlo, mille lodi
    Rapportando da ogn'un ne' suoi verd'anni.
    Sette volte nel ciel girata è omai
    La sorella del sol, da che per Flori,
    Misero pazzo, da te stesso in bando   35
    Vai noioso agli amici, e in odio penso
    Fino del ciel, né qui d'intorno è sterpo,
    Tronco o sasso che molle dal tuo pianto
    Non sia tornato mille volte, dove
    La più parte del tempo tra quest'erbe   40
    Corcato piangi e gridi.
    Ahi caro amico in quale
    Stato (lasso) or ti veggio?

Androgeo

I am without a soul; I have no heart; I have no life. O death, O nymph,
O heavens! Run, you woods! Meadows, do you not see who is killing me?
Ah, nymph! Oh! heavens, take up your arms!

Serrano

How great, Love, is your power! Who could doubt it who sees this man's
pitiful case? For, whenever he is deprived of the sweet sight of his nymph,
his soul and wits abandon him, and from his mouth issues naught but this
"Flori, I am without a soul!" and a stream of other nonsense. But in her
beloved presence he returns to what he once was, so sage and courteous
that with his sweet words and music and his wise counsels he drew shepherds and nymphs from many miles around to hear and see him, winning
great praise from all who knew him, even in his tenderest years! Seven
times now has the Sun's sister[37] rotated in her heaven since you became
a wretched madman, an exile from yourself, a burden to your friends—
hateful, as I think, even to the gods. Nor in all these woods is found a
single branch, a single trunk or stone, which has not been drowned in
tears by you a thousand times, for you delight to pass the greater part
of your days here, lying in this fair glade, weeping and moaning. Dear
friend! Alas, in what state do I see you?

SCENA QUARTA

Melampo Vecchio, Serrano, Androgeo

Melampo

Non può l'uom ricordar memoria grata   1
In doloroso stato (quanto voglia
Sia pur virile, e saggio)/[7r]
E non sentir al cor mill'aspre punte.
Qui s'io non erro molte gioie io ebbi   5
Ne la mia gioventù con Tirsi, al tempo
Che venivamo ad onorar de' boschi
Il riverito Dio. Vecchio, e spogliato
Di molte spemi, solo, or qui mi trovo.
Ah tempo, tempo,   10
De l'uom fiero nemico, invida sorte,
Di perturbar mai sempre
Vaga gli altrui contenti,
Com'a l'instabil tuo voler soggiace
Il corso uman, che senza ordine o legge   15
Travolvi e giri a tuo piacer crudele?
(Lasso) che'l pianto a pena frenar posso,
Lo stato de' mortali or discorrendo.

Serrano

Melampo io ti saluto. Forse vieni
Sì di buon'ora al sacrificio nostro?   20

Melampo

Serrano, figlio caro, il ben trovato.
Benché debole il piè questa mia salma
Grave da gli anni a pena portar possa,
Pur vengo ad onorar così degn'opra.
Misero Androgeo, ancora   25
Di lui non m'era accorto. O quante volte
La mia figlia Licori
Rammentando il tuo amor verso costui
(Che pur non esser tuo fratel m'afferma)
Mi pose dentro al core   30

SCENE FOUR

The aged Melampo, Serrano, Androgeo

Melampo

No man, however so wise and strong, can remember past happiness in times of misery without a thousand sharp blades stabbing at his heart.[38] This, if I recall right, is the site of many a pleasant hour that I spent in my youth with Tirsi, when we would come here to worship the revered god of these woods; and now I find myself here once more, a poor old man, alone and stripped of my greatest hopes. Ah, time, fiercest enemy of man! And you, cruel fate, ever eager to devastate our joys! How is it that our human course of life should lie subject to your unstable whims, dancing without sense or scheme at the dictates of your cruel will? Alas! I can barely restrain my tears, thinking thus on our mortal state.

Serrano

Melampo, greetings! Are you come here so early in the day perhaps to attend our sacrifice?

Melampo

Well met, Serrano, dearest boy! Though these aged feet are weary, and I can barely drag along this poor body, weighted with the years, yet still I have come to honor so worthy an endeavor. Wretched Androgeo! I had not remarked him there. Oh, how often has my daughter Licori recalled your love for this poor shepherd, who I hear is not even truly your brother. What she has told me has left me eager to know more.

    Gran desiderio di saper s'è vero
    Ch'ei viva sconosciuto.

Serrano
              Troppo è vero./[7v]
    Ma benché sconosciuto, egli ne viva
    Forestier qui tra noi, che'l padre mio
    Già diciott'anni fa trovollo avolto   35
    In ricchi panni entro a solinga piaggia
    Ove scorrea talor rapace stuolo
    Di passaggeri infidi;
    È tanto nondimen da ogn'uno amato
    Ch'altro pastor di lui più non fu mai.   40
    Il mio buon genitor per figlio l'ebbe,
    Gelinda e io come fratel l'amiamo.

Melampo
    L'età quasi conforme esser dovea,
    E UGUAL[3] età produce amor sovente.

Serrano
    Era egli piccioletto, né cred'io   45
    Ch'a un anno fosse giunto, com'ha detto
    Più volte il padre mio pria che morisse,
    Ne l'avanzava io d'un mese a pena
    Allor che fu trovato. Nè più mai
    Fu chi un sol giorno scompagnati ancora   50
    L'uno da l'altro ne vedesse insino
    Che fu morto il mio padre, anzi commune,
    Se commune anco seco io tengo il resto.
    Allor la cura a lui lasciai del gregge
    E d'ogn'altra mia cosa seco sempre,   55
    Le mie voglie partendo e ogni pensiero,
    (Lasso) e mi duol che dal mio buon volere
    Nacque la sua ruina.

Melampo
              Raro pure
    NASCE da buon pensier cattivo effetto.
    Qual fu questa ruina?

Is it true that his parentage is unknown?

Serrano

All too true, alas! But although he lives here in our midst as a stranger—
for some eighteen years ago, my father found him, richly swaddled, lying on a bleak plain oft traversed by rapacious and treacherous passing
gangs—yet is he loved by all here more dearly than any other shepherd.
My father always regarded him as a son, and Gelinda and I love him as a
brother.

Melampo

You must be near alike in age, and such equality often fosters love.

Serrano

He was no more than an infant (not yet a year old, as my father often
told me before his death) and I was almost the same age at the time when
he was found. And from that time, we did not spend so much as a day
outside one another's company, until the time of my father's death. *Our*
father, I should rather say—and, just as we had a common father, so I
hold all else in common with him, for, on our father's death, I entrusted
to his charge our flocks and all my other goods, and shared with him my
every desire and care. Alas! It pains me cruelly that from this love of mine
there sprang his ruin.

Melampo

Strange that from such a good motive such ill effects should derive! But
what was this ruin of which you speak?

Serrano

Ei ben sovente/[8r]   60
Si ritrovò con Fronimo, di Flori
Fratello, insieme a le campagne, ai paschi,
E de la dolce vista anco di lei
Potea goder ben spesso, onde s'accese
Di troppo caldo e smisurato affetto.   65

Melampo

Dunque Amor fu la sua ruina?

Serrano

A punto.
AMOR che d'ogni mal solo è cagione,
Misero, a tal l'indusse.

Melampo

Anzi ch'AMORE
Ogni pace ogni bene al mondo apporta.
Segui; non gradì Flori questo affetto?   70

Serrano

Ella solo attendendo a' canti, a' suoni,
Il vano stuol seguìa con l'altre ninfe
De la gelata Dea, nulla curando
De l'affetto d'Androgeo; sorda e cieca
Al suo pianto, a suoi preghi, ancor che seco   75
Ragionasse talor semplicemente.
Ma le parole egli stimando dolce
E cara ricompensa al suo languire
Sperava, amava, e la servìa tacendo;
De l'armonia, e del lume   80
Degli occhi, e de la voce
Cibando l'alma aventuroso a pieno.
Or ch'ella lo disprezza e fugge, in pianto
Stando mai sempre immersa per la morte
De la ninfa Amaranta sua compagna,   85
Ei si distrugge e pere, poco avendo
Di vita omai, s'oggi non impetriamo
Grazia nel sacrificio che per lui

Serrano

As he pastured our flocks, he was wont to meet in the fields with Fronimo, Flori's brother, and often, too, would feast his eyes on the sweet sight of the sister. And in this way there was kindled in him an ardor all too fierce and excessive.

Melampo

So Love was his ruin?

Serrano

It was indeed. Love, the cause of all ills, was what brought the poor wretch to this pass.

Melampo

Nay, rather the source of all peace and good in this world! But continue. Did Flori not look kindly on this love?

Serrano

She, caring only for song and music, followed with the other nymphs in the idle train of the icy goddess, and Androgeo's love was nothing to her; deaf and blind she proved to his tears and pleas. Sometimes she would deign to speak with him, meaning nothing by it, but he, deeming her words a sweet and precious recompense for his pining, was silently filled with hope as he loved and served her, his happy soul drinking in her sweet harmonies, the light of her eyes, and her voice. And now she spurns him and evades his sight, plunged into a grief beyond measure at the death of her companion Amaranta; and he wastes away and perishes. Little of life can remain to him now if our prayers cannot win some grace for him at the sacrifice that is to be performed for him—

Far si deve, e per Flori ch'ambi vanno/[8v]
Per disugual cagione errando pazzi.   90

Melampo
Con gli Dei nostri, unito Amor insieme,
Se fu cagione di duol, fia ch'oggi apporti
Forse altrettanta in ricompensa gioia.
L'ordine posto a intender vado, a dio.

Serrano
Dentro dal cor fin da principio, anch'io   95
Che questa Flori vidi al tempio santo
Di Pale nostra Dea, con l'altre ninfe,
Calde brame portai d'esserle grato;
Onde sovente qui d'intorno vengo
E fingo trattenermi con Licori,   100
Ninfa assai graziosa; ma diverso
È il cor dal viso ch'io le mostro. In somma
Il pensar che sarebbon tratte al vento
Le mie parole, e ogn'opra con costei,
Ch'a vano amor con questa ninfa morta   105
Attendeva, sprezzando ogni pastore,
E quel rispetto, ch'a l'amico mio
E mio caro fratel portato ho sempre;
Fin qui le fiamme mie tener m'han fatto
Entro al petto nascose, di me stesso   110
Fidando a pena, or io di novo sento
Ch'amo più che mai fessi.

Androgeo
                    O cielo, o ninfa!
Io non posso giocar; deh quanto, quanto
Sei tu spietata Flori,
A' miei gravi dolori non avendo   115
Pur poca di pietate. O amore, ahi cielo.

Serrano
Come parla, meschino, anco talora
In quest'empie sciagure qual fea saggio.

for him and for Flori, for both are now, though for different causes, equally wandering in their wits.

Melampo

If Love was the cause of this sorrow, perhaps that same Love, joining his forces with those of our gods, may today bring a joy that can compensate all woes. I shall go to inform myself of the arrangements that have been made. Farewell.

Serrano

I too, since the first time I saw this Flori at the holy temple of our goddess Pales[39] along with the other nymphs—I too have been possessed of a warm desire to find my way into her good graces. Hence I come often to this place, feigning to dally with her friend Licori. And a most charming nymph Licori is, though my dalliance with her is mere seeming and does not come from my heart. But I knew that all my words and deeds would be thrown away on Flori, who spurned the advances of all shepherds, infatuated as she was this other nymph, now dead; and I also held back on account of my feelings for this my dearest friend and brother. For these reasons, I have always kept the flames of my passion hidden within my breast, barely entrusting my secret even to myself. But now I feel my love burns more fiercely than ever.

Androgeo

O heavens! O nymph! I can jest and play no longer. Oh, Flori, Flori, what cruelty is yours! Not an ounce of pity, even for my bitterest anguish? O Love! Ah, heavens!

Serrano

Hark how he talks, poor creature! Even in the depths of his anguish, he can sometimes speak as he did when sane.

[*9r*] *Androgeo*

Orsù cielo, non vuoi? Ten ridi Amore?
E tu ninfa, mi sprezzi? Io non ho il core   120
Non ho spirto, o Amor, la ninfa mia.

Serrano

Ecco, torna al suo pianto, al vaneggiare.
Deh Amor, Amor, oimè le finte larve
Di tue dolcezze amare, e che non ponno?
Ma non molto lontan parmi vedere   125
Flori al sepolcro a canto in terra stesa,
L'altra che in piedi or leva esser de' certo
Licori. Andar le voglio incontra, forse
Ella m'avrà veduto; par che voglia
Discorrer seco stessa gravi cose.   130
Forse or di me si pensa. Ah nè sa quanto
E'l mio desir dal suo diverso. Voglio
Qui fermarmi ad udirla, poscia infine
Scoprirommele. Intanto fia che gli occhi
Si compiacciano almeno, benché lungi,   135
Di vista amata e cara.

SCENA QUINTA

Licori, Serrano, Androgeo

Licori

O miseria de l'uomo, in qual si voglia   1
Stato non avien mai ch'egli dir possa
D'esser contento in questa vita un giorno.
Ahi che d'Arcadia le allegrezze tutte
Spariron bene al chiuder de' begli occhi   5
De la casta Amaranta.
Ma sfortunato Androgeo,/[9v]
Che di morte l'error convien che purghi.
Ora qual gioia ha il cor, mentre la lingua
Di questo Androgeo il caro nome esprime?   10
Si compiacquero sempre gli occhi miei
De la sua vista (lo confesso) e anco
Talora m'augurai d'esser io Flori,

Androgeo

Come now, heavens, do you resist? So, Love, do you mock me? And you, nymph, will you spurn me? No heart I have, no spirit. O Love! My nymph!

Serrano

And now, see, he returns to his weeping and his raving. Alas, Love! How great the power of your bitter phantoms of sweet delight! But what is that I see there not far off? It looks to be Flori, lying beside the tomb of her love, and that other nymph now getting to her feet must doubtless be Licori. I must go to speak with her. She may, indeed, have seen me— though she has the air of one pondering grave things. Perhaps she is thinking of me, little knowing how ill-matched are our desires. I shall wait here and listen awhile, before I discover myself. And as I wait, my eyes can at least from far off delight in the vision of her I so love and cherish.

SCENE FIVE

Licori, Serrano, Androgeo

Licori

O wretched mortals! Whatever our state, we cannot be said to be truly happy, not even for a single day. Alas! For all the pleasures of Arcadia fled hence when chaste Amaranta's lovely eyes closed in death. Ah, hapless Androgeo, condemned to pay the price of death's error! . . . But what pleasure my heart feels when my tongue utters that dear name of An- drogeo! I must confess that my eyes ever delighted in his sight. Some- times I have even wished myself in Flori's place, to be loved by so noble

Perché pastor così gentil m'amasse,
Ma non s'estese il mio pensier più inanzi.   15
Ora Amor quali sono queste fiamme
Ch'io sento al cor? Io che di caccie vaga,
Di selve, e di Diana, infastidita
Fin di me stessa, or da più caldo foco,
Da stral più fiero, e da più forte laccio   20
Che pungesse, annodasse, o ardesse mai
Misera, stretta, arsa, e piagata sono.

Serrano

Dal ventilar de le vicine frondi
Perdute assai parole, ho pur nel fine
Compreso che d'Amore ella si lagna,   25
E io ne deggio esser cagione. Ah, certo
Ben sarei troppo ingrato e sconoscente
S'io non gratificassi di parole
Almen chi tanto m'ama, io vo' scorprimi.
Buondì Licori, ove sì sola vai   30
Facendo copia a queste dure pietre
E insensibil arbori di tanta
E sì fatta beltà, di cui, da l'ora
Che queste luci mie restar digiune,
(Lasso) mi vo struggendo in mille guise.   35

Licori

Ben trovato Serrano. Se di questa
Mia beltà che tu di' giudici avranno/[10r]
Ad esser queste piante e questi sassi,
Cosa a udir non avrò già che mi spiaccia,
Quindi è che volentier seco dimoro.   40
Ma tu perché ti struggi se lontano
Qual vicino, e non men che fratel t'amo?
E chi non deve poi
Di grazia amarti, se d'Arcadia tutta
Più d'altro sei gentil, modesto e saggio?   45
Se di mia vista gli occhi tuoi non pasci,
Qual'ella sia, come bramar sì fingi,
È perché sai che nel fallace mondo
Esser non possiam mai felici a pieno.

a shepherd—though further than that point my thoughts did not proceed. But now, Love, what are these flames I feel at my heart? I who was ever devoted to the hunt, the woods, Diana, and chary of all ties—now, poor wretch, by a fiercer fire, a sharper arrow, a stronger noose than ever wounded, bound, or blazed, I find myself chained, burnt, and pierced quite through.[40]

Serrano

Although the rustling of these leaves has robbed me of many of her words, it is clear to me from what last she said that she is complaining of love. And I must be the cause! Ah, but I cannot be so boorish and ungrateful as not to offer some solace, at least with words, to one who so dearly loves me. Let me reveal myself. *[to Licori]*[41] Licori, well met! Where are you bound, all alone? Will you lavish your peerless beauty on these hard stones and insensible trees, when I have been pining in anguish since the moment I was deprived of your sight?

Licori

Serrano, greetings! If the sole witnesses to the beauty you attribute to me are indeed to be these dumb trees and plants, then at least I shall not be troubled with unwelcome compliments. That is one reason why I so enjoy their company. But why all this pining, when you know that I love you as a brother, whether you are far from me or near? And, indeed, who could fail to love you—the most noble, modest, and mannerly of all the shepherds of Arcadia? If you cannot feast your eyes on the sight of me— for what it is worth!—as you so claim to desire, it is because in this treacherous world of ours our desires are never satisfied.

Ciò che non voremmo, abbiam davante;   50
Ma quanto il nostro cor brama, di rado
Vien che gli occhi lo godano; e di questo
Ben io posso far fede.

Serrano
                    Ahi dunque, lasso,
Più non m'ami Licori? E son venuto
De gli occhi tuoi sì tosto a schivo?   55

Licori
Non intendo così, voleva dire
Che le cose del mondo insomma tutte
Sono⁴ fallaci e brevi, e che'l disio
De l'uomo s'assomiglia a la vaghezza
Di ben debole fior. Non hai, Serrano,   60
Cagion di dubitar già ch'io non ami.
Amo, e amo pur troppo, ah non amassi!
Pur Dio volesse, e così amata fossi
Da chi non m'ama amando chi non l'ama.

Serrano
Non intendo Licori il tuo parlare.   65
So ben che t'amo; io amo tanto ch'io/[10v]
Scordo me stesso⁵, e ogn'altra cosa cara.
Ma dimmi: come Flori impetra tanto
Di tregua al suo dolore, al vano pianto?

Licori
Vano a punto ben dici. La meschina   70
O nel sonno o nel duol sta così immersa
Fa buona pezza là tra l'erbe stesa
Non è qui intorno penso arbore o sasso
Che non si svella e franga per pietate;
Qua per tempo venimmo, e'l sacerdote   75
M'ha detto che nel fin del sacrificio
Ella tornerà saggia e del pastore
Primiero che vedrà farassi amante.
O sommi eterni Dei
Aspirate a costei   80

What we would not see is ever before us, while our eyes can rarely delight in what our heart longs for. How well I know this!

Serrano

Ah then, alas! you no longer love me, Licori? Have I so soon become distasteful to your lovely eyes?

Licori

That was not what I meant. All I intended to say was that, ultimately, the things of this world are nothing but passing illusions, and man's desires no more than the fragile beauty of a flower in bloom. Serrano, you need have no fear that I am not a prey to love. I love all too dearly. Would that I did not! Unless God willed that I should be loved by him who loves me not, and who in turn loves one who loves *him* not.

Serrano

Licori, I do not understand your speech, but I do well know that I love you, and my love is such that I forget myself and all else dear to me. But tell me: How is it that Flori appears to have found such peace from her suffering and vain tears?

Licori

Vain indeed! The poor creature is quite immersed in sleep or sorrow; for some time now she has been couched there in the grass. But I think there is not a tree for miles around that has not been wrenched from its roots by pity for her, or a stone that has not been shattered to its core. We came here before dawn, and the priest told me that with the sacrifice she will regain her wits, and will fall in love with the first shepherd who meets her gaze.[42] O eternal gods on high, breathe your grace into her,

Sí che omai sieno sgombre
Le tante orribil' ombre
Che l'alma d'Amaranta ancora vaga
Che la compagna sua l'ami d'intorno
Le va pingendo e ben sovente a lei   85
Scoprir si de' tal con sembiante adorno
L'alletta, strugge, e sol di pianto appaga.

Serrano

Io ben sapea del sacrificio, ch'anco
Si farà per Androgeo,
Ma de l'oracol l'ultima risposta   90
Già non aveva inteso; anco Melampo
Il vecchio padre tuo poc'ora è giunto.

Licori

Ben n'ho piacere.

Serrano

                    Io vado
Perché invitati sien molti pastori,
Onde fra tanti un sì felice sia/[11r]   95
Che con la vista sua risani Flori
Beando sè, deh fosse Androgeo questi.

Licori

Molti pastori stranieri quinci intorno
Dei più nobili e giovani d'Arcadia
Invitati già sono, anzi per darti   100
Carico di condurli insieme uniti
Ieri fosti cercato lungamente.
Io di guidar le ninfe avrò la cura.
Ma forse Androgeo è quegli che là veggio
Meschin, tra l'erbe steso, al ciel rivolto?   105

Serrano

Egli è; Licori a dio.

Licori

Io non vedeva l'ora che costui

that she may be freed from those ghastly phantoms that Amaranta's soul
yet conjures all around her, still intent on ensnaring her companion's
heart even after her death. For often the dead nymph must appear to her,
and in so lovely a guise that she is drawn to the image and yearns for it
with a longing that only her tears can assuage.

Serrano

I had heard tell of the sacrifice, which has been ordained for Androgeo,
as well as Flori, but this last response of the oracle is new to me. Your aged
father Melampo, too, is come; he arrived here but a short time since.

Licori

I am pleased to hear it.

Serrano

I must leave. I have to ensure that many shepherds are invited to the sacrifice, so that one may be so fortunate as to catch the eye of Flori, curing
her and at the same time securing his own happiness. Would that Androgeo were that one!

Licori

Many shepherds have already been invited here from all around—some
of the noblest youths of Arcadia. Indeed, yesterday you were sought far
and wide to accompany these strangers hither in a party. I have been
charged similarly to act as escort to the nymphs. But is that Androgeo
whom I see there stretched out on the grass, poor creature, staring up at
the heavens?

Serrano

It is indeed. Licori, farewell!

Licori

At last he is gone!

Mi si fossi dinanzi a gli occhi tolto.
M'è venuto sì a noia che non posso
Più rimirarlo a pena; grande certo   110
È il mutamento mio. Pur poco dianzi
Gli faceva buon viso, e volontieri
Seco talor mi trattenevo, essendo
Tutto accorto, piacevole e modesto,
E mostra assai d'amarmi; sì perché anco   115
Ben spesso fatto mi venìa, che seco
Potea veder Androgeo, al quale ho sempre
Calda inclinazione avuta, ancora
Ch'ella sia stata al petto entro nascosa,
Parendo a me che di seguire avea   120
Solo desio le sagge e caste voglie
Di Cinzia, che l'amare, e amar pastore,
E pastor sconosciuto a me non fosse
Convenevole cosa. Or non so, come
Tutta son esca, e zolfo, il core è un foco;/[11v]   125
Si strugge l'alma per desio soverchio
Di poterlo veder. Ma ecco a punto
Qual bella occasione (Amor lodato)
Avrò di poter seco oggi scoprire
Queste mie nove passioni, essendo   130
Solo rimaso. Oimè, ma non so forse
Poi ch'ogni detto sarà vano? Essendo
Egli fuor di se stesso, mentre lunge
Da la crudel sua Flori si ritrova,
D'ogni buon sentimento intanto privo   135
Restando? Pur voglio tentar mia sorte.
Androgeo, Dio ti salvi! Qual tua stella
Quivi ti tien da' tuoi compagni cari
Disgiunto, in vista sì pensoso, e fino
Da te medesmo astratto, osservatore   140
Poco lieto del ciel ch'attento miri?

Androgeo
Io non posso cantar, son privo d'alma
Senza cor, senza vita.
Non mi pregar più ninfa.
Cantate voi pastori, e tu ciel canta.   145

He has become such an unwelcome presence to me that I can scarcely bear the sight of him. I am strangely changed in my feelings for him. Only a little while ago, I looked kindly on him, and would happily dally in his company, for certainly, he is a wise, mannerly, and modest youth, and to all appearances quite in love with me. Besides which, seeing Serrano was often a means to see Androgeo, for whom I have always nursed warm feelings, though I would never own them, for it seemed to me that, having pledged to follow the chaste and seemly rules of Cynthia, it was not for me to love—and still less to love a shepherd, and a shepherd of unknown descent! But now—I know not how—I suddenly find myself all ablaze! My heart is on fire, and my soul consumed with an overwhelming desire to see him. And now, through Love's good graces, I find myself furnished with the perfect opportunity to reveal this new passion of mine to its object, for he is here, alone. But, alas! my words will all be in vain, for when he is out of sight of cruel Flori, he is out of his wits and quite deprived of reason. Yet I shall venture my luck. *[To Androgeo]* Androgeo, greetings! What baleful star keeps you here, an unhappy watcher of the heavens, far from your dear companions, and seemingly so wrapped in care as to be oblivious even of yourself?

Androgeo

I can sing no longer. I have lost my soul, my heart, my life . . . Plead no more, nymph! Let the shepherds sing, and the heavens!

Deh non vedete chi m'uccide, o ninfa
O ninfa, o selve, o cielo!

Licori

Quanta per lui pietà m'affligge l'alma.
Ah ben diss'io, che non trarrei risposta
Conforme a la richiesta. Egli si strugge,   150
Misero, e si consuma,[6] più che mai
De sensi privo; deh foss'io pur quella
Che sanar lo potessi, che sì cruda
Già non sarei qual la mia cruda e troppo
Semplice, e ingannata, amica Flori./[12r]   155
O quanto è male, che un pastor sì degno
In sì florida età debba morirsi
Senza rimedio. Deh mal aggia quegli
Ch'introdusse giamai tra queste selve
Questi fra ninfe vani amori e ciancie.   160
Deh Amore al cocodril ben simil sei
Che fuggi chi ti segue, a chi correndo
Da te s'invola impiumi l'ali e'l segui.
Ma poiché dal mio Androgeo non m'aviene
Di poter pur sperare un guardo solo,   165
Che'l terrei guiderdon di tanto affetto,
Son risoluta almen poich'or son sola
Quivi restata di baciarlo, e poi
D'averlomi sognato fingerommi;
E sarà così a punto s'egli è uscito   170
Di se medesmo e non c'è alcun che vegga
Quanto vo' far. Forse averrà ch'in queste
Belle e soavi labra il miele[7] io colga
Di mischiar con l'amaro che m'attosca.
O me beata s'egli avien ch'io possa   175
Dei miei spirti fugaci un sol raccorre,
O breve stilla de l'algente ghiaccio
Sugger, di ch'egli ha'l cor formato e l'alma
Contra ogn'altra che Flori, da temprare
Quel sì cocente ardor che'l cor mi strugge.   180
Cari amati rubini
Elette perle ond'io
Solo appagar potrei l'alto disio,

Do you not see who is killing me? O nymph! O nymph! O woods! O heavens!

Licori

Oh, how piteous a case! Well did I know that I would receive no answer relating to my question. Poor soul, he is quite consumed with longing, and more bereft of reason than he ever was. Oh, would that I were she who has the power to cure him! I would not be so cruel as is my cruel friend Flori—cruel and yet innocent, all too innocent, and sadly deceived! O what an evil, that so worthy a shepherd can be dying in the flower of his youth, without remedy! A curse be on Him who introduced these vain loves and follies here among these glades, where we nymphs wander! Love! You are indeed like a false crocodile! Ever do you flee those who seek you, but when you see one who tries to evade you, then do you unfurl your wings and give chase! But since it seems that I cannot hope for the merest glance from my dearest Androgeo—so little do I ask as a return for my great love!—I am resolved at least to profit from having found myself here alone with him to steal one kiss. And then I shall pretend that I have dreamed it—and it shall be, indeed, as though it were no more than a dream, for he is quite unaware of what is passing before him, and there is no one here as a witness. Perhaps on those fair lips, I shall cull sweet honey to mingle with the bitter venoms that are poisoning me. How blessed I shall consider myself if I can retrieve from those lips but one of the vital spirits that have flown me, or suck one brief drop of water from that searing ice that seals his heart and soul against all but Flori, to temper with its moisture the burning flames that are consuming my heart! Sweetest beloved rubies and choicest pearls, which alone can quench my fierce desire!

Siepe amorosa oimè d'acuti spini
Com'avida contende ogni ben mio/[12v]   185
Mentre vi afiso il guardo,
Di fuori impalidisco, e dentro io ardo.
Beatissima me, non punto invidio
(Sacra Diana) i tuoi piaceri quando
Nel Monte Latmio in Caria ti godesti   190
Del tuo vago fanciullo addormentato.
Ma deh lassa, che faccio? Oimè non veggo
Che de l'onestà mia le leggi offendo?
S'alcun ben non mi vede o può saperlo,
Non mi vedrà quest'aria e questo cielo?   195
E non lo saprò io? Ah non fia mai.
Sprezza Licori ardita quel pensiero
Che di cieco desir t'accende e tenta,
Indegno, d'appagar la parte umana.
Dunque esser ebra sì dovrò che poco   200
Prezzi d'onesta donna quel tesoro,
Ch'esser le de' più de la vita caro?
Priva del qual nè donna è più, nè viva?
Sgombrin questi pensieri impuri, e vili.
Tu Amor lacera il core, affliggi l'alma,   215
Che travagliata, consumata, e morta
Prima, crudel, m'avrai che d'atto pure
Men che onesto il mio onor macchi giamai.
Nè tu santa Diana mai chiamarmi
Potrai de le tue leggi oneste e sante   220
Empia profanatrice; anzi ti chieggio
Perdon di questo audace mio pensiero,
E d'aver io vil donna e abietta ninfa
Rimproverato a[8] te, celeste Dea,
Col bello Endimion picciolo scherzo.   225

[13r] *Androgeo*

Misero oimè, di ch'è l'alma mia?
Ov'è il mio cor? dove i miei spirti? E'n quale
Parte, è la vita mia? Ditelo cieli,
Rispondete voi selve, arbori, piante
Quercie, erbe, fior, augelli, pesci, e fere.   230
Io non posso giocare

Thicket of love, whose piercing thorns, alas! stand between me and my heart's longing! Gazing on him, I feel my visage grow pale while within I am all aflame! O most fortunate of women to be able to gaze thus! Sacred Diana, I envy you not those pleasures you enjoyed as you feasted your eyes on Mount Latmos in Caria on your lovely sleeping boy.[43]

But, wretch that I am, what I am doing? How can I thus disregard my honor? What if no mortal eye can ever see me or will ever discover my secret—will it not be known to the air around me and the heavens above? And to myself? Ah, let it never be! Shameless Licori! Spurn that vain thought that is inflaming you with blind desire and dishonestly tempting you to satisfy your earthly senses. Am I so inflamed with passion that I have become careless of that treasure that every honest woman should prize more than life itself? Without which, indeed, she is neither truly alive, nor worthy of the name of woman? Cast aside these impure and base thoughts! And you, Love, tear at my heart as you will and plague my soul—better by far that I should be ravaged, consumed, and slain by your hands than that any act less than honest should ever stain my honor! Nor shall sacred Diana ever have just cause to reproach me as an impious profaner of her honest and revered laws. Rather, Goddess, I ask pardon for the boldness of my thoughts—that I, a humble woman and abject nymph, should have had the temerity to reproach you, a celestial divinity, with your brief dalliance with the fair Endymion!

Androgeo

Oh what ails my soul, wretch that I am? Where is my heart? Where my vital spirits? Where lies my life? Tell me, O heavens! And you, O glades, trees, plants, oaks, grasses, flowers, birds, fishes, beasts of the woods! I can no more compete in shepherd games,

Nè men so più sonare.
Voi pur ridete mari, fiumi, e fonti
Laghi, rivi, e tu ninfa, o cielo, o ninfa.

Licori

Come vaneggia, misero, mai sempre,   235
E le sembra d'udir ch'altri l'invite
A giochi, a suoni, e con le piante, e fere
Forsennato ragiona, ritornando
Infine al cielo e a la sua ninfa ingrata.
Voglio partirmi, trappassando l'ora   240
Che dovea qua venir Fronimo, e pure
Portar vo' meco almen del mio pastore
Gentil questo zendal di seta, ond'egli
Cinger soleva il delicato fianco.
Forse che gioverammi il mirar cosa   245
Da gli occhi e da le man veduta e tocca,
Che m'han repente il cor legato e acceso.
Condurò meco Flori a la capanna;
Intanto il suo dolore, e la mia fiamma
Novella e così ardente   250
Mitigando verrò, se pur Amore
Tanto poter di farlo mi concede.
Flori, non più sospir, dammi la mano
Dolcissima sorella; andiamo, o Flori.

Flori

O Morte, deh Amaranta,/[13v]   255
Vieni, o Morte, e m'uccidi, io non ho vita.
Cielo, Amaranta, Morte!

Licori

Non la finiremo oggi s'io la lascio
Mirar ne l'urna; che sì come Androgeo
Non torna in sè giamai se lei non vede,   260
Così, a l'incontro, s'ella non si leva
Dal rimirar quel marmo ch'in sè chiude
D'Amaranta gentile il casto velo,
Mai da saggia non parla, e mille volte
S'avien che sola resti qua ritorna.   265

nor can I make sweet music. And still you mock me, O seas, rivers, springs, lakes, grassy banks. And you, O heavens! O nymph!

Licori

Poor creature, how he raves! Always hearing himself called to sweet games and music, always conversing madly with the trees and wild creatures of the woods, and drawn back ever to the heavens and his ingrate nymph. I must go, for the hour is now past when Fronimo was to come here. Yet I shall take with me as a token from my lovely shepherd this silken kerchief, with which he is wont to sheathe his sweet flank. Perhaps it will ease my pain to look upon something dwelt on by the eyes and touched by the hand that so swiftly inflamed and imprisoned my heart. I shall take Flori with me to the shepherds' hut, seeking on the way—if Love will permit me such solace—to temper both her pain and, with it, this new and ardent flame of mine. *[To Flori]* Flori, sigh no more! Give me your hand, sweetest sister. Come, Flori.

Flori

O death! Amaranta, come to me, and death, come kill me. I live no more. O heavens, O Amaranta, O death!

Licori

We shall never see the end of this today if I allow her still to gaze on the urn. For if Androgeo is driven from his mind if he does not see her, she, by contrast, can only recover her wits when she is dragged away from the sight of that tomb which encloses the chaste mortal remains of fair Amaranta. And I have seen a thousand times that, whenever she is left alone, she finds her way back here.

Or ecco, vo' levarla di tal vista
E tornerà quanto mai fosse saggia.
Flori sorella, andiamo. O Flori, Flori!
Questi satiri, oimè, questi silvani
Faranci qualche mal. Flori corriamo!   270

SCENA SESTA

Satiro, Flori, Silvano, Androgeo

Satiro

Questa fiata a fè non fuggirai.   1
Corri Silvano piglia, è una,⁹ corri
Non lasciar fuggir l'altra, o questa è mia.

Flori

Dolcissima sorella, anzi signora,
Ov'ora lassa, oimè, ti veggio estinta   5
E fredda in sen d'un aghiacciato marmo.
O Amaranta, o ninfa, o cielo, o morte!

Satiro

Non valerà chiamar la morte, o 'l cielo
Dopo tanto cercar n'ho pur colto una.

Silvano

O male aggian le ninfe, ho tanto corso/[14r]   10
Che posso trarre a pena il fiato: penso
Ch'abbiano l'ali a' piedi poscia ch'elle
Non corrono, ma volano.

Satiro

                    Tuo danno.
Io ci son pur venuto tante volte,
Ch'oggi non fia questo viaggio indarno.   15
Io vo' condurla in qualche antro riposto
Od ombroso cespuglio, e ivi poscia
Goderla a mio bell'agio. O com'è bella!
Io starò ben. Silvano, mi rincresce
Che la tua dapocaggine levato   20

Now I shall take her away from here, and she will at once be restored to her right mind. Flori, dearest sister, let us go. But O Flori! Flori! These satyrs I see, these wild men, will surely do us some harm. Flori, let us run from here!

SCENE SIX

Satyr, Wild Man,[44] *Flori, Androgeo*

Satyr

This time you will not escape, by my faith! Run, comrade! Catch that one! Run! Do not let that other go! Ah, this one is mine!

Flori

My dearest sister—nay, I should say my lady—where, alas! do I now see you lying dead and cold, enclosed in this chill marble! O Amaranta! O nymph! O heavens! O death!

Satyr

Little good will it do you to call on death or the heavens! After all my questing, at last, I have one in my hands!

Wild Man

A curse on these nymphs! I have run so hard I am quite out of breath. They must have wings on their feet. They do not run—they fly!

Satyr

All the worse for you. I have come here so often before: this time, at least, let the journey not be in vain! I want to take her to some hidden cave or shady grove, where I can enjoy her at my leisure. O how lovely she is! I am well set up! Friend, I am sorry that your lack of prowess should have deprived

Oggi t'abbia di man tanta ventura
Di poterti goder quell'altra ninfa.

Silvano

Io non so qual malanno abbiano a' piedi.
Dico c'ho corso più che mai facessi
In vita mia. Ecco che fa la morta.   25
Ma o come è bella, a fè che starem bene.

Satiro

Non vi pensare or suso, io son contento;
Farem come la gatta che scherzato
Buona pezza col topo, alfin se'l mangia.

Silvano

Mi contento, facciamo come tu vuoi.   30
Ma perché sta dogliosa, e semiviva?

Satiro

Non sai forse l'astuzie de le ninfe
D'Arcadia e i vizî loro? Fa la morta
Acciò noi la lasciamo e fuggir possa,
Ma fia scarso il disegno questa volta.   35
Piglia Silvan; levianla in qualche parte
Solinga, che non giunga alcun pastore
Che n'involi la preda e ne dia morte.

Silvano

Alto ninfa! O che vedo? Questa è Flori,
Quella ninfa che va per Amaranta/[14v]   40
Morta sì addolorata; o ch'è ben pazza
Se dietro a morta e femina si strugge.
Or l'ho riconosciuta, è vero, è quella
Ninfa tanto a' pastori ingrata, e fiera
Contra le fere in caccia, da Diana   45
Sì favorita, e che riporta sempre
Di correr, di ferire, al canto, al suono
Tra le ninfe di Arcadia altero vanto;
E ch'anco a noi fa tanti danni e mali.

you of the happy chance of being able to enjoy that other nymph.

Wild Man

Blast them! What is the secret of their speed? Never in my life have I had to run so hard! Ah, this one is playing dead! But, oh, how lovely she is! What a time we will have of it, by my faith!

Satyr

Do not fret yourself. How happy I am! We will make like a cat who, having long played with her mouse, finally gobbles it up.

Wild Man

I am content: just as you please. But why is she so doleful? She seems half-dead.

Satyr

Do you not know of the cunning of these Arcadian nymphs, and their vices? She is playing dead, in the hope that we will leave her, and she may flee. But her little plan will not work this time. Take her, friend; let us carry her off to some lonely place, where no shepherd ever ventures, for else we risk losing our prey and meeting our death.

Wild Man

Come, nymph, on your feet. But what is this that I see? This is Flori, that nymph who is so grieved at Amaranta's death—mad indeed, to so destroy herself in mourning a woman, and a dead one. Yes, it is indeed she—that nymph so ungracious to all shepherds, and so fierce a hunter of beasts! That nymph so favored of Diana, who carries the palm among all her peers in running, hunting, singing, and playing—and the author of countless injuries to us and all our sort.

Oggi pagherà il tutto. Alto Silvano,[10]   50
Voltian di qua, che tornerà in cervello.

Flori

Oimè! cieli, ov'è il core?

Silvano

Chi sarà quel che colà steso a terra
Rimira il ciel? Qualche astrologo infermo?

Satiro

Sostienla ben, che par che si risenta.   55

Flori

Misera, dove sono? Ah traditori,
Di far torto v'è lecito a le ninfe
Dunque di Delia? A questo modo? Lascia,
Làsciami dico! O Cinzia, dammi aita
Contra questi deformi mascalzoni!   60

Androgeo

Fuggitte che v'ammazzo! Ah traditori,
Troppo onorati ladri sete, e troppo
Ricca preda è per voi questa, e gentile.

Silvano

Corriam, che s'ei ci giunge, siamo morti.

Satiro

Ben te'l diss'io ch'eravam troppo lenti.   65

Flori

Pastore, io ti ringrazio de l'avermi
Da così roze mani e sì rapaci
Tratta. Se mai da me si potrà tanto,
M'ingegnerò dartene in qualche parte
La ricompensa, e quando anco pur fia/[15r]   70
Che per me non si possa altro offerirti
Che ricca volontà d'animo grato,
Resta almeno sicuro che Diana

Today she will pay the price for all she has done to us! Come, friend, let us take her from here, for she will come back to her senses. *[They carry her off.]*

Flori

O woe! O heavens, where is my heart?

Wild Man

But who is that youth lying there on the ground and gazing at the heavens? Some infirm astrologer, perhaps?

Satyr

Hold her firmly! She seems to be regaining her senses.

Flori

Alas! Where am I? Ah, traitors! Do you then think you have the right to injure a nymph sacred to Delia?[45] And in this manner? Let me go! Let me go, I say! O Cynthia, lend me your aid against these monstrous knaves!

Androgeo

Away from here, or you are dead! Traitors! Keep to your own! You aim too high in your pillaging; she is too rich and noble a prey for you.

Wild Man

Run! If he catches us, we are dead!

Satyr

I told you we were being too slow! *[They exit.]*

Flori

Shepherd, I thank you for having saved me from the grasp of these creatures, so crude and rapacious. If I am ever in a position to do so, I shall do my utmost to return your services. And if it so happens that I cannot offer you anything but the rich store of goodwill of a grateful heart, then rest assured that Diana

Quest'atto tuo saprà sì generoso,
Qual come Dea cortese mai non suole   75
Merto lasciar andar senza il suo premio.

Androgeo

Ringrazio il ciel leggiadra ninfa e bella,
Anzi regina mia, ch'a tempo giunsi
C'ho potuto esser degno di servirti,
Se dimandar servigio pur si deve   80
L'essermi solo mosso per salute
De la mia vita istessa, del mio core,
De l'alma mia che nel tuo petto vive.

Flori

Che alma? che core? Ah bene
Ora ti riconosco.   85
Perché non m'han più tosto divorata
Questi immodesti satiri, e straziata
Mille rapaci fere, prima ch'io
Mi ti vedessi inanzi? Io ben pensava
Ch'ormai chiarito fossi quanto io poco   90
Curo il tuo amor, quanto ti fuggo, e sprezzo,
E de l'audacia tua fossi pentito.
Rèstati che del mar fien dolci l'acque,
Amaro il mele, senza fiori il maggio,
La terra il ciel di chiare stelle ornata,   95
E coltivato il ciel da roze mani,
Pria che l'affetto tuo pregi, o ch'io t'ami.

Androgeo

Deh vita del cor mio, fermati un poco,
Non fuggur così presto,
Lascia ch'io affisi il guardo ancora un poco/[15v]   100
Negli occhi dolci tuoi, pria che'l disio
Uccida l'alma mia, che sì vien meno.
Ah per Dio non fuggir, non fuggir; resta,
O lascia ch'io ti segua,
Ch'intanto meco avrà forse il duol tregua.   105

Il fine del primo atto

will hear of this noble deed of yours—and that gracious goddess is not wont to let any deserving soul go unrewarded.

Androgeo

I thank the heavens, O fair and gracious nymph—nay, my queen!—that I arrived in time to be able to have the honor of serving you, if I can speak of having served you, when what moved me was the good of my own life, my heart, my soul, which all dwell within your breast.

Flori

What soul, in faith? What heart? Ah, now I recognize you! O, why did those shameless satyrs not rather devour me, or a thousand fierce beasts tear me apart than that I should have to suffer the fate of seeing you before me? I should have thought by now that it would have been quite clear how little I care for this love of yours, and how avidly I flee and scorn you! Why have you not yet repented of your boldness? Be assured that the ocean's waters will be sweet, apples bitter, May flowerless, the earth adorned with stars, and the heavens tilled by rustic hands[46] before I welcome your love or love you in return.

Androgeo

O, life of my heart, stay a while! Do not flee so soon. Let me gaze a little longer into your sweet eyes, before desire kills my fainting soul. O God! Do not flee! O let me follow you, and find a moment's solace from my pain.

End of act one

[16r] ATTO SECONDO

SCENA PRIMA

Licori sola

Licori

QUANTA E' la forza d'un verace affetto.   1
Poco stimando vita, or ne veniva
Scossa la tema dei selvagi mostri
Per dar aita a la mia amica Flori,
Od egual sorte oggi passar con lei.   5
Quando giù la incontrai da questo colle
Fuor di periglio, ma novello affanno
Mi giunse al cor de la sua libertate,
La cagion mi diss'ella, gli umil preghi,
Le parole cortesi, i supplici atti   10
Del suo fedel amante, e insieme anco
L'altera sua risposta.
Ahi crudel ninfa ingrata!
Ingrata Flori, e pazza
Ben più di lui che troppo t'ama, ingrata.   15
Da così belle man foss'io pur stata
Liberata, e da bocca sì soave
Pregata, che già mai tanta ventura
Sprezzata non avrei. MA raro amore/[16v]
D'egual desio colma duo cori amanti,   20
E quando così sia com'è in effetto,
Lassa, che sperar posso? Debbo, e voglio
Procurar di sanar Androgeo e Flori,
E lasciar quel seguir c'ha il ciel disposto.
Il proprio ben di lor vo' che mi mova,   25
Non di me l'interesse; CHE colui

112

ACT TWO

SCENE ONE

Licori alone

Licori

Oh how great is the power of true feeling! He rushed forward, careless of his own safety and casting aside all fear of those savage beasts, determined to save my companion Flori or to suffer the same fate as she. But when I met her just now at the foot of this hill, safe from danger, her account of her salvation was a source of new anguish for me. She recounted all that had occurred—the humble pleas, the courteous words, the supplicating gestures of her faithful lover, and then her haughty response. Ah, cruel, ungrateful nymph! Ungrateful Flori, and mad—far more so than him who loves you too well, ungrateful creature! Oh, would that such fair hands had saved me! That such a sweet mouth should have addressed its prayers to me! I should never have scorned such good fortune! But it is rare that Love chooses to fill two loving hearts with corresponding desires. And, alas, given that this is how things stand with us, what hopes have I? My duty and my sole desire must be to do all I can to cure Androgeo and Flori and to let whatever follow that the heavens decree. I must think only of their good, not my own interest, for no one deserves

Mal del nome d'amico allor si vanta
Ch'altrui servendo al proprio ben sol mira.
Attenderò che'l sacrificio segua,
Da Fronimo intendendo la cagione   30
Del suo tardo venire, al sacerdote
Raccomandando l'uno e l'altro insieme.
Ma ecco Urania. A dio sorella, a dio.
Ove v'andavi sì pensosa in vista?

SCENA SECONDA

Urania, Licori

Urania

A dio Licori. Uscita   1
Da fiera pugna son poc'or avuta
Con una tigre, la cui strana forma
Nel rimembrarla ancor m'empie d'orrore;
E da lei vinta al fin rimanea morta   5
Se da Serrano, che di là passando
La fera uccise al mio periglio, scampo
Non m'era dato. Egli salvommi; ahi lassa,
Ch'anzi m'uccise il core.
Oimè, forse megl'era una sol morte/[17r]   10
Che ad ogn'ora patirne mille, e mille.

Licori

Novo accidente forse,
Urania, ora t'astringe
Di non poter godere
Del degno tuo liberator cotanto   15
Dono ch'è stato il ritornarti viva?
O d'Amor lusinghier l'invitta possa
Le già caste tue brame a cangiar sforza?

Urania

Ah ch'è ben novo l'accidente e strano,
Quando in poc'ora nel perder me stessa   20
Danno mi si fe'l don, morte la vita.
Avvivando la spoglia, uccise il core

the name of friend who seems to serve others while thinking only of his own advantage. I shall await the sacrifice (but what can have delayed Fronimo in coming to inform me of the time for it?), commending these two poor souls in all good faith to the kind offices of the priest. Ah! Here is Urania. Greetings, sister, greetings! Whither were you bound, so enveloped in thought?

SCENE TWO

Urania, Licori

Urania

Greetings, Licori! I have just escaped from a fierce struggle with a tigress, the memory of whose strange form still fills me with terror.[47] And I should certainly have died under the assault had I not been saved by Serrano, who was passing by and killed the beast. He saved my life—but, alas! in doing so, he slew my heart. And maybe a single death would have been better than the thousand deaths I must now endure.

Licori

Have you suffered some strange accident, Urania, which prevents you from enjoying the great gift your worthy savior bestowed on you when he returned you to life? Or are the mighty powers of that sly god Love imprinting a new pattern on your once chaste desires?

Urania

A strange accident indeed is that which has befallen me! In the briefest of spells, as I lost myself, the sweet gift that had been given me turned sour, and life turned to death. Licori, Serrano slew my heart at the same

Serrano; egli, Licori, questa vita
Liberando fe' l'alma prigioniera.

Licori

Come al varcar del tempo, che se'n fugge   25
Di rapid'onda in guisa, de' mortali
Varian l'umane cose.
Costei, poc'anzi serva
Di Delia, ora d'Amore
Soggetta è, sì ch'in nove fiamme il core   30
Par se le strugga. O folle,
FOLLE chi a l'uom prescrive
Fermo desire un giorno,
Ch'ei vago gira a par de l'ore e vola.
Ami dunque Serrano, Urania?

Urania

                          L'amo.   35

Licori

Sarem compagne in egual danza. Or dimmi
Allor dove n'andavi, che tra l'erbe
(Al tuo ben cieca talpa) non scorgesti
Quella rete d'Amor che tanti allaccia?
Non t'ha forse con l'altre/[17v]   40
Filli invitata al sacrificio d'oggi
Che qui per Flori celebrar si deve?

Urania

Da Gelinda, e da Filli già invitata
Venìa per ritrovarmi a l'altre unita
In sì pietoso officio. Ma qual danza   45
È questa ov'ambe a ritrovar n'abbiamo?
Ami forse ancor tu Serrano?

Licori

                       Io l'amo.
Dunque non lo sapevi?

time that he restored my body to life, and, freeing my life, he took my soul prisoner.

Licori

Just as time flees in its passing like a rapid stream, so do the fates of us mortals change from hour to hour. This poor creature, until so recently a votary of Diana, is now a slave to Love and feels strange flames melting her heart within. O what folly it is to predict that any human desire will last so much as a day! Our desires wander at will and flit past with the passing hours. [*To Urania*] So, you love Serrano?

Urania

I do.

Licori

Then we are companions in the same dance![48] Now tell me, Urania, where was it you were going when—blind as a bat to your own best interests!—you stumbled into the trap that Love had set for you and in which He catches so many. Did not Filli invite you along with the other nymphs to the sacrifice which is due to be performed today for Flori?

Urania

I was indeed invited by Gelinda and by Filli, and I was coming to join the other nymphs for this most pious of duties. But what do you say of our being companions in the dance? Do you too love Serrano?

Licori

I do indeed. Did you not know?

Urania
>   Aimè, pur or non lo sapessi ancora.
>   Misera me, qual più conforto resta   50
>   Urania a le tue pene?

Licori
>   Non più sospir; ben l'amo Urania, ed egli
>   Finge d'amarmi, ma dentr'ambi fiamma
>   Disugual (forse) n'arde i cori e l'alme.
>   Quella dogliosa danza in cui fa poco   55
>   Ti dissi che doveamo esser compagne
>   Quella è (se tu nol sai) dond'Amor trae
>   Mille seguaci suoi cattivi, e presi,
>   Miseri, nella quale ogn'uno ardendo
>   Agghiaccia, e in ùn piangendo ride, e gioia   60
>   E duolo a un tempo prova, e tristo e lieto,
>   Tra speranza e timor se stesso leva
>   Talora in cielo, e poi repente abissa.
>   Ma perché l'ora intender cerco quando
>   Dovrò trovarmi al sacrificio, vado   65
>   Fronimo ricercando, onde non posso
>   Ora il mio core a pien scoprirti. Andiamo,
>   Che tra via parlerem; nè temer, ch'io
>   M'adoprerò per te.

Urania
>   Io ti ringrazio
>   Ma se dal cor tanto umor m'hai tolto/[18r]   70
>   E con la tua promessa a pieno resa
>   Contenta, un poco ora ti ferma ancora
>   (Cara Licori) e dimmi, se fu vero
>   Che'l gran Titiro a Flori discoprisse[11]
>   (Quando morta Amaranta ancor non era)   75
>   Un giorno le sue fiamme, e ch'ella altera
>   Negasse di gradire un tanto affetto.

Licori
>   Fu vero, e allor io poco era lontana.

Urania

Would that I were still so happily ignorant! Alas, Urania! What hope can there be for you now?

Licori

Sigh no more, Urania! I do love Serrano and he feigns to love me. But deep within both of us, I suspect, a different love is burning our hearts and souls. That doleful dance in which I said we were to be companions is (as perhaps you know) the dance in which Love leads a thousand victims bound and captive. Poor wretches! As they dance they freeze and burn, and laugh and weep, caught up in joy and misery together, and prey at the same time to hope and fear; one minute they are in the heaven of ecstasy and the next in the abyss of despair. But I am afraid I cannot reveal my heart to you entirely, as I am searching for Fronimo to tell me the precise time I need to be at the sacrifice. Come along with me, and we can speak as we go. And fear not! I am resolved to help you in this.

Urania

Licori, I thank you. Your promise lifts a great fear that was weighing on my heart and reassures me quite. But, dearest Licori, stay a while and tell me if it is true what I hear, that the great Titiro once revealed his love to Flori (before Amaranta had passed from this life) and that she haughtily refused to return the love of this lofty suitor?

Licori

It is indeed true, and I was nearby when it happened.

Urania

In cortesia nàrrami come e dove.

Licori

Il finto ardor del gran Titiro Flori   80
Più volte di sua bocca udito avendo,
Sotto l'ombra d'un faggio un giorno assisa
Seco, così le disse (allor ch'ei pure
Fingea d'ardente brama aver il core
Consunto e l'alma, d'accostar le labra   85
Al seno, a gli occhi, e a la bocca amata):
'Titiro tu sai ben che l'uomo in petto
Più d'un cor già non ha. Se dunque è vero,
Come creder debb'io che m'ami, avendo
Come già mi dicesti, il tuo donato   90
Ad Amarilli, a Fillide, a Licori?
Se'l core è un sol, se una sol cosa data
Già non si deve più pigliar, com'io
Mai crederò che'l tuo languir sia vero?
Se a mille una sol cosa doni e togli,   95
E tolta la ridoni, e poi donata
La ripigli di novo e a mille a un tempo
Involi doni, e ancor donato furi?'
Ed ei rispose: "Flori, io te sola amo.
E se le luci tue ch'arsero il core/[18v]   100
Che in questo petto già serbava, e ch'ora
Vive nel tuo, mirar potesser entro
A questo seno mio,
So che l'imago tua vedrebbon sola
Star, per mano d'Amor nel mezo incisa.   105
Non t'ho (crudel) giurato mille volte
Ch'io t'amo più d'ogn'altra ninfa? Ah cara,
Cara Flori crudel, queste mie voci
Addolorate, il mesto suon ch'or odi
De' miei sospiri ardenti, il grand'affetto,   110
La mia fè di gradire omai ti piaccia."
"Deh quanto" (ella rispose) "mal s'accorda,
Saggio pastor, il tuo parlare a quello
Che sì di farmi creder t'affatichi.
Non sai che POCO parla chi molto ama?   115

Urania

Pray tell me how and where this occurred.

Licori

It was not the first time that Flori had heard from Titiro's own mouth his false confessions of love.[49] They were sitting together one day in the shade of a beech tree, and he was feigning that his heart and soul were consumed with desire for her and that his lips longed to kiss her breast and eyes and mouth, when she said to him:

"Titiro, you know full well that no man's breast harbors more than a single heart. If that is the case, then how can I believe that you love me when you have given your heart—as you yourself have confessed—to Amarilli and to Filli and to Licori? If the heart is a single thing, and that thing, once given, should not be taken back, how, then, can I believe that what you say of your languishing is sincere, when you give your one heart to a thousand nymphs, and then take it back, give it again, and take it back once more, only to give it anew? When you steal your gift back from all thousand of your loves and no sooner give your heart than you snatch it back again?"

"Flori, I love you alone," he replied, "And if the sweet rays of your eyes, which set ablaze this heart of mine (that heart that first lived within my breast but now lives in yours)—if those eyes could look into my inner self, it would see nothing but your own image, etched within by the hand of Love. Oh cruelest of nymphs! Have I not sworn to you a thousand times that I love you more than any other? Ah, sweetest, sweetest cruel Flori, let these doleful tones of mine and the wretched sound of my burning sighs bend your will at last to reward the great love and faith that I bear you."

"Ah!" she replied, "Wise shepherd, how your speech gives the lie to that of which you are seeking to convince me. Do you not know that he who loves much speaks little?

Tu che ragioni assai poco amar devi."
"Ahi Flori" (egli soggiunse) "ardo, e ne gli occhi
Scorgi il foco (ben so) che'l core avampa
In ardente fornace." "Mal si tempra
Fugace e debil fiamma," ella rispose,   120
"GRAND'ardir poco amor dimostra;" e poi,
"CHI può dir com'egli arda è in picciol foco."
"Ahi ninfa, anzi d'Amor nimica, e mia
Ladra gentil" (Titiro disse), "omai
Fa quest'alma felice, le tue labbia   125
Accostando a le mie, sì ch'ella traggia
Dolce ristoro al suo digiun, soave
Ambrosia ond'ella si nodrisca e viva,
Ch'allor sarò beato." Ella sorrise,
E gli additò di certe note inciso/[19r]   130
Un faggio, e disse: "ivi leggendo credi."
E si partì qual già solea vezzosa.

Urania
    E quali eran le note incise poi?

Licori
    Queste: "Più d'altra ninfa,
    Flori scontenta e fida." Di sua mano   135
    Eccone inscritti mill'arbusti intorno.
    A Filli e a Gelinda
    Ieri carico diedi ch'ancor elle
    Con l'invitate ninfe di buon ora
    Fossero al fonte degli abeti, ov'io   140
    Stata sarei con Flori per dir loro
    Ciò che avessimo a far; ma qua venendo
    Di là passai, né v'eran giunte ancora.

Urania
    A l'ombra mi cred'io staranno assise
    Del platano vicino al sacro tempio,   145
    Ove dicean voler fermarsi, e preghi
    E voti offrir ché'l boscareccio Dio
    Benigno arrida ai desir nostri; e poscia,
    Di fiori inghirlandate,

You speak much; I must conclude that you love little."

"Ah, Flori," he said, "I burn for you and I know well that you can see in my eyes how ardently the flames of my love are blazing away, consuming my heart in their fiery furnace."

"A feeble and flickering flame is difficult to temper," she replied. "The bolder the lover, the lesser the love. He who can describe how he burns can only be consumed by the puniest of fires."

"Ah, nymph—or rather, enemy to Love!" Titiro said. "Sweet robber of my soul! Now fill my soul with delight: bring your lips close to mine, so that I may find sweet respite from my long fasting, and my starving soul may be succored and restored to life by the ambrosia of your kiss. Then alone shall I be happy!"

She smiled at this and pointed to some lines inscribed on a nearby beech tree, saying "Read, and believe." Then she vanished as flightily as was her wont.

Urania

And what were these words on the tree?

Licori

These: "Flori, faithful and unhappy above all other nymphs." See! They are written in her own hand on a thousand trees all around.[50] Yesterday, I charged Filli and Gelinda to make their way with the other invited nymphs to the fountain of the fir trees in good time, saying that I would come there with Flori to instruct them on what they needed to do. But I passed the fountain on my way here and did not see them there.

Urania

I imagine they will be gathered in the shade of the plane tree close by the sacred temple, where they said they had arranged to meet to offer prayers and vows to the woodland God, to make him well disposed to our wishes. Then, garlanded with flowers,

Dicean voler fermarsi a pié del monte,   150
Dove con Flori esser dovevi all'alba
E ivi espor de l'opra il modo insieme.

Licori

Ben per questo stupisco che vedendo
La mia nel gire a lor troppa tardanza
Non vengano a cercarne la cagione.   155
Ma l'indugio di Fronimo ogni colpa
N'abbia; or andiam che'l cercheremo, e in tanto
I nostri amor consiglieremo.

Urania

                   Andiamo.

[19v] SCENA TERZA

Serrano solo

Serrano

Ho parlato a Damon, che l'ora quando   1
Il sacrificio far si debba attende
Da Fronimo, ch'ei cerca, e m'ha promesso
Farmi sapere a la capanna il tutto.
Intanto un cane, il mio bastone, e l'arco   5
Diedi a Leggiadro, mio pastore, e dissi
Che dietro al colle al mio tugurio, unito
Entro a un vago pratel riposto unisse
I pastori più giovani d'Arcadia,
Che'l mio fratello Androgeo ritrovato,   10
Saría con lor, dov'ho pensato insino
Al far del sacrifico trattenerli
Con la lotta e col corso, in pregio dando
Lor questi doni che ballando io vinsi.
Non gli ho però scoperto con inganno   15
Operar questo, a fin ch'io sol tra pochi
Mirato sia da Flori, ch'a me stesso
Fin vo celando un così van pensiero.
Ma dove Androgeo ito sarà? Pur quivi
Fa poco lo lasciai tra l'erbe steso.   20

they intended to make their way to the foot of the mountain where you had said you would go with Flori at dawn, so that you could there together resolve what was to be done.

Licori

I am surprised, then, given that I am so late in arriving, that they have not come to seek me, to learn the reason. But it is all due to Fronimo's lateness. Let us now go to seek him, and as we go we can consult about our loves.

Urania

Yes, let us go.

SCENE THREE

Serrano alone

Serrano

I have spoken to Damone, who has gone to find out the time of the sacrifice from Fronimo, and has promised to come back afterwards to the hut to tell me. Meanwhile, I gave a dog, my crook, and my bow to my shepherd Leggiadro and told him to gather together all the youngest shepherds of Arcadia, including my brother Androgeo, in that pretty little meadow that lies behind the hill adjoining my humble abode. There, I told him, he is to keep them until the sacrifice is over, competing in games of strength and speed for the prizes I will give, which I in my turn won in the dance.[51] What I did not tell Leggiadro was that this plan of mine was a trick to ensure that I should have few rivals in catching Flori's eye at the sacrifice—for, to tell the truth, I am reluctant to admit even to myself that I am capable of such a base thought. But where can Androgeo have got to? I left him here but a moment ago, lying on the grass.

Misero, avrà veduta la sua ninfa,
E fatto saggio a l'orme care dietro,
Corso sarà di fera ingorda al fine
Per esser preda; vo' cercarlo e meco
Tenerlo finché 'l sacrificio segua,/[20r]   25
Che ancor che io qualche a la sua Flori inganno
Tenda per conseguirla, del mio core
A paro io l'amo; e se di lei disporre
Le voglie a senno mio potessi, solo
De la crudele egli saría signore.   30
Ma ben è ver che (s'altri esser marito
Le die) che bramo esser io quegli, e quando
Esser non possa, divenir già pazzo
Non voglio, ch'altre ancor ninfe saranno
Che non mi sprezzeran (forse). E pur oggi   35
Una da morte tolsi, e se non meno
Ragionan de la lingua gli occhi e'l viso
(Com'altri par ch'affermino), mi credo
Ch'al suo partir col scintillar soave
De' begli occhi dicesse ne la fronte: 40
"Leggi Serrano il cor; mio dir ti posso
Liberatore, e omicida a un tempo."
Ma di farle risposta allor mi tolse
Il sacerdote là giungendo. Or ecco
Che di qua vien a punto, è forse seco   45
Darello? o erro? A fè ch'egli è. Ma[12] quando,
Quando ciel leverai sì infame mostro
Da l'umano consorzio. Ricoprirlo
Ah perché degni? E tu perch'ampia terra
(Troppo vil peso) il suo mortal sostieni?   50
Voglio ad udir le sue bugie qui starmi
Ascoso dietro un pezzo, o che bel fusto!

[20v] SCENA QUARTA

Damone Sacerdote, Darello, Serrano

Damone Sacerdote
   Io t'ho inteso Darello. Tu vuoi dire   1
   C'ha in seno Flori accolto ogni veleno

Poor wretch—he must have seen his nymph and, returned to his senses, set himself to run behind her dear footsteps, at the risk of falling prey to some ravening beast. I shall seek him out and keep him with me until the sacrifice has taken place. For even if I may have designs on his Flori, whom I hope to win through this trick, yet still I love him as my own life; and if I could dispose of her feelings at will, then I would want nothing more than that he should be that cruel nymph's lord and master. But if another man is fated to be her swain, I would wish to be that man— though if this is not to be, I certainly do not wish to remain mad with love for her, for there are other nymphs, perhaps, who will not despise my suit. Only today, in fact, I saved the life of just such a one; and if it is true what some say, that the eyes and the face can speak as loud as the tongue, then I can well believe that the soft sparkling of her eyes as we parted was clearly saying, "In my visage, Serrano, read my heart. I may truly say that you are at once my savior and my undoing." But the arrival of the priest prevented me from replying. Ah! And there he is again, as I speak. But is that Darello with him? Can I be mistaken? I do believe it is! Ah, heavens! When, when will you remove this infamous monster from our midst? How can you bear any longer to countenance his presence? And you, wide-spreading earth, why do you still sustain his miserable carcass? Let me hide a while here, the better to hear his lies. Oh, what a fine figure of a man!

SCENE FOUR

Damone, Darello, Serrano

Damone

I understand, Darello. You are telling me that Flori harbors venom in her breast,

Degli Dei detrattrice, onde se'n ride
Superba e, insomma, che le sante leggi
Di Pan Dio nostro sprezza, e nulla stima   5
Pale, e tien anco tutto il mondo a vile.

Darello

Così dissi, e l'affermo, anzi prometto
Tutto provar s'ella negarlo ardisce,
Né mi movo per odio, ma per zelo
De l'onor degli Dei. Voi pur andate   10
Che da l'orgoglio suo, da l'alterezza,
Dal fasto, e con che parla e con che sempre
Risponde, a pien vi chiarirete, spero.

Damone Sacerdote

Vado, e farò quanto mi si conviene,
Ché s'a l'onor mondan l'uom così mira,   15
Le sacre cirimonie in cui s'onora
Pan Dio de' boschi in quale stima avransi?

Darello

Non mancate. Avrò pur con la mia lingua
Più che pestifer angue di veleno
Colma, e di rabbia, oprato sì ch'a terra   20
Gli ordini andran del sacrificio santo,
A la natura mia conforme oprando.
Vado in cos'altre ancor simile a punto
Di mie voglie a impiegar il malign'uso.

Damone Sacerdote

Forse di qua meglio sarà ch'io vada./[21r]   25
Ma che va seco stesso borbotando
Colui fra' denti? Sarà vero forse
Quanto di lui si dice ch'è maligno?
Mi par gran cosa ch'una ninfa insomma
Tal sia qual'egli Flori m'ha dipinta.   30
Anzi che segua il sacrificio seco
Voglio parlar e intender da molti altri
Lo stato suo, le cirimonie sacre
Tardando intanto, altre ragion rendendo

that she blasphemes against the gods, and laughs their powers to scorn in her pride; that she despises the holy laws of our god Pan, cares nothing for Pales, and holds the whole world in contempt.[52]

Darello

> That is indeed what I said, and I hereby reaffirm it; indeed, I am happy to swear that I shall prove it if she dares to deny it. And do not think that I am motivated by hatred; rather, my motive is pure zeal for the honor of our gods. Go to her—for her pride and haughtiness and the worldliness of her speech and the manner of her replies will, I hope, leave you in no doubt of the truth of what I am saying.

Damone

> I shall go, and shall do my duty. For where someone is so intent on worldly vanities, what hope can there be that the sacred ceremonies held in the name of Pan, god of the woods, will be given the respect that is their due?

Darello

> Do not fail to do as you say! *[Aside]* Ha! Then I shall have ensured, with my evil tongue, more venomous and malign than that of any serpent, that all the plans that have been made for this holy sacrifice will have been in vain. For such is my nature. Now, I must go to find some further outlet for my fell designs.

Damone

> This is perhaps the best way to go. But what is Darello muttering about over there? I wonder whether it is true what they say of him, that he is ill-intentioned. I can scarcely believe that any nymph could be as wicked as he paints Flori. I shall speak to her before the sacrifice and question others on her state, postponing the ceremony on some other pretext.

Perché tal vadi in adoprarmi tardo.   35
Ma ecco suo fratel Fronimo a punto.
A tempo giungi, per alcuni miei
Disturbi penso trattenere al tardi
Gli sacrificî nostri.

Serrano
                    O pur mi spiace
Tanti intoppi fra' piedi; avevo il tutto   40
Accommodato, or voglio udire il resto.

SCENA QUINTA

Fronimo, Damone Sacerdote, Serrano

Fronimo
Damone ben trovato fino al core.   1
Quest'indugio m'incresce; da le ninfe
Vengo a punto che stanno a pié del monte
E del venire attendon l'ora e dove.
E peggio è che di sotto a questo colle   5
Ho trovata Licori, che cercando
M'andava, e Urania seco, e ho lor detto
Che a l'urna d'Amaranta quindi a poco/[21v]
Tutte insieme si trovino con Flori,
Ch'io trovarei Serrano intanto, e gli altri   10
Giovanetti pastore, e l'altar fatto
(Come dicesti) sopra l'urna; il pazzo
Vi guideremo ancora.

Damone Sacerdote
                    Or non importa.
Così conviemmi, tu Fronimo intanto
Ritroverai Serrano, e tra voi dato   15
L'ordine, drizzerete ivi l'altare
Il mio venir poscia attendendo; ch'io
Vado, e in serviggio degli Dei fornita
Cert'opra verrò e spero il ciel benigno.

But there is her brother. Fronimo, you have arrived just in time. I am thinking of postponing the sacrifice due to an unexpected occurrence.

Serrano

[*Aside*] How vexing, to have all these new obstacles thrown in my path. I had planned things so well! Now to hear the rest.

SCENE FIVE

Fronimo, Damone, Serrano

Fronimo

Damone, well met! I am sorry from my heart for all this delay. I am come this moment from the nymphs, who are all gathered at the foot of the mountain, waiting to be apprized of the hour and the place. What is worse, I encountered Licori and Urania just now at the foot of this hill, looking for me, and I told them all that they should go directly to Amaranta's urn, along with Flori. Meanwhile, I said I would go and find Serrano and the other younger shepherds, and that once the altar was made (according to your directions) above the urn, we would lead the mad shepherd there as well.

Damone

No matter. These arrangements will do well. You, Fronimo, seek out Serrano and go about setting up the altar while you wait for me to arrive. I have a service I need to perform in the name of the gods. When that is done, I shall come to you; and may the heavens look benignly on this enterprise.

Fronimo

    Tanto farò, dando a le ninfe aviso   20

    Di questo, a dio.

Damone Sacerdote

          A dio.

Serrano

          Damon, Damone![13]

Damone Sacerdote

    Chi mi chiama? O Serrano io ne veniva

    Per ritrovarti e Fronimo anco insieme

    (Al quale ho già parlato) e a darvi l'ora

    Del sacrificio ch'andrà tardo penso.   25

Serrano

    Il tutto ho già sentito, e di Darello

    Anco le false accuse, che buon pezzo

    Fa m'ero dietro a quei ginepri ascoso.

    O maligno Darello, avida arpia

    De l'altrui bene, empio pastore e vile!   30

    Damon (credimi pur) son tutte folle[14]

    Le finte di costui chimere e ciance.

    Flori fu (come intesi) sempre umile,

    A' nostri Dei sempre devota, e grata

    Nel conversar; quanto di mal può dirsi   35

    Forse[15] è, che sua virtù s[t]im' ella troppo,

    E quindi altera il mio fratel disprezza,/[22r]

    E ogn'altro pastor che l'ama e segue.

    D'amor virile insomma sprezza i nodi,

    La face schiva, le saette, l'arco   40

    E d'Imeneo dic'ella il duro giogo.

Damone Sacerdote

    Do (Serrano) gran fede ai detti tuoi;

    Nondimen mal poss'io

    Pagar il mio dover a un testimonio

    Sol dando fede, da più parti ancora   45

Fronimo

> I shall do as you say and shall advise the nymphs of what is happening. Farewell.

Damone

> Farewell. *[Fronimo exits.]*

Serrano

> *[Emerging from behind thicket]* Damone, Damone!

Damone

> Who is this who is summoning me? Oh! Serrano! I was just on my way to find you, to inform you and Fronimo (with whom I have just been speaking) about the time of the sacrifice, which looks set now to start late.

Serrano

> I have already heard all this, for I have been hiding for some time now behind that juniper thicket. I also heard Darello's false accusations. Oh that malign creature! That ravening harpy, ever ready to sink his teeth into others' happiness! Vile, impious shepherd! Damone, believe me, they are all lies, that man's empty, feigned slanders. I have always heard that Flori is nothing if not humble and properly respectful of our gods— and entirely affable, what is more, in her speech. The worst that might be said of her is perhaps that she prizes her virtue a little too highly, and thus haughtily disdains my poor brother and all other shepherds who love her and court her: in short, that she scorns the love of men and shrinks from Hymen's sacred torch, his bow, his arrows—what she would call his yoke.

Damone

> Serrano, your words carry much weight with me, but I would be failing in my duty if I listened to one sole witness. I must investigate the matter

Ne cercarò, e poi su'l tardi a voi
Sarò per far quant'ho già detto, a dio.

Serrano

Orsù, ben veggo i miei disegni sparti
E le castella andar di vetro a terra,
Che in mente cressi poco dianzi in aria.   50
Misero stato uman sù che fondato?
Sopra lieve alga oimè, ch'a lo spirare
D'irato Borea men da turbo in aria
Sospinta piuma si rivolve e gira.
Quanto a Leggiadro[16] imposi sarà in vano.   55
Frettoloso partì Fronimo, e giunto
Colà esser deve ov'avisai ch'a bada
Fosser tenuti i pastorelli in giochi,
E lor qui seco conduran per fare
L'altar, e insomma ogni mia speme è vana.   60
Lascia d'amar Flori, Serrano, e Amore
Lascia, lascia esto amaro, e non amore.
Amor non è già quel ch'io sento; io erro
E solo, e vo' che sia fraterno affetto
Che di desir mi colmi, ch'alfin segua   65
Il sacrificio e'l mio fratel si sani
Con Flori amica (e non amante) insieme,/[22v]
Quel tutto fa che vuol l'uomo; di ghiaccio
Mi sento pur il cor ch'or or ardea.
Ah non è vero, in desiando l'alma   70
Vaneggia, io sento ch'amo; la ragione
Ben (de' sensi mal grado) sorge, e vuole
Che così sia; ma non è in fatto, debbo
E voglio, e debbo procurar d'Androgeo
La salute e di Flori senza inganno,   75
E poscia Amor renderà forse in fine
A lo mio merto il guiderdone uguale.
Licori alfin non mancherammi, ed altre
Ancor. Ma che? Non mi rammento ch'oggi
Quella a cui diedi aita,   80
Mi mirò dolcemente?
Amerò quella, e se non quella un'altra;
E dirò a questa, a quella: "io t'amo sola."

further, and then shall come to find you and Fronimo, as we have arranged. Farewell.

Serrano

Ha! Now indeed I see all my plans coming to naught and the fragile castles my mind had spun in the air plummeting to earth. Oh, on what fragile foundations does this miserable life of ours rest? Alas, on shreds of seaweed wafted around on a storm-tossed sea, more unstable than feathers whirled around in the wind. I cannot see how Leggiadro can now carry out my plans. Fronimo left in haste, and must already have arrived at the meadow where I had told Leggiadro to assemble the young shepherds and distract them with games. Now they will bring them all back here to set up the altar. Ah well! It seems all my hopes are in vain. Serrano, cease to love Flori! Cease, indeed, to love at all (if such a bitter thing even deserves to be called by so sweet a name).[53] But it is not love that I feel; I have been in error. Henceforth, let the only object of my desire be the good of my brother. May the sacrifice proceed, and may my brother be healed, and may things then go just as he would wish with my friend Flori—my friend, note that I say, not my beloved. My heart, which was only now ardently burning, I now feel to be of ice . . . But no! It is not true. When desire grips us, our minds err. I am still in love. I feel it—even if my rekindled reason would deny my senses and tell me I love not. . . . Yet it is not so. I must and shall and *must* seek the good of Androgeo and Flori, foregoing all deceit, and then perhaps Love will in the end give me some reward for this forbearance. After all, there is always Licori, and there may be others . . . But how could I have forgotten? Only today, that nymph I saved looked so sweetly on me. I shall love her—or if not her, another, and whoever it is, I shall tell her that I love her alone.

E dirò il ver; che sola amo colei
Con cui talor ragiono; ma poi vero   85
È ancor ch'a un'altra inanzi mi dà il core
Mille volte giurar che da me sola
È amata, ed è mia cara donna, e Dea.
Ma non frodo però del viril sesso
L'uso in picciola parte   90
Lunge da lor tutte le scordo. A un tempo
Trovato Androgeo, e co' pastori insieme
Qui verrò. Vado. Pan guidami, e quanto
Io deggia oprar tu mi ragiona, e inspira!

Il fine del secondo atto

And this will be the truth! For I do love only that nymph to whom I am speaking at a given moment—although then, perhaps, when I find myself in the presence of another, my heart will prompt me to swear a thousand times that she alone is my beloved and my dear lady and my goddess. But then, faithful as I am to the custom of my sex, when they are out of sight, all are out of mind. Enough. I shall find Androgeo and bring him together with the other shepherds to this spot. Pan, be my guide: inspire me and instruct me what I must do.

End of act two

ATTO TERZO

SCENA PRIMA

Leggiadro solo

Leggiadro

   Non so da qual pensier spinto Serrano   1
   Oggi di questi doni si privasse
   Sì di leggier, che di se stesso cari
   Al paro li teneva, ben sovente
   In essi vagheggiando il suo valore.   5
   Mira in aspetto com'è fiero il cane,
   Polito l'arco, le cui fila attorte
   Furo prim'opra di verginea mano,
   E di strana fattura il bel bastone.
   Sembra duo serpi aviticchiati insieme.   10
   E s'io talor m'assido e lo depono,
   Nel ripigliarlo poi mi scuoto tutto
   Che proprio parmi avelenati serpi;
   Né so se la natura meglio, o l'arte,
   Abbia ridotto in disusata forma   15
   Un legno di ginepro, a l'altrui vista
   Certo meraviglioso; ne la fine
   Mira che punta di forbito acciaio.
   S'amor fu del fratel gran lode merta,/[23v]
   Ma qual si sia cagione alta la stimo.   20
   Tutti (com'ei mi disse) i giovanetti
   A la lotta e al corso giù invitai
   A piè de colle, in quel pratel riposto
   Donde ora parto in aspetarli stanco.
   Trattenuti gli avrà nov'ordin forse   25
   Del sacrificio. Eccoli a punto, e seco

ACT THREE

SCENE ONE

Leggiadro alone

Leggiadro

Whatever can Serrano have been thinking of, giving those gifts away so casually, when they were things he has always prized as dearly as life itself? How often he would delight to gaze on them, seeing in them a reflection of his own prowess. See how keen this dog is and how brave! And look at how exquisite this bow is, with its cord strung by a virgin hand! And this fine crook, strangely fashioned to look like two snakes wound around one another. Sometimes when I sit down and lay it aside a while, I feel shocked to the core when I take it up again in my hand: I could swear I was really holding a handful of poisonous snakes. In truth, I do not know whether it is nature or art that can have rendered this juniper branch in so cunning a form, but either way it is quite marvelous. And that spike of polished metal at the end![54] If it was fraternal love that inspired him to this generosity, then indeed he is deserving of all praise for this fine action—but whatever his motive, I am sure it was a noble one. I invited all the young shepherds, as he instructed me, to compete in games of strength and speed there in the little meadow that lies at the foot of the hill. But I grew tired of awaiting their arrival, and am now come back here. Can it be that they have been detained by some new arrangement connected with the sacrifice? Ah! There they are—and

Fronimo; di che cosa vi ridete[17]
Capi sventati? Forse
Vi sembro al cane e a l'arco
Novo Ateone, o Apollo? od al bastone   30
L'antico sposo de la bella Aurora?

SCENA SECONDA

Fronimo, Giovane Pastore, Leggiadro

Fronimo

   Più tosto lor devi sembrar novello   1
   Narciso al torto ed aureo crine e al viso.

Giovane Pastore

   De la vaga Ciprigna anzi l'amato
   Lo stimavamo a l'arco e ai sembianti.

Leggiadro

   Lasciamo le parole. Or dite pure   5
   La cagion del tardar.

Giovane Pastore

           Noi venivamo
   Ma Damone incontrandone ci disse
   Che s'era l'ora differita al tardi
   Del sacrificio, e ch'a Serrano ancora
   Detto l'aveva; onde partito a pena   10
   Da noi, che venivamo verso il colle
   Ov'aspettarne giù dicesti al piede
   Per narrarti la cosa, giunse a noi/[24r]
   Fronimo che qua seco n'ha condutti.

Leggiadro

   So che i giochi farem tra noi proposti,   15
   E questi doni in ricompensa avremo?

Fronimo

   Non importa, Leggiadro, di Serrano

with them Fronimo. Why are you laughing at me, cloth-heads? Do you take me for some new Actaeon[55] or Apollo, standing here with my dog and my bow? Or does my crook make you think of lovely Dawn's ancient spouse?[56]

SCENE TWO

Fronimo, Young Shepherd, Leggiadro

Fronimo

Nay—they must think you a new Narcissus, looking at your rippling blond locks and beauteous face!

Young Shepherd

No, rather we were convinced that he was the object of the beautiful Cypriot goddess's love,[57] to judge by his appearance and that bow at his side.

Leggiadro

That's quite enough! Tell me, why were you so late in coming?

Young Shepherd

We were just coming to meet you when we encountered Damone, who told us that the sacrifice had been delayed and that he had already informed Serrano of this. And as he left us, we were just setting off again to join you at the foot of the hill, as you had instructed us, to tell you of the change, when we met Fronimo, who told us to come along here with him.

Leggiadro

But the games we had proposed will still proceed. Shall we still be awarding these same prizes, I wonder?

Fronimo

Leggiadro, do not fear: I well know

Il generoso core assai m'è noto.
Serberansi tai giochi ad altro tempo,
L'altar facciasi intanto a l'urna sopra   20
D'Amaranta gentil ch'abbiamo l'agio,
Ch'io stimo ben ch'ei fatto sia per mani
Giovinette. A Serran l'incarco diedi,
E pensai favorirlo conoscendo
Ch'ama Licori, di trovarla, come   25
Quella ch'a noi dovea condur le ninfe
E di farle saper l'ordine posto.
Alto, ponianci a' fatti. Ah pastorelli
Sù, ch'io vi veggia un poco; inanzi a gli occhi
Esser v'imaginate ora di quelle   30
Che nel cor fisse avete. Tu Leggiadro
A quel fronzuto faggio il cane lega
E, deposto il bastone e l'arco, sagli[18]
Quell'orno e taglia a terra. Intanto voi
Ite incrociando i verdi rami, ch'io   35
V'insegnerò com'adattar gli abbiate.

Un Pastore
Allegramente, or via mi segua ogn'uno.

Un Pastore
Vorrei che si cantasse. A che sospiri
Leggiadro? sei già stanco?

Leggiadro
                              E che ti pare?
Tai colpi a pena Ercole fatto avrebbe.   40
Ma lasso che altri colpi
Ora prov'io nel cor per man d'Amore.

[24v] Un Pastore
Che ragioni d'Amor?

Fronimo
                     Dev'egli dire
Ch'insano Ercole venne per amore.
Or via cantiamo, che propizio il cielo   45

Serrano's generous heart. Let the games be postponed until some other time, and let us meanwhile profit from this delay to begin erecting an altar above the urn of sweet Amaranta, for this seems to me a task that requires young hands. I had allotted the task to Serrano, thinking to do him a favor, as I know that he loves Licori, and I thought this would give him an opportunity to meet her. For she has been chosen to conduct the nymphs to this spot, and he would have needed to speak to her to inform her of the new arrangements for the sacrifice. But enough of this! Let us get to work. Come along, shepherds, let me see what you are made of! Imagine that that special nymph I know each of you has fixed in his heart is here watching your prowess. And you, Leggiadro, tie your dog to that leafy beech tree, and laying aside your crook and bow, climb that ash tree and cut us down some branches. You, shepherds, meanwhile, can start weaving these green fronds together; I will show you later how we shall be using them.

A Shepherd

With great pleasure! Come, lads, follow me, and let us to work.

A Shepherd

How about a song? But Leggiadro, why are you sighing? Tired already?

Leggiadro

What do you think? It is a task for Hercules! *[Aside]* But more than the blows I am to inflict on this tree, I am wracked by the blows that Love is inflicting on my heart.

A Shepherd

What are you saying about love?

Fronimo

He was doubtless pointing out that Hercules was driven mad by love.[58]
But come, let us have a song, and may the heavens

Aspiri al canto nostro, ma invochiamo
Pale cantando e Pan.

Un pastore
                    Or via.

Un pastore
                              Sù tutti.

Leggiadro
     Ecco, ecco chi vien, làsciali il cane!

Un pastore
     Tò, tò Licisca piglialo!

Fronimo
                         Non fare
     Non lo slegar, férmati.   50

Un pastore
                              Che vorresti?

Un pastore
     Darello?

Fronimo
                    O ben trovato.

Un Pastore
                              A dio Darello.

Un pastore
     Una fune Darello, ove ne vai?

SCENA TERZA

Darello, Fronimo, Giovane Pastore, Leggiadro

Darello
     Ben trovati pastori. A l'urna intorno   1
     V'adoprate per far l'altare forse?

look kindly on us: let us call on Pales in our song and on Pan.[59]

A Shepherd
   Come, to work!

A Shepherd
   Rouse yourselves!

Leggiadro
   Wait, wait! See who is coming! Set the dog on him. *[Darello approaches.]*

A Shepherd
   Go on, Licisca, get him!

Fronimo
   No, stop! Do not unleash the dog!

A Shepherd
   Darello, what do you want?

Fronimo
   Well met!

A Shepherd
   Darello, greetings.

A Shepherd
   Darello, what are you doing with that rope?

SCENE THREE

Darello, Fronimo, Young Shepherd, Leggiadro

Darello
   Well met, shepherds! What are you doing, all gathered around the urn?

Seguirà il sacrificio? Pur inteso
Avea (né dove so) ch'andava in nulla.

Fronimo

Ben tu'l vorresti, oggi si fa del certo   5
E altro non volendo andar te'n puoi.

Darello

V'ha bisogno di me l'opra? ch'io resti?

Fronimo

No no, va pur.

Darello

            Si farà dunque certo
Il sacrificio?

Fronimo

            Al tuo dispetto certo.

Darello

Mi raccomando.

Un Pastore

          Su la forca.

Un Pastore

             In vento.   10

Fronimo

Deh, come d'astio colmo e di rancore
Parte, e nel sen mille ceraste asconde
Sotto finta bontà. Costui non altro
Oprando mai ch'empie nequizie, fatto
S'è odioso in modo appo ciascun ch'io penso/[25r]   15
Che men odiata sia da l'uom la morte.

Un pastore

Làscialo andar, che senza lui più bello
Sarebbe il mondo. Or via, cantiam.

Are you setting up the altar? Is the sacrifice to go ahead then? I thought
I had heard a rumor that it was to be abandoned.

Fronimo

I am sure you would like that to be the case! But it is to go ahead. If that
was all you wished to know, then you can leave this moment.

Darello

Am I not needed for this task? Should I stay?

Fronimo

No, no—no need.

Darello

You are quite certain that the sacrifice will go ahead?

Fronimo

Quite certain—whether you like it or not.

Darello

I wish you luck with it.

A Shepherd

And I wish you the gallows!

A Shepherd

In the wind.

Fronimo

Look at him, going off filled with spite and rancor, and harboring a thousand serpents in his breast, despite all that feigned goodwill. His constant malice has made him so universally hated that Death is hardly less
loathed.

A Shepherd

Let him go. The world would be a better place without him. Now—a
song!

Fronimo
    Cantiamo.

Leggiadro
    Vedi quai disperate ei va facendo,
    Férmati che l'udiamo.

Fronimo
            Taci.

Un pastore
                Ferma.   20

Darello
    Misero, ah che giovato
    M'han l'ordite mie folle?[19] Avrò pur lasso
    Scoperto a pien l'iniquità ch'io serbo
    Entro al core. Damone oggi avrà forse
    Scorta di Flori l'innocenza e io   25
    Perduto il nome. I machinati inganni
    Miei dissipati caderanno; alfine
    Seguirà il sacrificio, e sani fatti,
    I pazzi goderan. Sol io meschino,
    D'ogni contento privo, andrò penando.   30
    Oimè! QUANTO s'inganna
    Uom che fuggir si pensa il suo destino.
    Ora m'accorgo che DI rado il cielo,
    E non mai, favorisce i rei pensieri.
    Da che nacqui del padre, dei fratelli   35
    Al mio sangue, che più? fin di me stesso
    Nemico fui crudele,
    D'uomo non ritenendo altro che il nome.
    Dunque fia dritto ben ch'a me medesmo
    Di me stesso ogni fallo or or pagando   40
    Con questo cinto mio dal mondo levi
    Uom de la vita indegno.
    E sarà giusto ancora
    Se del riposo altrui conforme io tenti/[25v]
    L'avida brama a ingorde fere e brutte,   45
    Che cibo lor questa mia carne torni.

Fronimo
> Yes, let's sing.

Leggiadro
> Look at him raving away there, though. Stop a minute so we can listen.

Fronimo
> Hush!

A Shepherd
> Tools down!

Darello
> Alas! What use has all my foolish plotting been? All I have done is to lay bare the malice that lurks within my heart. Perhaps Damone has already discovered Flori's innocence, in which case my reputation is ruined. All my machinations will come to naught. The sacrifice will go ahead and those lunatics will be restored to health and will bask in their sanity, while I alone, poor wretch, will be left lamenting, stripped of all pleasures. Oh how we deceive ourselves, when we think to escape our destiny! I realize now that the heavens rarely or never reward evil thoughts. Since I was born, I have always been the cruelest foe of my father, my brothers, my own blood—what do I say? Even of myself! I have been a man only in name. It is only right that I should now be forced to pay in my own person for all the ill I have done myself and to use this girdle of mine to rid the world of a man who is unworthy of life. It is only just if I, who in life preyed on others' repose, should now in death be fodder for wild and ravening beasts.

A dio prati, a dio campi, a dio pastori,
Veloce ad essequir vado, a dio mondo.

Fronimo

Non s'ha potuto insomma udir parola,
Pur ne la fin compreso ho che si parte   50
Disperato. Già parmi di vederlo
Divenir Parca di se stesso e'l filo
Troncar, infame e 'ndegno,
Che al sconcio velo suo quell'alma unita
Tien, ch'in vita oprar ben già mai non seppe.   55
E vederlo anco parmi
Già pendente da un selce offrir (ben degno
Cibo di lor) a' corvi e a' cornici
Quell'odioso corpo che tra noi
Regnò qual loglio e avena entro al buon grano.   60
O (s'è molesto al buon talora uom reo
Per voler degli Dei) de' nostri falli
Condegna e acerba sferza. Ma si canti
E s'attenda a l'altar, ch'è indegnitate
Il parlar di costui.

Leggiadro
                          Sì, sì.

Un pastore
                                    Cantiamo.   65

         Sommi possenti Dei
Ch'udite ogn'or tanti angosciosi omei
Di due pastori insani
E i lor desiri vani
Soli quetar potete; il prego umile   70
De' nostri cori non abbiate a vile.
Deh sien da noi lontani
Tanti dolor, sorga pietate, e omai/[26r]
Sgombrin (vostra mercè) tant'aspri guai.
         Alma che sciolta dal mortal tuo velo   75
Quinci forse t'aggiri
E di Flori i sospiri

Farewell, meadows, farewell pastures, farewell shepherds. Let us be swift to execute this justice. Farewell, world!

Fronimo

Well . . . that was all quite inaudible, but from what I caught of the end of his speech, he seems to be going off in desperation. I can imagine him now becoming a Parca to himself,[60] and snapping off that wretched and unworthy thread of life that keeps that soul that never learned to do a shred of good united to his vile mortal shell. I see him now hanging from some willow tree, offering as a worthy banquet to the carrion crows that hated body that lurked in our midst like some noxious chaff or weed among the healthy grain. If it is true that the gods sometimes send evil men to vex us as a punishment, what a harsh and deserved scourge he has been for us! But let us sing and attend to the altar, for to speak of him is a waste of words.

Leggiadro

Indeed!

A Shepherd

Let us sing!

Chorus of Shepherds

O highest and most mighty gods, who hear at all hours the anguished laments of two poor mad creatures, you who alone can quiet their vain raving desires, we beg you, do not despise the humble prayers of our hearts. Banish these great sorrows from our midst; let pity come to our aid, and through your mercy bring an end to these bitter woes we suffer.

Oh soul who, freed from your mortal veil, perhaps still haunts this spot and listens to Flori's sighs,[61]

Odi, deh ti ricovra omai nel cielo
E se pietoso zelo
Ti punse, omai (benigna) con amore   80
Unita, oggi 'l favore
Degli alti Dei n'impetra, ond'abbia pace
Ella che di dolor per te si sface.

Fronimo

Or ch'è fornita l'opra andar possiamo.
Tu, come conscio a pien del fatto e anco   85
De le contrade resterai, Leggiadro,
Acciò di qua pastore alcun passsando
Narrar la cosa lor tu possa, e teco
Trattenerli fin tanto che torniamo.
Del tuo padrone a la capanna intanto   90
Andaremo, ov'ei disse che ridotti
Tutti gli altri pastori, la venuta
Del sacerdote, de le ninfe, e nostra
Attenderebbe. Il suo bastone intanto
Le sarà consegnato, l'arco, e'l cane.   95

Leggiadro

Fate come vi pare.

Un Pastore

        Andiamo.

Leggiadro

            Andate.
Come chi in ùn fra tema e speme attende
Cosa bramata, e d'acquistarsi incerta,
Tal son io tra mestizia e gioia, avendo
Fra poco a saziar l'avida vista   100
Nel desiato mio bel sole, in cui
Sì raro avien ch'affisar possa il guardo./[26v]
O felice, o beato
Leggiadro, anzi scontento e infelice
Misero amante. Oimè, dove condotto   105
M'avea di poca vista incerta speme?
Chiamerò dunque aventuroso (ahi lasso)

we pray you now make your return to the heavens. And if the urge to pity has touched you, now, benign soul, united with Divine Love, plead with the other gods that she who is torn apart with grief for you may find peace.

Fronimo

Now that the task is completed, we may go. Leggiadro, since you are fully informed of the business at hand and know these parts well, you remain here, and, should any shepherd pass by this spot, explain to him what is happening and keep him here until our return. Meanwhile, we shall go to the hut of your master Serrano, whither he is supposed to be returning to await us, along with the priest and nymphs, once all the shepherds have been assembled. And let us take his crook back to him too, as well as his dog and his bow.

Leggiadro

As you will.

A Shepherd

Come, let's off.

Leggiadro

Farewell. Like the man who awaits something for which he has been yearning, but which he dreads may yet escape his grasp, torn between hope and fear, so I wait here caught between sadness and joy, knowing that my avid gaze will soon be able to sate itself in the sight of the lovely sun of my desires, on whom I so rarely have the chance to rest my eyes. Oh happy, oh fortunate Leggiadro—but yet poor, wretched, miserable lover. Alas! What has become of me, led astray by the uncertain hopes raised by one fleeting glimpse? Who am I am calling happy and fortunate? One who, poor wretch, lives unrecognized in a stranger's house,

Chi sconosciuto in altrui casa vive,
Servo d'amor poco gradito, e novo
Tantalo, e più infelice?   110
Poiché mirar non lice
A me pur del mio vago
Cibo soave l'odorata scorza.
Ben le viv'io vicino, ma timore
E riverenza (di verace affetto   115
Certo segno) non lascia ch'opri cosa
Ch'io mi possa pensar purché le spiaccia.
O mia Gelinda cara,
Cara Gelinda amata.

SCENA QUARTA

Alessi, Leggiadro

Alessi

Giovanetto pastore, i tuoi riposi   1
Mi rincresce sturbar. Sapresti dirmi
Se questa strada al fiume Lampeo porta?

Leggiadro

Non m'è disturbo. In maggior cosa bramo,
E di più forza oprarmi per pastore   5
Qual tu mi sembri nobil e gentile./[27r]
Ben la strada conduce al Lampeo infine,
Ma in più giri partita anco al Ladone
A l'Erimanto adduce. Qui potrai
Meco posarti alquanto e ti prometto   10
Poi venir teco ove più a gir t'aggrada.
Seguirà intanto un sacrificio, e spero
Ch'a doler non t'avrà l'esser rimaso.

Alessi

È questo il loco ov' a seguir ha forse
Un sacrifico per sanar duo pazzi?   15

Leggiadro

È questo, ecco l'altar, n'hai forse nova?

an unrewarded slave to Love, and a new Tantalus[62]—or unhappier still than him! For I am not even permitted to gaze on that sweet nectar of my eyes, that fragrant creature, even though I dwell alongside her. The fear and reverence she inspires in me—a sure sign of true affection!—prevent me from venturing anything that I fancy might displease her. O my darling Gelinda! My darling, beloved Gelinda!

SCENE FOUR

Alessi, Leggiadro

Alessi

Young shepherd, forgive me if I trouble your repose. Can you tell me whether this path leads to the River Lampeus?[63]

Leggiadro

What you ask is no trouble. On the contrary, I only wish I could assist you in some greater way: you have the air of a noble and well-bred shepherd. Indeed, this path does eventually lead to the Lampeus, but there are forks off to the Ladon and the Erymanthus. Why not rest here a while? After that, I promise to accompany you wherever you wish to go. Meanwhile, there is due to be a sacrifice here. If you choose stay for it, I hope you will have no cause to regret your decision.

Alessi

Ah, is this the place then where a sacrifice is to take place to cure two poor mad creatures?

Leggiadro

Precisely—there is the altar. Have you then already heard something of this?

Alessi

   N'intesi ben, ma non a pien, da certi.
   Or ben ch'io vada per fermarmi u' bagna
   Il . . . il patrio mio terreno, ingombro
   D'alti pensier il petto, di ferita   20
   Mortal piagato, da mia sorte lasso
   Straziato a torto, rimarrommi. Forse
   Trovar potrei ne l'altrui mal conforto.
   Sono questi i pastori?

Leggiadro

                 Eccoli, e seco
   Le ninfe e'l sacerdote. Ritirianci.   25

Alessi

   Non veggo pazzi, quai saranno?

Leggiadro

                 Quelli[20]
   Che segue dietro al sacerdote, vòlto
   Verso le ninfe, di pallor di duolo
   Il volto ingombro, è'l pazzo.

Alessi

   E la ninfa qual'è?

Leggiadro

               Quella ch'in mezzo   30
   A le due ninfe inanzi essangue viene,
   Col viso asperso d'animata neve.

[27v]SCENA QUINTA

Sacerdote, col coro d[i] pastori guidato da Fronimo e Serrano,
e coro di ninfe guidato da Licori

Damone Sacerdote

   Tutti v'accommodate in giro, accolti   1
   Pastori e ninfe a l'urna intorno, e quando
   M'udirete agli Dei nostri quei doni

Alessi

I have indeed heard some vague rumors of it. Although I am headed to where the river . . . bathes my native land,[64] I shall interrupt my journey as you ask. My heart is oppressed with grave concerns, and I am wounded to the quick and cruelly savaged by fate, but perhaps I can find some comfort in others' woes. Are those the shepherds?

Leggiadro

Indeed, and with them the nymphs and the priest. Let us retire.

Alessi

I do not see the afflicted ones. Which are they?

Leggiadro

See there. The man following the priest and turning towards the nymphs with his face full of sorrow—he is the mad shepherd.

Alessi

And the nymph?

Leggiadro

She who walks before the two leading nymphs, pale as death, with her face as if adrift with living snow.

SCENE FIVE

The priest Damone, with chorus of shepherds led by Fronimo and Serrano, and chorus of nymphs led by Licori

Damone

Come, nymphs and shepherds, gather round the urn, and when you hear me offering up to the gods the gifts that you are bearing, then step for-

Ch'in man tenete offrir, trattevi inanzi
E umili a l'altar sopra voi prima   5
Pastori appresentategli, e voi poscia
Ninfe seguite a far l'istesse offerte,
Chiedendo quel di che informati sete.
Poi tutti insieme nei cor vostri i nomi
Loro lodate in dolci canti, intanto   10
Riverente ad udirmi ogn'un si ponga.
Tu Serrano mentr'io le preci movo,
E teco insieme Fronimo, spargete
Di vin spumante al foco santo sopra
Quelle tazze che in man serbate piene.   15

Serrano
Ambi tanto faremo.

Fronimo
                          Eccoci pronti.

Damone Sacerdote
Tu Dio di queste selve,
Di queste piagge e campi,
Ch'entro di noi mortali
Scopri i desiri ardenti/[28r]   20
L'alta pietà ch'abbiamo,
Deh mira a duo pastor miseri insani,
Fa che t'abbiano a ceder di bontate
Uomini rozi e vili,
A la nostra pietà la tua pietate   25
Pietosamente omai socorra. O Dea
Tu de la quale è il pregio,
Somma benignitade anco rivolgi
A noi, pietosa il divin guardo. E ambi
O Dei celesti, insieme l'alte posse   30
Vostre colà si scoprano ov'intenti
I desir nostri aspirano, e benigni
Intanto di gradir vi piaccia queste
Picciole che porghianvi umili offerte.

But, if I am not mistaken, these sudden streaks of lightning, flashing across the sky, augur some happy event, and this sound of thunder off to my left fills my heart with joy and hope. Now let each go his own way, for the holy sacrifice is made. You, Licori, now is the time to do what I have ordained. You too, Serrano.

Licori

Flori, sit here a while and wait for me. When I have escorted these nymphs down from the hill, I shall return to share with you certain thoughts of mine.

Flori

Go—I shall await you. [*Aside*] If I recall right, on that day in April when it is our custom to honor the goddess, I would always come here early and eagerly, along with the other nymphs, to attend the sacrifice. Today, though, I know not why, I was reluctant to come to this spot, although I did at last, constrained by the entreaties of my dear friend Licori—more than a friend, a sister. But—again, I know not why—as soon as I came here, I felt so sweetly consoled that not one of those troubles has disturbed me that previously so strangely consumed my soul. Perhaps the hymns offered up by the priest at the altar—which, I now see, stands

Che chiude il casto velo de la mia   105
Cara compagna, vergine Amaranta,[21]
Che m'avranno sottrata/[29v]
Dal peso, onde venían meno gli spirti?
Ma da qual forza occulta
Tiranneggiato è'l cor dentro al mio petto?   110
E in esso qual novello duce in schiera
Con nova legge guida i pensier miei?
Ne la mia mente quai novi desiri
Sorgono? e quali brame in questo seno
Germogliano improvise?   115
Oimè chi mi trasforma? e chi cangiata
M'ha da lo stato mio
Primiero? Ahi chi da gli occhi il velo toglie
Ch'adombrato ave lor finora il lume?
Ma caro velo e amato.   120
E chi quell'ombre sì noiose fuga
Che'l mio pensiero sì angosciosamente
Tormentavan, da morte a me dipinte?
Ma care ombre e amate.
Ahi che da sonno[22] (quasi) grave scossa   125
Tutte le cose mie passate ho in mente
E qual'uom che nel sogno orride larve
Scorse, desto ancor teme, e sta dubbioso
Se vere o finte siano state l'ombre
Che poco dianzi vide,   130
A pena dando a se medesmo fede,
Tal io di meraviglia colma in forse
Resto, se pur fu vero
Che a donna, e morta, follemente dietro
Errassi un sì gran tempo,   135
O pur nel sonno immersa
Lontan dal vero, cosa abbia veduta./[30r]
Ma a che dubbiar? Amai purtroppo, è vero,
E viva e morta la più chiara ninfa,
Per grazia e per virtù, ch'unqua Diana   140
Seguisse in selva o 'n prato.
Né già con brame più d'affetto calde
Alcun amante il suo pregiato oggetto

above the urn that encloses the chaste remains of my dear companion, the virgin Amaranta—perhaps these hymns had some secret virtue that banished the burden of sorrow that so oppressed my spirits?

But what is this hidden force that I now feel rising with irresistible power within my breast, marshaling my thoughts to its commands like some strange new inner tyrant? What are these unwonted desires surging within me? What mysterious promptings are germinating suddenly in my heart? Alas! What force is so changing me? Who has transformed me from my previous state? Who has rent that veil from before my eyes that had so long concealed the light from them? (But what a dear veil and how beloved!) Who is it that banishes from my thoughts those dark shadows that so threateningly loomed over them, painted in my mind by the hand of death? (But what dear shadows and how beloved!) Alas! As though suddenly stirred from deep sleep, I find myself besieged by the things of my past, just as the man who has conjured ghastly horrors in his sleep still fears them at the moment of his waking, and cannot tell whether the shades that haunted his dreams are real or false, doubting even the evidence of his own senses; just so, I remain wondering, filled with strange marvel. Can it be true that I erred so long in folly for the sake of another woman, and a dead one? Or have I been dreaming and imagining to myself things that have never been?

But what do these doubts avail me? I loved, alas! it is true, alive and dead, the most glorious nymph—glorious in grace and virtue—that ever followed Diana in the woods or meadows. Nor has any lover ever followed the object of his longing with keener desire;

Seguì, né meno in terra
Cosa mortal fu mai più riverita;   145
Ma così pure, e così oneste, furo
Le voglie mie, che stanchi e mille e mille
Dei più degni scrittor verrebon prima
Che adombrar pur potessero una parte
Cel mio candido, vero affetto santo.   150
Ma quanto fida ed altretanto pazza
(Lassa) ben fui, che a l'impossibil dietro
(Di me stessa nimica), incontro al cielo
Ho pugnato finora, non mirando
Che s'a morte ella cesse, e di natura   155
Tali sono le leggi, che chi nasce
A tal necessità soggetto nasce,
Dovea quetar il duolo
Al voler di chi 'l mondo a un cenno regge.
Ora non più cordogli, non più folle.²³   160
Ben fa (ti prego Amor) ch'ami e non scordi
La beltà, le virtù che mi destaro
Lunge dal volgo errante a vera gloria;
Ma sia qui fine a le schiocchezze, al pianto,
Ed ai prefissi su nel cielo eventi,   165
Questo cor mio s'acqueti.
Ma come oimè s'acqueterà, s'io sento/[30v]
Tutt'ora dentro al seno
D'inimici pensieri armate schiere,
C'han l'alma posta in nova guerra acerba?   170
E solo stanno a depredarla intenti?
Già felice la veggio prigionera,
Già, già la veggio serva
E parmi udir che resa
Gridi: "mercè, vinta mi chiamo, e presa."   175
Le braccia stese a pena
Sopra l'altare i' avea, due tortorelle
Donando anch'io tra l'altre
In sacrificio, quando dentro l'alma
Sentî rasserenarsi aura improvisa   180
Di celeste favor, sgombrando forse
Le nebbie sue.²⁴ Né così quete ha l'onde
Il mar, quand'Eolo i suoi prigioni affrena,

nor was ever mortal thing so revered as this nymph was by me. But my desires were so pure and honest that a host of the noblest poets would weary before they could describe the least part of my candid, true, and sacred love. Faithful I was, certainly—but also quite mad, as, alas, I now see. For I was pursuing the impossible, an enemy to myself, battling against the heavens. I should have considered that, if my Amaranta had ceded to death, then this was the law of Nature, to which all who live are subject; I should have eased my sorrow, thinking that this was the will of Him whose merest gesture rules all earthly things. Now, no more sorrow, and no more follies! O Love, I beseech you that I may still love and shall not forget the beauty and virtue that spurred me to leave the vulgar crowd in pursuit of glory; but let all my folly and weeping now cease, and let my heart accept with tranquility those events that have been ordained on high.

But, alas! how shall my heart be tranquil, if even now I feel marshaling within my breast armed hordes of enemy thoughts, which are throwing my soul back into fresh turmoil? Oh pity! They are quite intent on disturbing my soul's peace. Once happy, I now see it a prisoner and reduced to servitude; I hear it surrendered and pleading, "Have mercy, I freely acknowledge my defeat."[65] Barely had I reached out my arms over the altar, as I stood with the other nymphs and offered up two turtledoves in sacrifice, when I felt my soul suddenly infused with the clear aura of celestial grace, which banished the dark mists in which it had been shrouded; the waters of the sea are no more tranquil when Aeolus[66]

Ed è sereno il cielo,
Come dentro a la mente   185
Quetarsi i miei pensier ch'eran sì erranti.
Ma non sì tosto a dietro ritirata
Fra l'altre, di questi occhi il guardo corse
Ad incontrar lume sereno e vago
Di duo bei soli a meraviglia ardenti,   190
Ch'io sentì l'alma già ferita, e 'l dianzi
Suo sereno turbarsi.
Tal da nube repente un lampo appare
La notte, e breve a pellegrin dimostra
Sentier, ch'annotta al suo sparir più forte.   195
Mi venne fatto di mirar pastore
Dopo l'offerta, non più visto ancora./[31r]
Questi con gli occhi che soavemente
Passaro scintillando a l'alma, dielle
Morte ad un tempo dolce, e dolce vita.   200
Egli in atto pietoso fiso il guardo
Tenea ne l'urna, e a le guancie sopra
Spargea dogliose lagrimette e rare,
Che non più belle o ricche mai serbaro
Chiuse conche nel mar Indico, pregne   205
D'umor celeste orientali perle.
M'accorsi allor ch'era già presa, e dissi
In silenzio a me stessa:
"Oimè da quell'umor soave e santo
Che veggo uscir da quei begli occhi fuore   210
Nova material avrò d'anco dolermi?
Da le lagrime altrui cagion prendendo
Di distillarmi eternamente in pianto?"
Misera, io ardo e tremo;
O doppiamente folle, erro e vaneggio.   215
Com'arder posso per cagion di pianto
Se d'acqua egli è formato?
E non speng'ella il foco, e non l'ammorza?
Ma che? son ebra? o da dovero sogno?
Uomo non è? non è costui pastore?   220
Forse non so quanto lontana vivo
Da cotali pensieri?
La fè ch'a Delia servo avrò scordata?

holds back his prisoners and the sky is clear than my once turbulent thoughts now were. But as soon as I stepped back from the altar with the other nymphs, my gaze was drawn to meet a serene and beauteous light that came from two lovely suns, burning with such marvelous ardor that I felt my heart at once wounded, and its former serenity turned once more to tumult. Just so sometimes, in the depths of night, a sudden flash of lightning will appear from some cloud, momentarily illuminating for the pilgrim a path that seems all the darker once this brief light has vanished. So, following the sacrifice, I found myself gazing upon the face of a shepherd I had never seen before. This man's soft gaze, sparkling with light, brought death to my soul—a sweet death, and, with it, a sweet life. With reverent mien, he was gazing fixedly on the urn, and on his cheeks could be seen a few sorrowing tears. Ah! In the seas of the far Indies, sealed shells, impregnated with celestial humors, never jealously guarded lovelier or more precious oriental pearls! I realized then that I had been taken prisoner, and said to myself in silence, "Alas! Will that sweet and sacred liquor I see issuing from those fair eyes be the source of new torments for me? Shall another's weeping be the cause of my eternally melting into tears? O poor wretch that I am! I burn, I tremble. O doubly foolish! Once more I am raving and wandering. How can I be burning on account of his tears, if these are made of water? Will not this water dampen and extinguish my flames?"

But how can this be? Am I drunk? Or am I indeed dreaming? Is he not a man? Is he not a shepherd? How far such thoughts should be from my mind! Have I forgotten the vows I made to Delia?

E d'Amaranta mia quegli atti cari?
Quelle dolci parole? il viso santo?   225
Gli occhi soavi suoi leggiadri e belli?
Né le promesse tante/[31v]
Avran più loco entro al mio petto infido?
Ah Flori, Flori, ove ne van guidati
Da sì poca ragione i tuoi pensieri?   230
Ma perché poca? anzi da molta e saggia
Ragione è scorta l'alma;
Già le piante²⁵ di morte ed oscur ombre
(Mercè dei nostri Dei) lasciate avendo.
Ma ecco che se n' viene seco stessa   235
Ragionando Licori, a questo faggio
Dietro vo starmi un poco.
Scoprirommele poscia, che mai l'ora
Non vedea che giungesse per nararle
I novi miei pensieri.   240

SCENA SESTA

Licori, Flori

Licori

Col girar de le sfere anco rotando   1
Va fortuna de l'uom gli umani eventi.
Il mio caro pastore Androgeo pazzo
Era fa poco, or più d'ogn'altro saggio
L'han veduto questi occhi, più che mai   5
Oltra misura grazioso e bello.
Saggia fatta sarà Flori anco spero,
E non fien vani i miei desiri e l'opre.
Ma chi sarà che per me poi s'accinga
Per piegarmi le voglie   10
Del mio sanato Androgeo? o gli racconti
Delle mie tante una sola pena almeno?/[32r]
Non per questo cred'io
Far alcun torto a la mia amica Flori,
Che di pastor straniero   15
Accesa la previde il sacerdote.

And all my dear memories of my Amaranta? Those sweet words of hers? That innocent face? Those soft, fair, clear eyes? And all the promises I made—do they have no place now within my treacherous breast? Ah, Flori, Flori, where are your wayward thoughts leading you, guided by unreason? But why unreason? Rather, your soul is being led by true and sober reason, having left behind the ways of death and darkness, through the grace of our gods. Ah, here comes Licori, speaking to herself as she comes. I shall hide a moment behind this beech tree and listen to what she is saying. But then I shall discover myself, for I am longing to share these strange new feelings of mine with her.

SCENE SIX

Licori, Flori

Licori [aside]

As the heavenly spheres spin in their orbits, so does the course of our human affairs proceed. My dear shepherd Androgeo was mad until a moment ago and now is saner than any other. I saw him with these eyes, charming beyond measure and more handsome than ever. I hope, too, that Flori will now have been made sane, and that my desires and deeds will not be in vain. But who will now come to my aid in bending the now cured Androgeo to my desires? Or who will reveal to him at least some small part of my woes? I do not think that in doing so I would be slighting in any way my friend Flori, for the priest foresaw that she would fall in love with a stranger shepherd.[67]

Flori

> O poter de gli Dei!
> Vo scoprirmele or ora.
> Licori!

Licori

> Flori cara,
> Dolce amica! Pur spero che con novi   20
> Pensieri troverotti, e più contenta.
> E come stai? Quali accidenti occorsi
> Ti sono mentre sola
> Qui stata sei? Narrami il tutto, e quale
> Cagion ti tien così tra mesta e lieta.   25

Flori

> Quella a punto c'hai detto ragionando
> Teco stessa poc'anzi.

Licori

> Misera me, m'hai tu sentita forse?

Flori

> Non t'arrossir, Licori. UMANA forza
> Poco val contra'l cielo. Incauta anch'io   30
> Mosso ho già il piè nel laberinto, dove
> Tardi, e non mai (se non per morte), uscirne
> Spera d'Amor verace servo e fido.
> Ma perché (quando Androgeo ancor amassi),
> Temi di farmi offesa per amarlo?   35
> Se di me puoi disporre
> Più che non puoi di te medesma ancora?
> Ah ch'io non amo Androgeo. Godo, godo
> Che tu l'ami; e m'accingo
> Ad opra tal che rimarrai contenta.   40
> Altro scalda il cor foco, e altro laccio
> Mi stringe, e da più forte/[32v]
> Rete è già l'alma colta.

Licori

> Non già volea celarti

Flori

O how great is the power of the gods! I shall reveal myself to her forthwith. Licori!

Licori

Darling Flori, my sweet friend! I hope I find you now refreshed in your
mind and happier. How are you? What new adventures have happened
to you as you rested here alone? Tell me all! What is it that makes you,
as you seem, suspended between sorrow and joy?

Flori

That same thing of which you were speaking just now, when you thought
you were alone.

Licori

Do not tell me that you heard what I was saying!

Flori

Do not blush, Licori. Our mortal powers cannot prevail against the heavens. I too have set my incautious foot within that labyrinth in which true
and faithful servants of Love are condemned to wander all their days, until death releases them. But, even if I *did* love Androgeo, why do you think
you would be wronging me by loving him? You know that you can dispose of me entirely—more so than you can of yourself. But, ah, I do not
love Androgeo! And it fills me with delight that you do! I shall do all I
can to insure that you are happy. It is another fire that burns my heart,
another chain that binds me; it is a tighter net in which my soul is en-
meshed.

Licori

Oh Flori, it was not that I wished to hide from you any of the secrets of

(O Flori) del mio core alcun secreto,   45
Poiché mai sempre i miei pensieri tutti
Solo dentro al tuo seno
Trovar fido ricetto.
Amo Androgeo (nol nego) quell'Androgeo
Che ha te, crudel, più de la vita sua,   50
Più de l'anima amata.
Ma dimmi tu qual'è ch'ora il cor t'arde?
(Gli Dei lodati) pur ti veggio Flori
Sanata, o amica cara.
Non mi posso saziar già d'abbracciarti.   55

Flori

Dolce amica Licori,
Non conosco chi m'arde; ma perch'io
Ora m'accorgo ben che per me fatti
Furono i sacrificî, e forse ancora
Per Androgeo; se'l senso a dentro scorgo   60
De le parole tue poc'anzi udite,
Se'l sacerdote al mio fratel promise
Di sanarmi, e di più, ch'io resterei
Di pastore straniero accesa, questo
Bastar ti de', ch'è troppo stato il vero.   65

Licori

Purché a la morte dietro non ti lagni,
Come solevi inutilmente, il tutto
Passerà bene alfine;
Ma qual stranier pastore
D'amor novello t'ha piagato il core?   70
Quegli che a l'urna appresso con Leggiadro
Si stava insieme è forse?/[33r]
Colui che qua guidato hanno le stelle
(E ch'Alessi è nomato s'io non erro)
Per far te saggia, e me felice a un tempo?   75

Flori

Ah come sana? se già in ogni parte
Piagata ho l'alma? Oimè Licori, quello,
Quello, è'l pastore ch'i' amo, e ch'io mirai

my heart; as ever—more than ever—I know my every thought can find its safest haven in your breast. I do love Androgeo, I cannot deny it— that same Androgeo who loved you, despite your cruelty, more than his life and soul. But tell me, what is the cause of your present ardor? Ah, but Flori, may the gods be praised that I see you now healed! Dearest friend, I keep wanting to embrace you!

Flori

Oh Licori, my sweetest friend, I know not for whom I burn. But if I have rightly discerned the sense of what you were saying just now, it seems to me that the sacrifice was performed on my behalf, and perhaps on Androgeo's too. If the priest promised my brother that I would be healed but would remain smitten by love for a stranger shepherd, you do not need to know more: his prophecy has proved all too true.

Licori

At least you are no longer yearning vainly for death, as you have been for so long. You will see that all will turn out well. But who is this stranger shepherd who has pierced your heart with a new passion? Could it be that shepherd who was standing by the urn with Leggiadro—Alessi, I seem to remember his name was? Is he the man who has been guided here by the heavens to make you sane and me happy at the same time?

Flori

Sane? How can you say it, when my soul is pierced through and through! Alas, yes, Licori, he is the man—the shepherd whom I love, and whom

Vagamente piangendo in atto starsi
Da inamorar Diana ancora e'l cielo.   80
È questo Alessi dunque, il mio pastore
(Lassa), e l'amato mio
Dolce nimico, il mio tiranno, e mago.
Egli, donno entro al sen, tutt'altre cure
Sbandite, siede ai pensier miei sol duce,   85
Che 'l seguon fidi ovunque ei move il piede,
Ed al qual porgerò fino ch'io viva
Largo d'affetto e d'alta fè tributo.

Licori

Al variar del volto or ben m'aveggo
Qual strale ha oprato Amor entro al tuo petto;   90
Ma dimmi sai tu forse
Di che piangeva il tuo novello amato?

Flori

Altro non so, se non che la pietate
Ch'ebbi allor del suo pianto, dal mio seno
Trasse il cor; che (novella quasi pianta)   95
Amor (allor cred'io presente) dentro
Al suo dolce inestò, dov'egli a punto
Perpetua stanza avrà, s'ei non me'l niega,
Sì come eterno la sua effigie bella
Avrà seggio ove dianzi era il mio core,   100
Unico di quest'alma
Gradito e caro obietto./[33v]
Ma in vasto (oimè) d'Amor pelago forse
Infelice sarò nocchiero, e questo
Allor fie quando ei, preso d'altro laccio   105
Partì tosto d'Arcadia, me lasciando
In dure Sirti abbandonato legno.

Licori

Bona nova di questo or io so dirti.
Da Serrano pregato e da Leggiadro
Rimarassi in Arcadia qualche giorno   110
Il tuo pastore, nel qual tempo in parte
Il tuo dolor disacerbar potrai.

I saw standing there weeping so gracefully that Diana herself and all the heavens would have fallen in love with him at that moment. It is this Alessi, then, who is my shepherd and (to my cost) my beloved sweet foe, my tyrant, and enchanter. He has invaded my mind and, banishing all other cares, has taken up his role there as lord of my thoughts, which henceforth have no choice but to follow him wherever he stirs. For as long as I live, my tribute of love and faith is due to him as my liege.

Licori

Ha! I can well see from your changing expressions how deep Love's arrow has gone. But tell me, what was the cause of your new love's weeping?

Flori

I know nothing of this. All I know is that the pity that I felt for him then, seeing him weeping, tore my heart from my breast, and Love, who I think was there looking on, transplanted it like some young sapling into his own sweet heart. And there it shall remain, if he will permit it to— just as to all eternity his lovely image will have its seat where my heart once was, the only dear object of this soul. But alas! Perhaps my destiny will be that of an unhappy helmsman trying to steer a path through the vast ocean of love. Perhaps he is already bound by another chain and will leave Arcadia directly, leaving me an abandoned ship caught between perilous tides.

Licori

I have good news for you on that count. Your shepherd is to remain in Arcadia for a few days, invited by Serrano and Leggiadro: a delay that will surely offer some respite to your suffering.

Intanto, seco io ti prometto fare
Per te, ch'amo di core,
Quanto per la mia vita (che non meno   115
Amo la tua) farei, ed altretanto
(Mi credo²⁶ certa) che per me farai.

Flori

Esser certa di questo puoi, che cara
Più di te non ho l'alma.

Licori

Sarà meglio ch'andiam, felice nova   120
Portando al tuo fratel di tua salute.

Flori

O Licori, chiamar pur vuoi salute
Il precipizio mio?

Licori

Taci Flori, che prima anco che salga
Ad allumar la cacciatrice Dea   125
Con la sua pompa in ciel la prima spera
Sarai, spero, beata.
E chi sa che dai guardi dolci tuoi
Sana se 'n porti l'alma.
Spera, spera. So ben che di Serrano,   130
Lieto, accettò l'offerta, e ch'anco spesso
Pieni dal sen mandava alti sospiri.

[34r] Flori

Ahi che di consolar l'alma pensando,
Licori, uccidi 'l cor; questi sospiri,
Quelle lagrime sue (se non lo sai)   135
Lo dinotano amante.

Licori

Ben saperemo il tutto; pur n'andiamo,
Che le ninfe aspettar ci devon tutte
Appo il fonte, vicino a la capanna
Del tuo fratel, di desiderio colme   140

And meanwhile, I shall do all I can to help you, loving you as I do from my heart, for your life and happiness mean as much to me as my own, and I know that you will do the same for me.

Flori

You can be quite sure of that, for you are dearer to me than my own soul.

Licori

But we should perhaps be going, to take the good news of your cure to your brother.

Flori

Oh Licori, you speak of my cure still, when I am plummeting into the abyss!

Licori

Hush Flori! For even before the divine huntress has risen to bathe the first sphere of the heavens in the splendor of her light,[68] you will, I hope, have attained your heart's desire. Even now, who knows whether your shepherd himself is still quite in his right mind, after the assault of your fair eyes? Hope! Hope! I know he seemed happy to accept Serrano's invitation; and I saw that he often sighed deeply.

Flori

Oh Licori, you are trying to console me, but instead your words will be my death! Do you do not know that those sighs of his, those tears, are signs that he is in love?

Licori

Well, we shall soon know all. But let us go, for the nymphs must all be awaiting us by the spring beside your brother's hut, filled with desire to

Di rivederti saggia e d'abbracciarti;
Che fu del sacerdote opinione
Che quivi alfin ne rimanessi sola,
Acciò gli spirti, poco dianzi tuoi
Smarriti per gran duolo e disgregati,   145
Potesser meglio unirsi e racquetarsi.

Flori

Facciam come ti par, ma o come intorno
Soave s'ode un suon di chiusa voce;
È un GRILLO, e sembra al canto ANGELO vero.

Licori

E odi, o che fischiar sonoro e grave,   150
Anco lungi si sente; è s'io non erro
Di TASSO che, destato,
In altrui desta meraviglia estrema.
Ma se da questo bosco d'improviso
Uscisse ad assalirle orso o leone   155
Come sarebbe bello, or che siam sole.

Flori

Per me non fuggirei se orso foss'egli
Simile a quello ch'una volta io vidi.

Licori

No, no, ci guardi il ciel di tal incontro.

Flori

O miracol a dir, non so se mai   160
Licori io te'l dicessi; in ripa d'Adria/[34v]
Figlio d'un gran LEONE
Un ORS' ATTO vid'io vincer di senno
Ogn' uom più saggio. Umana avea la forma,
Benigno il gesto, il portamento grave,   165
E note aprìa celesti e 'n guisa dolci
Ch'assai vi perderìa nettare e ambrosia.
Io l'inchinai (o mia ventura) come
Cosa divina, e come
Di natura e del cielo ultima possa.   170

see you restored to sanity, and to embrace you. For the priest ordained that you should remain here a while alone, so that your vital spirits, which not long ago were wandering in their great pain, should have a chance better to mend and calm themselves.

Flori

As you wish. But hark how all around there suddenly echoes a sweet sound from some hidden voice! It is but a cricket *[GRILLO]*, and yet from its sweet tones, it seems an angel *[ANGELO]* singing.[69]

Licori

And hark at that grave and sonorous whistling, which could be heard from far off. If I guess rightly, it is a badger *[TASSO]*, awoken from its rest and now awakening marvel in all around it. But what if some bear or lion were to leap out of this wood to attack us?[70] What a fine thing that would be, alone here as we are?

Flori

I should not flee, if it were a bear like one I once saw.

Licori

No, no—the heavens preserve us from any such encounter!

Flori

It was quite miraculous! Licori, I am not sure I have ever told you. On the banks of the Adriatic, I once saw the son of a great lion *[LEONE]*, a bear fit *[ORS'ATTO]* to outdo in its wisdom even the wisest of men. It had a human form, with a benign aspect and a grave demeanor, and the tones of its voice were quite heavenly and sweeter than nectar and ambrosia. Oh my good fortune in seeing it! I bowed down before it as a thing divine and the proudest creation of nature and the gods.

Licori

    Dai pastori d'Alcide,
    Gloriosi seguaci, quelle note
    In suon flebile udite a reitirare
    In ripa al Bacchiglione,
    E che resero lor famosi tanto   175
    (Mentre di gemme d'ostro e d'or lucenti
    In ricca compariro ampia capanna
    Che de le meraviglie una è del mondo).
    Erano[27] Flori quelle voci forse
    Di quest' ORS' ATTO, a far stupire il mondo?   180

Flori

    Sì, sì, le udisti dunque? Erano quelle
    Compartite tra lor sì saggiamente
    Da quel Leucippo che cantò de l'alma
    CALISA i veri pregi sì altamente.
    Ma se presente à ciò ti ritrovaste,   185
    Che ti parve Licori poi di quelle
    Due verginelle ninfe, anzi divine
    E celesti sirene, per cui solo
    Il Bacchiglione altero
    L'arena ha d'or, di puro argento l'onda?   190

[35r] *Licori*

    Che me ne parve? E che ti posso dire?
    Scemerebbe ogni lode il suo gran pregio.

Flori

    Mille cori allettar, mill'alme ingombre
    Render d'alto stupor le vid'io, mentre
    Fra molta turba de pastori eletti   195
    Co l'armonia del lor soave canto,
    E con maniere oneste, entro a l'interno
    Le discordie de' sensi ivan quetando.

Licori

    Non più si trattenian, che l'ora è tarda.

Licori

Can it be that these were the same sweet tones heard faintly echoing on the banks of the Bacchiglione by the glorious shepherds who follow Alcides?[71] Those same tones that won them fame, at the time when they appeared in that rich and mighty hut that is now one of the wonders of the world, embellished with jewels and purple and burnished gold?[72] Is it of this bear fit [ORS'ATTO] to stupefy the world that you are now speaking?

Flori

So you heard those sweet notes, so wisely distributed among the shepherds by that Leucippo who sang so nobly of the virtues of the lovely Calisa?[73] But Licori, if you were present at that event, what did you think of those two sweet virgin nymphs—rather, divine and celestial sirens—whose singing turned the sands of the proud Bacchiglione to gold and its waters to the purest silver?[74]

Licori

What did I think? What can I say? Their performance was such that no praise could do it justice.

Flori

I saw a thousand hearts enchanted by them and a thousand souls filled with the utmost wonder, as amid the throngs of noble shepherds, with the harmony of their sweet song and the grace of their manners, they soothed every discord of the senses.

Licori

Come, let us be off, for it is getting late.

Flori

> Ora via caminian. Così in andando　　　　　　　200
> Ad Eco potrem anco addimandare
> De l'avenire alcuna cosa. Or via,
> Tu Licori incomincia.

Licori

> I decreti del ciel chi può saperli?
> Ma nondimen per compiacerti or odi:　　　　205
> Si disconviene a me, ch'a Delia servo,
> Fortunata seguir d'almo pastore
> E aventurosa orma felice?

Eco

> 　　　　　　　　　　Lice.

Licori

> Tarderò a conseguir l'onesto fine
> Che brama il cor prigion d'Amore?

Eco

> 　　　　　　　Ore.　　　　　　　210

Licori

> O me felice! Altro saper non bramo.
> Tu pur (Flori) incomincia, ch'io t'ascolto.

Flori

> Ninfa, se la memoria di tua sorte
> Mai sempre in cor d'egregio amante viva,
> Colma d'alta pietà, di grazia, or dimmi,　　215
> La grazia acquisterò che può bearmi
> In terra? Un giorno a le mie pene tante
> Onesto fine dando omai?

Eco

> 　　　　　　Mai.

Flori

Indeed, let us be on our way. And as we go, we can ask Echo what the future holds for us.[75] Licori, you start!

Licori

Who can know what the heavens destine for us? But to please you, I shall ask something. Is it wrong for me, when I am a votary of Delia, to follow this shepherd so fair?

Echo

Dare!

Licori

Shall I have long to wait before my wretched captive heart can at last rest at peace in Love's bowers?

Echo[76]

Hours!

Licori

Ah! What happiness! I have nothing more to ask. You go ahead, Flori, and I shall listen.

Flori

Nymph, may the memory of your sad fate live forever within the hearts of noble lovers! Gracious and merciful nymph, tell me—shall I ever attain that pleasure that alone can give a foretaste of heavenly bliss on earth? Shall there be an honest end to my sufferings ever?

Echo

Never!

Flori

Oimè poca pietate a le mie pene
Non avrà dunque (lassa) alcuno?

Eco

Uno.   220

[35v] Flori

Uno ben basta, ma fia Alessi.

Eco

Sì sì.

Flori

Non so se più lieta o dogliosa andarmi
Possa di tua risposta, ninfa, quando
Felici in uno e sfortunati eventi
Mi prometti, confusa rispondendo.   225

Licori

Andiamo, che felice avranno fine
(Flori) i desiri tuoi, pur stanne lieta.

Flori

Lieta allor potrei star ch'Alessi meco
Dedicandosi a Cinzia castamente,
Di mutuo nodo avinto,   230
In pari fiamme ardesse meco; allora
Ben sarei lieta.

Licori

Andiamo.

Il fine del terzo atto

Flori

Alas! Then will a shred of pity for my sufferings be had by no one?

Echo

No, one!

Flori

If he is Alessi, one is all that I need!

Echo

Indeed!

Flori

Nymph, I know not whether your replies should give me sorrow or joy. Your confused answers promise me at the same time happy events and sad.

Licori

Flori, let us go. You will see that all will turn out well for you in the end. Trust, and be happy.

Flori

For me to be happy, my Alessi would have to be beside me, burning along with me in mutual desire and vowing himself chastely to Diana. Then, then, would I be happy!

Licori

Come, let us go.

End of act three

[3 6 r]ATTO QUARTO

SCENA PRIMA

Leggiadro solo

Leggiadro

Felice avuto ha il sacrificio fine,   1
Son da Serrano mio padron mandato
A spiarne il successo, ed ho incontrata
Flori con la compagna, e saggia e lieta,
A cui dett'ho che dai pastori tutti   5
Sono aspetate, e nova ancor lor data
Che Androgeo saggio è ritornato, ch'ambe
Lo sapevano, e mostran gran contento.
Tutti insomma ne godono. Serrano
Poi s'è scoperto giù in andando meco   10
Ch'ama Flori, e ch'Amor prodigo il fece
Di quei doni, ma scorto ho ch'egli alcuna
Da dovero non ama, ch'altre ancora
Loda, albergando a un tempo dentro al petto
Mille vani pensieri.   15
Misero me, che'l più fedel non vive
Amante di me in terra, poi che corro
Tacito e riverente in grembo a Morte.
Da pastor passaggero la beltate/[36v]
Mi fu dipinta di Gelinda, e corse   20
L'imago da l'orecchie al cor sì tosto
Che pria che pur me n'avedessi (o Amore)
Divenni Amante, il ricco gregge, e 'l mio
Vecchio padre lasciando per potere
Godere di lei la dolce vista almeno.   25
Oimè! Nè pur di quella anco talora

ACT FOUR

SCENE ONE

Leggiadro alone

Leggiadro

So, the sacrifice had a happy outcome. I was sent by my master Serrano to see what had happened, and met Flori with her companion, sane and happy. I told them that the shepherds were awaiting them and that Androgeo too had returned to his right mind; this they already knew and were delighted it was so. Everyone, then, is happy. Serrano, meanwhile, revealed to me just now that he was in love with Flori and that it was Love that had made him so prodigal with those gifts of his. But I could tell that he does not love her—or anyone—truly, for he has flattering words, too, for other nymphs and harbors a thousand vain whims together in his breast. While I, poor wretch, the most faithful lover on earth, am rushing headlong towards death, unable to break my wonted silence and reverence towards my beloved. A passing shepherd described to me the beauty of Gelinda, and the image he evoked raced so swiftly from my ears to my heart that before I had even realized it (O, the power of Love!), I found I was a lover.[77] And, leaving my rich flocks and my aged father, I came here, so that I might at least enjoy the sweet sight of her—

Le fameliche brame del mio core
Saziar ardisco a pena.
Ma (lasso), ahi caro, caro, di che 'l padre
La patria, il gregge, e ogn'altro ben lasciai,   30
Servo d'amor ingrato, a che ti lagni?
Scerner dunque dovrai sì male il bene?
Il bel volto di rose, il sen di latte
Con alcun guardo anco talor non godi?
In lei sola ridotti rimirando   35
Di mille Ninfe i pregi alteramente
A quei begli occhi, anzi a quei soli inanzi
Rischiarando (felice) i pensier foschi?
Ahi, pur si parta ogn'altro van consiglio;
Lascia Leggiadro pur la patria, il padre,   40
Il gregge, e le ricchezze. Se d'Amore
Verace servo sei,
Perché sì ti disdice
Il servire? Ah, pur servi
La tua ninfa, il tuo core.   45

[37r] SCENA SECONDA

Fronimo, Leggiadro

Fronimo
Gli Dei lodati! Androgeo sano in tutto,   1
Tal anco spero Flori tra le ninfe.
L'ho già vedut'al fonte, ove si stanno
Tutte insieme danzando, nè pur volse
Licori a pena ch'io la salutassi.   5
"Bàstiti" (disse) "ch'ella è già sanata.
Qui goduteci un pezzo a te verremo,
Fronimo: non sturbar nostri piaceri."
Io vo' trovar per raccontarle il tutto
Damone. Ma chi viene? A dio, Leggiadro.   10

Leggiadro
Fronimo, mi rallegro, ch'ottenuto
Avrai l'intento tuo.

but, alas! I barely now dare to feed my burning desires even with a look.

Ah, but why then, my dear Leggiadro, did you leave father, homeland, flocks, and all else for her? Ungrateful servant of Love, why do you complain, when you are so inept at acting in your own interest? Why do you not snatch at least a glance of that lovely rosebud face, that milk-white breast? In her you can see assembled in all their glory the charms you would seek in vain in a thousand other nymphs. If you would only allow yourself to gaze on her fair eyes, which shine like suns, you might at least find some respite from your dark brooding. But ah! Banish all other vain thoughts, Leggiadro! What does it matter that you left your home, father, flocks, and riches? If you are a true servant of Love, why should you disdain to serve? Serve! Serve your nymph, serve your heart.

SCENE TWO

Fronimo, Leggiadro

Fronimo

The gods be praised! Androgeo is quite cured, and Flori too, I hope. I saw her just now among the other nymphs, by the fountain, where they are all gathered together dancing, but Licori would hardly allow me even to greet her. "Content yourself that she is cured," she said. "When we have dallied here a while, we shall come to you, but, for now, Fronimo, do not disturb our pleasures." I want to find Damone, to tell him what has been happening. But who is this? Leggiadro, greetings!

Leggiadro

Fronimo, I am delighted that you have achieved that for which you were hoping.

Fronimo

             Io ti ringrazio.
Per qual cagion solo e pensoso vai,
Leggiadro? Forse Amore
N'è la cagion?

Leggiadro

                 No'l nego.   15

Fronimo

    Penso che tu mi beffi. Non so ancora
Qual'è la ninfa tua. O forse Amore
Pur oggi t'ha ferito?

Leggiadro

    Non solo un giorno intiero
Da che suo servo femmi   20
Lasciò Amor di ferirmi,
Ma brev'ora, un momento,
Ove posso anco dire
Ch'oggi Amore m'ha ferito.

[37v] *Fronimo*

    Io per te mi offerisco in quanto vaglio   25
E con l'effetto più che co'l consiglio;
Che ben so io che in giovanetto core
Ov'Amor fatto è donno
Raro ha loco consiglio.
Il nome de la ninfa or fammi udire.   30

Leggiadro

    Duo mesi e anni duo fanno oggi a punto,
O mio Fronimo, ch'io
Per la bella Gelinda sconosciuto
Ardo, servo d'Amor più d'altro fido.

Fronimo

    Per Gelinda sorella di Serrano?   35
    Del tuo padron Serrano?

Fronimo

Thank you. But, Leggiadro, what are you doing here, alone and brooding?[78] Is Love the reason?

Leggiadro

I cannot deny it.

Fronimo

Are you teasing me? I do not yet know who is your nymph—or has Love wounded you only today?

Leggiadro

Love has not let a day pass without wounding me since I became His servant—not a day, not the briefest of hours, not a moment. So, yes, I can say that Love has wounded me today.

Fronimo

I am entirely at your service in anything I can do for you, though I think that I may be of more use to you in deed than in counsel—for I know that in a young heart, when Love has taken possession of it, there is little room for counsel. Come, tell me the name of your nymph.

Leggiadro

For two years and two months exactly from this day, my dear Fronimo, I have burned for the fair Gelinda, who knows nothing of my love: I am Love's most faithful servant.

Fronimo

For Gelinda, the sister of Serrano, do you mean? Of your master Serrano?

Leggiadro

 Quella a punto è ch'io amo.

Fronimo

 Diffìcil fia l'impresa, quando pure
 L'otteniamo anco al fine,
 Perché (come tu sai)   40
 Ella è sola a Serrano unica suora,
 Che di gregge è sì ricco e di terreno.

Leggiadro

 Io t'intendo. Vuoi dir che parrà strano
 A Serrano di dar la sua sorella
 Ad un suo servo, qual'io pur gli sono.   45

Fronimo

 Questo temeva a punto.

Leggiadro

 Mal abbia chi fu il primo a prezzar l'oro,
 Cagion che la ragione è bieca e torta.
 Dunque mia fè, l'affetto (a la bellezza
 De la mia ninfa eguale,   50
 Che al mondo non ha pare)
 Non si dovrà prezzar sovra tesori,
 Sovra[28] stati ed imperi? Ahi, volgo errante!

Fronimo

 Errante volgo e cieco, volgo ignaro,/[38r]
 Che l'abuso seguendo   55
 De l'ignorante mondo
 Nel van disio s'invoglie
 Di Mida, ogn'or non raffrenando ancora
 Con l'essempio del fin de l'infelice
 Le sue sfrenate voglie.   60

Leggiadro

 Ho pur udito dir ch'è sol felice
 E ricco a pien chi è povero di brame.
 Io che sol un disio tengo nel core,

Leggiadro

She it is, indeed, whom I love.

Fronimo

Then our task is a difficult one, even if you succeed in winning her love, for, as you know, she is the only sister of Serrano, who is so rich in flocks and land.

Leggiadro

I see what you are saying. You mean that it would seem odd to Serrano to give his sister to one who is his servant, as I am.

Fronimo

That is just what I fear.

Leggiadro

Cursed be he who first began to prize gold, and so twisted and warped all our values![79] So my faith and the strength of my feeling—equal to the beauty of my nymph, which has no peer in this world—are not to be valued above wealth and power and influence? Ah, how wrong the vulgar horde is to think this way!

Fronimo

Wrong, and blind, and ignorant! Following the common error of the world, it allows itself to be possessed by the same vain desire as Midas, little thinking of the unhappy fate to which his greed led him.[80]

Leggiadro

I have heard it said that the only truly happy man, and the only rich one, is the one who is poor in desires. Since I have only a single desire,

D'esser caro a Gelinda,
In questo modo sarò dunque ricco   65
E per moglie otterrolla.

Fronimo

Dove non è virtù manca ragione.
L'irregolate brame
(Come poch'or dicemmo)
De le ricchezze insomma   70
D'ogni più bel pensiero il lume abbaglia.

Leggiadro

Quando in richezze egual fossi a Serrano
Allor sarei de l'uno e l'altro ancora
Sposo e parente indegno?

Fronimo

Allor non temerei, ch'a tua bellezza   75
A la virtù, al valore
Fosse aggiunta ricchezza.

Leggiadro

Or che del cor t'ho le mie fiamme aperte
Fia ben ch'io ti palesi ancor lo stato.
Dunque saprai ch'Amor mi fè soggetto,   80
Non fortuna, ch'al par d'ogni pastore
Mi diè ricchezza, ed è mio padre TIRSI.
Non pria le di costei rare bellezze
Sentî lodar, che ratto venni, ed era/[38v]
Morto il suo padre allor di poco, ov'io   85
M'accommodai co'l suo fratel per servo.
Il ritrovar maggior la sua bellezza
Che non mi fu dipinta, e la pietate
Ch'io ebbi allora al suo paterno duolo,
Ahi quanto accrebbe a le mie fiamme forza!   90
Ella piangea sovente, e 'l morto padre
Con aggraziate voci in van chiamava,
E vagamente sospirava, al vento
De' quai s'accese il foco onde tutt'ardo.

to win the affection of Gelinda, this should make me rich and therefore in a position to win her.

Fronimo

Where there is no virtue, reason is dead, and, as we were saying, every fine thought is extinguished by the uncontrolled desire for riches.

Leggiadro

But if I were as wealthy as Serrano, should I still be considered unworthy as a brother to him and a husband to Gelinda?

Fronimo

Ah, I should have no fear then, if to your native qualities of beauty, virtue, and valor could only be added that of wealth.

Leggiadro

Now that I have confided in you the desires of my heart, let me also apprize you of my condition. Know then that it is love that has reduced me to this servile state, and not fortune, which endowed me with wealth to rival that of the noblest shepherd. My father is Tirsi. When I heard the beauty of this nymph of mine praised, I came here at once; her father had recently died, and I found employment with her brother as his servant. Her beauty was far greater in reality than in description, and this and my pity for her bereavement caused the flames of my love to burn still more fiercely. She would often weep, and vainly call for her lost father in the sweetest tones; and I would see her sighing, and her sighs would fan my flames still higher. I am all ablaze!

Fronimo
> Di Tirsi tu sei figlio?   95

Leggiadro
> Unico figlio a Tirsi io sono, e vero.

Fronimo
> O Amor, qual meraviglia
> Non opra il tuo sapere?
> Qual'avanza altra forza il tuo potere?
> Di quel Tirsi famoso per ricchezze   100
> E per ingegno (da Melampo, padre
> Di Licori, tenuto in tanto pregio
> E sì sovente nominato) dunque
> Sei figlio? Andiamo, che per opra mia
> Tua fia Gelinda pria   105
> Che Febo sormontando i gradi saglia
> In cielo un'altra volta
> Ad allumare il mondo,
> E già parmi vedere
> Il tuo padron Serrano e la sorella   110
> Goder dentr'ambi a sì felice nova,
> Recandosi l'averti a gran ventura
> Per cognato e per sposo.

Leggiadro
> Ecco, non è costei che sì pensosa/[39r]
> Viene, da sé disgiunta in vista Urania?   115

Fronimo
> Sì, mira, il crin discioglie. Da la danza
> O da la caccia stanca tornar deve,
> Nè s'è accorta di noi. Vogliamo udirla?

Leggiadro
> Ogni indugio m'annoia. Pur facciamo
> Come ti par. O come ella sospira!   120

Fronimo

You are Tirsi's son?

Leggiadro

His true and only son.

Fronimo

Oh Love, what marvels you work in your wisdom! What other force can equal your power? So, Leggiadro, you are the son of that famous Tirsi— famed both for his wealth and his wits—whom Licori's father Melampo so often praised so highly? Come, I shall deliver Gelinda into your hands before Phoebus rises again through the ranks of the heavens to light the world. I can already see your master Serrano and his sister filled with joy at such a happy discovery. Both will consider it their great good fortune to have you as their brother and spouse.

Leggiadro

But who is that coming towards us, so pensive and caught up in her thoughts? Is it not Urania?

Fronimo

Yes. Look, she is loosing her hair from its braids. She must be returning tired from dancing or hunting; and she has not noticed us here. Shall we listen to her?

Leggiadro

I am impatient for action—but let us do as you wish. See how she sighs!

Fronimo
> Ritirianci qua dietro a questa quercia.
> Io giurerei ch'ella è d'Amor mal concia.

Leggiadro
> Tosto ci chiariremo.

Fronimo
>   Or qui fermianci.

SCENA TERZA

Urania, Fronimo, Leggiadro

Urania
> O Amor, Amor, qual non apporti duolo?   1

Fronimo
> No 'l dissi?

Leggiadro
>   Cheto! O, sarà bello.

Fronimo
>   Segui.

Urania
> Amor, dei miei riposi e del mio bene
> Invidioso e avaro, io non ho pace
> Avuta al core un'ora   5
> Da che per te mi fu levata a un tempo
> La ragione e 'l consiglio.
> Non prima vidi Flori e l'abbracciai
> Ch'io partî senza far motto ad alcuna;
> Pur incontrar pensando in queste selve   10
> Il mio pastore amato.
> Ah, non più sono Urania! Questa chioma
> Mille volte ho disciolta, e poi di novo
> Racconcia ancora, dal consiglio preso
> Da l'onde cristalline di più fonti,/[39v]   15

Fronimo

Let us retire behind this oak tree. I would swear that she has been the victim of Love's mauling.

Leggiadro

We shall soon see.

Fronimo

Here, let us stay.

SCENE THREE

Urania, Fronimo, Leggiadro

Urania

[Aside] Ah, what pain love brings with it!

Fronimo

Did I not say?

Leggiadro

Hush. We are in for a treat!

Fronimo

Go on.

Urania

So, Love, it seems that you could not abide to see my former tranquility of mind and my happiness. Be assured that I have not had a moment of peace since you stole from me at one and the same time my reason and my judgment. As soon as I had seen Flori and embraced her, I left without a word to any of the other nymphs, hoping I might find my beloved shepherd in these woods. Ah, I am no longer the Urania of old! A thousand times I have loosed these tresses and then once more tied them up, following the counsel of the crystal waters of each pool I come to along the way.[81]

E pur novellamente mi compongo
Ancor; ma d'acque (oimè) tanto lontana,
In cui possa fidar l'avide brame
Ch'io tengo di sembrar vaga al mio sole?
Ove il crin mirerò partito in nodi   20
In questo bianco velo accolto dietro?
E qual facciano effetto sopra il viso
Le più minute anella? O come belli
Son questi fiori e verdi! Ancor vo' farne
Ghirlanda, ch'addattarli con colori   25
Che altrui possan mostrar maggior vaghezza.
Difficil fora più senza consiglio
Che unirli in giro; vo' intracciarli insieme
Con verde alloro o mirto.
Oggi parea cortese ogni arboscello   30
Invitarmi a pigliar de le sue frondi,
Ov'io tante n'ho colte
Da le lusinghe loro, o dal loquace
D'Amor silenzio, che n'ho 'l sen ripieno.
O questa è bella, mira! E' sempreviva,[29]   35
La terrò da donare al mio Serrano,
S'oggi avien che l'incontri (o me beata!).
Havrà Licori forse il buon officio
Fatto, che mi promise, ond'anco spero
Da chi desia il mio core esser gradita.   40
Ecco fornita la ghirlanda. Voglio
Sopra 'l crine addattarla. O mi sta bene!
Potessi almen vedermi. Taci, taci!
Ch'a fè mi veggo dentro a l'ombra. O Dio!
Scerno del corpo l'ombra sol, né scorgo/[40r]   45
La vaghezza dei fior ne la ghirlanda.
A quella quercia colà sotto forse
Meglio vedrommi.

Fronimo
                    Ora sian ben scoperti.

Leggiadro
Non s'è accorta di noi. Schivianla.

And now I feel the need once more to adjust my appearance—yet, alas! there is no water to be seen anywhere about. Who, then, shall help me in my burning desire to make myself lovely for the man of my dreams? Where can I see how my hair looks now that it is braided and caught up behind my head in this white veil? And who can tell what the effect will be of these little ringlets around my face? Ah! How lovely these flowers are, and these leaves! I shall make a garland of them, weaving them together with leaves of laurel and myrtle, for to match the colors harmoniously without a mirror or other counsel would be a difficult task. Every bush I passed today seemed courteously to proffer its leaves to me as I passed, and, bidden by their whispered flattery, or by Love's loquacious silence, I have picked so many that my bodice is quite full of them. Oh, see how lovely! It is sengreen; I shall keep it to give to my Serrano if I should chance to encounter him today. (Ah, what bliss if I do!). Perhaps Licori will already have done the good office for me that she promised, so that I may hope to see my love returned by the man my heart has chosen. Ah, here is the garland finished. Now to put it on my head. Oh, I am sure it must look charming. If only I could see it! But quiet, quiet! Here is a pool. If I stand out of the sun, I think I should be able to see myself . . . O Lord, all I can see is my own shadow, however I twist and turn. I cannot see the lovely flowers or the garland. But perhaps if I stand beneath the shadow of that oak tree over there, I shall be able to see myself better.

Fronimo

No! Now we shall surely be discovered.

Leggiadro

No, she has not noticed us. Let us pull back a little.

Fronimo

Taci!

Urania

O no 'l diss'io che qui, dov'è dai rami   50
Tolta ai raggi del sol l'entrata, ch'io
Meglio vedrommi? Ecco non sol la forma
Ma il movimento e i gesti
Tutti de la persona:
Ecco il braccio, la mano, il piede, e 'l capo   55
De la ghirlanda ornato, il dardo e l'arco.
Ma quali forme sono
Queste, che quinci intorno
S'aggirano pian piano?
Qui pur son sola, ne v'è alcuno. Forse   60
Amor vuol appagar questi occhi almeno
Digiuni del suo obietto
Di cara vista amata?
Il mio Serrano è certo, e seco Amore
Trasformato in pastore.   65
Chi ha tempo non l'aspetti, si suol dire.
Vo' gradire la pietate
Che ha di me avuto Amore.
Saluterollo e scoprirogli almeno
L'onesta fiamma ch'entro il petto m'arde.   70

Leggiadro

Non possiam più fuggir.

Fronimo

Taci, Dio buono!
Ecco si volge. Abbàssati, ch'ardire
Più le darà di ragionar (mi credo)
Un'ombra sola. Or odi.

Urania

Ben diss'io che quell'ombra giovanetta/[40v]   75
Era Amor trasformato, e sì discosta
Insomma oggi m'aspira
Benigno Amore e 'l cielo.

Fronimo
> Hush!

Urania
> Did I not just say that if I stood here, where the branches cut off the rays of the sun, I would be able to see myself better! There I am! And not just my outline: I can see every movement and gesture, clear as day. There are my arms, my hands, my feet, my head, crowned with its garland, my bow, my arrows. But what are those other shadowy forms I see creeping round behind me? I am quite alone: there is no one here. Maybe Love wants to reward these poor eyes, bereft of their object, with at least some shadowy semblance of his dear form? But yes! It must be my Serrano, and with him Love in the guise of a shepherd! Let me seize the occasion Love has so kindly set before me—for, as the saying goes, he who hesitates is lost. I shall greet him, and confess directly the honest flames that burn within my heart.

Leggiadro
> There is no escape now!

Fronimo
> Be quiet, for God's sake! Look, she is turning. Get down, quickly, for she will certainly be happier to unburden herself to a single apparition. Now listen!

Urania
> I was right! That younger shade, who has now vanished, was surely Love in a transfigured form. It seems that Love is looking kindly on me today,

Convien ch'ardisca. Urania, ardisci omai!
Sciocca, che temi? Or via.   80
Del mio Serrano, ombra felice amata,
Che l'alma sotto ammanti
Forse di lui che riverente adoro,
Ecco t'inchino, e porgo
Taciti preghi nel silenzio, quale   85
Invocando si dee cosa divina.

Fronimo

Qual pastor sì spietato
Ninfa gentil sarebbe
Che 'l tuo Amor non gradisse e non t'amasse?

Urania

Oimè!

Fronimo

                    Non fuggir, ninfa. Ecco noi siamo   90
Del tuo pastor l'un servo e l'altro amico.
Ferma, che siam per darti
Ogni aita e consiglio.

Urania

Misera, che val più celarmi, quando
Son da lor stata udita?   95

Fronimo

Non t'arrossir d'esser accesa, o ninfa,
Che RATTO in cor gentile Amor s'accende.
Sei giovanetta, e bella, e in questa etate
Ben si conviene amare.

Urania

D'onesto foco in seno ho acceso il core,   100
Non lo nego, pastore.

and the heavens are prompting me to take courage and declare myself. So, then, what are you waiting for, Urania? Take that leap! *[To Fronimo]* O happy and beloved image of my Serrano, you who perhaps cloak beneath your shadowy appearances that soul that I so adore, I humbly kneel before you and offer up tacit prayers to you in my heart, honoring you with that reverence all divine things deserve.

Fronimo

Gentle nymph, what shepherd could be so cruel as to deny you and refuse to love you in return?

Urania

Alas! What is this?

Fronimo

Nymph, do not flee! I am a friend of the shepherd you love, and this man is his servant. Stay, gentle nymph! We are at your service, for any help or counsel we can offer.

Urania

Oh, I am lost! What can it serve to conceal myself, when they have heard everything I have said?

Fronimo

Nymph, you should not blush at the fact that you are burning with love, for the noblest hearts are always the quickest to catch fire.[82] You are young and beautiful; it is only right that you should love at this age.

Urania

Shepherd, I cannot deny it: My heart burns in my breast with an honest flame.

Leggiadro

    Se (come inteso abbiam) per Serrano ardi,
    Chiara è la fiamma tua, leggiadra ninfa,
    Ch'è 'l più gentil pastore oggi non vive.

Urania

    Già voi m'avete udita. Amo Serrano/[41r]   105
    E cosa non è al mondo ch'io più brami
    Che d'esser riamata, e che non sdegni
    La mia fede, l'affetto,
    E se non sposa, esser gli possa serva.

Fronimo

    Cred'io, ch'Amore oggi qui intorno vago   110
    Di ferirci s'aggiri,
    E d'impiagar si goda dolcemente
    Ninfe e pastori insieme.
    Leggiadro è anch'ei ferito
    A sta d'Amor malconcio   115
    Per la bella Gelinda, e ti preghiamo
    A piegar la sua grazia ch'or n'andiamo
    Per chiederla a Serran, ch'a l'incontro
    N'offeriamo per te d'officio degno.

Urania

    Ho già più volte udita   120
    La tua bella Gelinda
    (Leggiadro) a sospirare,
    ma mi negò d'amare,
    di rose il vago volto allor spargendo,
    Ch'io le dicea, "so ch'ami, ancor che 'l neghi."   125
    Or vado, e mi dà il core
    D'operar cosa al tuo desio conforme.

Leggiadro

    Piaccia al ciel d'aspirarti
    Benigno a mio favore,
    Cortese ninfa, e a noi per te c'inspiri   130
    Cosa far che t'agradi.

Leggiadro

Lovely nymph, if, as it seems, it is for Serrano that you burn, then yours is a noble flame, for there is no more worthy shepherd than he living.

Urania

Ah yes, you have heard me! I do love Serrano, and my greatest desire is that he should return my love and not scorn my faith and deep affection, and that, if I cannot be his wife, I may at least be his handmaid.

Fronimo

I do believe that Love must be wandering here nearby, eager to pierce us with his arrows, and delighting in his sweet wounding of nymphs and shepherds both. Leggiadro too has been smitten and is quite worn down by love for the fair Gelinda. We pray you, do what you can to advance his case with her, for we are just now going to ask Serrano for her hand in marriage. We, in return, will be happy to serve you in any way we can.

Urania

Many times, Leggiadro, I have heard your lovely Gelinda sighing— even though she would always assure me she was not in love, with her fair face blushing like a rose. But I would tell her "I know that you are, even if you will not confess it." I shall go now. My heart is quite inclined to act in your best interests.

Leggiadro

May the heavens inspire you to this kind deed, courteous nymph—and us to do whatever may please you.

Urania

Amor il voglia.

Fronimo

Spero, che tutti sarem lieti infine.
Vo' compir con Damon quanto gli debbo,
E poscia ritrovar la mia sorella/[41v]
Per udire il successo ed abbracciarla.   135
Andiam, Leggiadro.

Leggiadro

Andiamo.

SCENA QUARTA

Tirsi vecchio solo

Tirsi

Misero vecchio afflitto,   1
D'ogni contento privo, orbo de' figli,
Ah che deggio più far? Ciel, perché vivo
De' cari figli privo?
Dal camin lungo, oimè, già stanco, il piede   5
Sostener può questa mia vita a pena
Dagli anni grave, e d'ogni affanno colma.
Fia meglio che tra l'erbe
Qui mi riposi alquanto. O figli, figli!
Anzi, più tosto, o Tirsi,   10
Meschino vecchio, abbandonato e solo!

SCENA QUINTA

Alessi, Tirsi

Alessi

Se dal tuo colpo, o Morte, ho il cor trafitto   1
E sì la piaga è fresca, che di sangue
Ho tinto il petto ancora, ah perché move
A danno mio di novo Amore il braccio,
E di già m'ha ferito?   5

Urania
> May Love look kindly on us!

Fronimo
> I hope we shall all have cause to rejoice together. Now, I want to fulfill my obligations to Damone and then to find my sister to hear what has happened to her and to embrace her. Come, Leggiadro.

Leggiadro
> Yes, let us go.

SCENE FOUR

The elderly Tirsi alone

Tirsi
> Poor wretched old man, bereft of all happiness, orphaned of my sons. Ah, what can I do? Heavens, why do I still live on, deprived of my dear sons? My aged feet, already weary from their long journey, can barely hold aloft this wretched frame, weighed down by the years and bowed with sorrows. Let me rest here on the grass awhile. O, alas! my poor children! Or better, alas, poor Tirsi! Wretched, lone, abandoned old man!

SCENE FIVE

Alessi, Tirsi

Alessi
> When Death has already pierced my heart—and the wound is still so new that the blood still stains my breast—ah, why, then, is Love now stirring to do me fresh harm? I already feel his arrows! Love, how did you

Ov'hai trovato a nove piaghe loco/[42r]
Entro al mio sen, Amore?
La sublime cagion de le mie spemi
(Lasso) cadde per man d'invida Morte,
Anco l'empia e rubella   10
Seco la messe mia mietendo in erba,
Ond'io scorgendo empî gl'influssi miei
Avea di non amar più mai giurato,
Quando di qua passando (per mio male
Penso) a quel sacrificio mi lasciai   15
Da un pastor giovinetto trattenere,
Ov'io la ninfa, per cui s'era fatto,
Mirai, d'alta pietà compunto il core,
Pensando che dentr'ambi egual cagione
N'affligevano i cori, in parte avendo   20
Il caso suo già udito, ov'ella ancora
Mirandomi talor sì m'ha conquiso
Che le fiamme d'Amore a mille a mille
Sorgon nel petto mio che omai può dirsi
Un'altro Mongibello.   25
Son da gli altri pastor pur sciolto alfine
Per qua tornarmi, ove di veder spero
Questa novella maga e omicida,
Che già m'ha trasformato, e che m'uccide,
E quando anc'oggi non mi venga fatto   30
Di rivederla in ogni modo, io resto
Da Serrano pregato e da Leggiadro
Qualche giorno in Arcadia, ove pur spero
D'effetuar quel desio sì ardente.
Oltra misura insomma son cortesi   35
I pastori d'Arcadia, senza pure/[42v]
Che mi conoscan; tutti fatto m'hanno
Mille vezzi ed offerte, il caso strano
D'Androgeo raccontandomi Serrano,
Atto a destar le tigri anco a pietate.   40
E certo ancor ch'ei sconsciuto viva
Senza saper da chi sia nato,[30] stimo
Che nobil sia, quanto è cortese e saggio.
Ma poi che ninfa comparir non veggio,
Da cui pigliar di chi mi strugge almeno   45

find any place for new wounds within my scarred breast? She in whom
all my highest hopes reposed was struck down by the hand of envious
Death. And as this cruel and unpitying foe had scythed down my harvest
when it was yet green, and I could see that a malign influence reigned
over my life, I swore that I would love no more. But then, as I was passing by this spot (as my ill luck would have it), I allowed myself to be detained by a young shepherd to watch the sacrifice. When I saw the
nymph for whom it was being performed, I gazed on her with my heart
full of the keenest pity, thinking that she was afflicted in the same way as
I, for I had in part heard the story of her trials. She sometimes met my
gaze, and I was so vanquished by her that the flames of Love are now
surging in my breast in their thousands as though I were a volcano. Finally, I left the other shepherds to return here, where I hope to see this
strange new enchantress and murderess of mine, who has already transfigured me with her magic, and is now set to slay me. But even if I do not
see her today, since I have agreed to stay on a few days in Arcadia, there
is still hope that this burning desire of mine may be fulfilled. I stay at the
invitation of Serrano and Leggiadro. The shepherds of Arcadia are certainly most courteous! Although I am entirely a stranger to them, they
have welcomed me with a thousand kindnesses and offers of help. And
Serrano has recounted to me the story of Androgeo, which is fit to inspire pity in the cruelest tiger. Although this man's identity is not known,
nor his background, he must surely be as noble in birth as he is wise and
courteous. Indeed, since no nymph is hereabouts from whom I might at
least seek some tidings of her for whom my heart yearns, to assuage its

Potessi nova consolando il core,
Androgeo cercarò, che meco brama
Dicea di star tutt'oggi. Pur fia bene
Ch'aspetti qui Leggiadro ancor un pezzo
Che mi disse incontrandolo poc'ora   50
Con Fronimo volere
Meco certe sue cose conferire.

Tirsi

Oimè, non passa alcuno a cui potessi
Addimandare almen nova dei passi,
O di Melampo mio sì caro amico;   55
Poiché, se insieme co 'l girar de gli anni
La memoria anco mia non s'è fuggita,
Questi contorni pur mi sembran quelli
Ove seco talor passai felice
Molt'ore liete in parlamenti grati   60
Al tempo ch'io venia per onorare
Ne l'età mia miglior con gli altri insieme
Nel Tempio santo Pan Dio nostro e Pale.
O memoria, o meschin vecchio, o miei figli!

Alessi

Odo voci da duol parmi interotte,   65
E sospir. Chi sarà ch'in flebil suono/[43r]
L'aria percota di dogliosi accenti
Quinci intorno? Fors'è colui che steso
Colà tra quei ginepri a terra giace?
Misero vecchio, alta sciagura forse   70
Tal lo spinge a dolersi. A dio, buon vecchio.
Qual cagion dal core ad ora, ad ora
Angosciosi sospir ti svelle, e 'l seno
Di caldo pianto irriga? A me discopri
I tuoi martir, che compatirli almeno   75
Ti prometto, quand'io
Dar non ti possa aita.

Tirsi

Deh, cortese pastor, dimmi, ti prego
Se questa parte dell'Arcadia è quella

pain, I shall search out Androgeo, who said he wished to spend the day with me. Or should I instead stay here to await Leggiadro, since he said just now when I met him with Fronimo that there was something he wished to talk to me about?

Tirsi

Alas, it seems that no one passes here from whom I could at least ask some news of my dear friend Melampo. For if my memory has not deserted me with the passing of the years, it was in this spot or hereabouts that I once spent many happy hours with him in pleasant conversation, at the time when I would come here in my youth to join the others in honoring our gods Pan and Pales in the sacred temple. O memory! O wretched old man! O my lost sons!

Alessi

I seem to hear doleful, broken words and sighs. Who can it be whose sorrowing tones so pierce the air hereabouts? Perhaps that man who is lying yonder among the juniper bushes? Poor old man! Perhaps it is some cruel blow of fortune that makes him so lament. Greetings, my good father! What is it that is wrenching these anguished sighs from your breast and furrowing your cheeks with hot tears? Reveal the source of your pain to me, that I may at least offer you compassion, even if I cannot be of any help to you.

Tirsi

Ah, courteous shepherd, pray tell me whether this part of Arcadia lies

Più vicina al gran Menalo, ove posto   80
Di Pan Dio nostro è il ricco tempio, e dove
Abitan (s'io non erro) duo pastori
Chiari di nome e ricchi di terreno,
Carino detto l'un, l'altro Melampo,
Ch'amai di cor quant[o] la vita istessa.   85

Alessi

Vedut'oggi ho Melampo, e di Carino
Inteso che qualch'anno è ch'egli è morto,
Per la cui figlia oggi son fatti a punto
Alcuni sacrificî a' quai pregato
Da un pastor giovinetto mi trovai   90
Di qua passando forestiero anch'io,
Né posso in questo altro ragguaglio darti.

Tirsi

Dunque è seguito il sacrificio?

Alessi

                              Or ora.

Tirsi

Misero me, qual più conforto resta
Tirsi, a le pene tue crudeli e tante?   95
Corse a l'orecchie mie ch'a far s'aveva/[43v]
Un sacrificio, in cui dovea trovarsi
Il fior di tutta Arcadia, e da più parte
Concorrervi anco altri pastori insieme,
Ov'io da le mie spemi rincorato,   100
Ch'ora tal nova avien che restin pure
Tradite, vi condussi questa mia
Greve salma e rugosa a lenti passi
Per camin così lungo, di trovare
Qualche pace sperando a' miei tormenti.   105
Ma s'è seguito omai, deh, che più spero?

Alessi

De l'aiuto divin non diffidare,
Amico mio, che LA pietà celeste

close by the great Mount Maenalus,[83] where the rich temple stands to
our god Pan and where, if I do not err, there live two shepherds rich in
fame and land, named Carino and Melampo? These men I once loved as
much as life itself.

Alessi

I saw Melampo today; as for Carino, I hear that he had died a few years
ago. Indeed, it was for Carino's daughter that there was today performed
a sacrifice, which I attended on the invitation of a young shepherd I had
met by chance as I passed through here, as a stranger to these parts.
More I cannot tell you.

Tirsi

So the sacrifice has taken place?

Alessi

Just now, yes.

Tirsi

Alas! Then what possible comfort can await you, Tirsi, for all your long
sufferings? I had heard that a sacrifice was due to be held, and that it was
to be attended by the flower of Arcadia, and also by shepherds from distant parts, who were coming here for this purpose. My hopes—now
dashed once more!—were raised on hearing this and I dragged my ancient body along the long road to this place, step by weary step, hoping
to find some solace for my torment. But if the sacrifice is already over—
ah, then, what more hope can I have?

Alessi

Despair not of help from on high, my friend, for the heavens in their

A' preghi nostri in ogni tempo è pronta,
Pur ch'onesti ed umili i preghi sieno.　　　　　　110
Impetrar qualche grazia dagli Dei
Forse volevi? E quel fascel che stringi
Tra le mani dolente è qualche dono
Che appresentar volevi al sacrificio?

Tirsi

Deh, non voler, pastor, ch'io rinovelle　　　　　115
(raccontando il mio danno) il mio dolore,
Che ben sai tu ch'ESSACERBATA piaga
Vie più tormenta. Ad ogn'or ben io bramo
Grazia aver dagli Dei, ch'ogni mortale
Del divino favor bisogna ha in terra;　　　　　120
Ma qua cagion altra mi trasse, e questo
Altro è che dono o pegno. Caro, o figlio,
O memoria crudel, misero vecchio!

Alessi

Pastor, sì mi trafiggi
Con questi tuoi lamenti l'alma e 'l core　　　　125
Ch'altrove bramo aver rivolto il piede/[43r bis]
Quando qua venni. Omai, deh, dimmi quale
Cagion ti move a lagrimar sì forte;
Che se l'uom per giovare è nato a l'uomo
Debbiam cercar l'uno dall'altro aita　　　　　130
E sperarla, che a AD uom che di ragione
Abbia pur picciol lume, unqua non puote
Alcun altra avenir cosa più cara
Che giovar ad altrui, se dichiarando
Cortese, e non del nome d'uomo indegno.　　　135

Tirsi

Ahi, che se questo cor capace fosse
D'alcun conforto, temprarei (confesso)
Gentil pastore, al tuo sembiante, al modo
Del grazioso tuo saggio parlare
In qualche parte almeno il mio dolore.　　　　140
Ma (lasso) l'alma mia

mercy are always attentive to our prayers when those prayers are honest and humble. Perhaps you were coming to the sacrifice in the hope of entreating some grace of the gods? Is that bundle you clasp in your grieving hands an offering of some kind?

Tirsi

Oh shepherd, do not ask me to relive my sorrow by recounting my pitiful tale, for you know that when a wound is reopened its pain returns all the worse. Certainly, I long for the grace of the gods, for all mortals have need of divine favor. But that was not the cause that brought me here, and what I carry is no offering or gift . . . O my son! O cruel memory! O wretched old man!

Alessi

Shepherd, your laments so pierce my heart and soul that I would wish that my feet had led me to some other place. But, I pray you, do tell me what is the cause of these bitter tears of yours. For we were put on the earth to help our fellow man, and must all seek to aid each other in our turn. Indeed, there can be no greater pleasure for any man who has the faintest glimmer of humanity than to help others, and show himself, in doing so, courteous and not undeserving of the name of man.

Tirsi

Gentle shepherd, if this heart had not gone beyond the point where it could feel any comfort, it would temper my grief in some part to look on your kindly face and listen to your gracious and wise words. Alas, though! My poor soul languishes so wretchedly beneath the heavy weight of my

Sotto sì grave pondo
Del duol langue meschina
Che 'l colpo solo attende
Fatale per uscir da questo rio   145
Carcer terreno, ed a un tempo
Da mille strazî insieme.
Ma perché al gesto nobile mi sembri,
E di spirto e di sangue, mi dispongo
A compiacerti, e me n'astringi quando   150
Mostri d'aver pietà de' miei dolori,
Ma pur che questo duolo che trabocca
Fuore dal cor per gli occhi non mi tolga
Di poter ragionar l'usata forza.

Alessi

In dir raccogli ogni virtute al core,   155
Et indi lo rinfranca, perché L'UOMO/[43v bis]
Allor del suo valor da saggio, quando
Del forte braccio di fortuna al colpo
Per schermo di prudenza il forte scudo
Gli oppone, e a quel non men resiste, quale   160
Ai riflussi de l'onde irate suole
Scoglio antico del mare, e spera, spera,
Che A L'uom più dolce non è cosa al mondo
De la speranza. Or segui
Prima che giunga alcuno a disturbarci.   165

Tirsi

Al quarto lustro un anno a pena manca
Che de la rota di fortuna in loco
Era sublime, quando in ima parte
Fui traboccato con troppo aspro modo,
Gioco di lei venendo. Er'io d'etate   170
Di più di dieci lustri oltre passato,
Padron de greggi assai, d'ampio terreno
Quanto pastor alcun dei miei contorni,
Nè padre ancora d'alcun figlio essendo,
Le dolcezze bramando di potere   175
Goder anch'io di questo nome figlio,
Dopo lungo pregar gli Dei mi diero
Un figlio. Oimè, meschino!

sorrow that it can await with eagerness only the fatal blow that will liberate it from this cruel earthly prison and its countless torments. But since you seem to me noble in blood and in spirit, I am disposed to do as you bid me, while the sympathy you show for my sufferings almost constrains me to do so. I shall speak, then—if this sorrow which spills from my soul through my eyes will allow me to speak as I am wont.

Alessi

In speaking, let your heart draw new energies, for the true test of a man's valor comes when he is struck by the mighty arm of Fortune and fights back with the hardy shield of prudence, resisting fortune's blows like a rock of ages resisting the stormy waves of the ocean. And hope, hope! For there is no sweeter thing in this mortal world than hope. Speak now, before someone comes along to disturb us.

Tirsi

Almost twenty years have now passed—there lacks but one year—since I became Fortune's plaything and was dashed from the peak of her favors to the very depths of misfortune in all too cruel a manner. I had already passed my fiftieth year and was as rich in flocks and land as any of the neighboring shepherds, but I was yet to become a father, and yearned only for my ears to enjoy the sweetness of those words "my son." And after long years waiting in vain, the gods granted me a son . . . Oh, alas! Poor wretch!

Alessi

RARO (come ti disse) e mai ne vanno
D'effetto vuote le preghiere oneste   180
Che si porgono giuste agli alti Dei.
LA celeste clemenza incontra noi
È pur troppo benigna. Or cessa il pianto
Pastore, e 'l resto segui.

Tirsi

Un figlio dico ebb'io (deh così mai   185
Avuto non l'avessi!). A un anno ancora/[45r]
Egli non era giunto, quando lieta
La madre sua il pargoletto pegno
(Dolce peso e soave) entro a le braccia
Tenea ristretto caramente seco   190
Scherzando del Ladon posta a la ripa.
Giunse d'infidi passaggeri un stuolo
Repente allor, sì che la vita a pena
Ella potè salvar, gettato a terra
(Ah cruda madre) il caro figliol; lasso,   195
Ch'in rimembrarlo solo esco di vita.
Troppo tenero furto a roze mani,
Oimè troppo pregiato,
Venne il mio caro figlio. Ahi figlio, ahi padre!

Alessi

Pon mente ch'oggi alta ventura scopro   200
Per Androgeo. La madre dunque tolta
Da le barbare mani, come suole
Timida (non già cruda) donna, il figlio
De le genti rapace lasciò preda?

Tirsi

Ahi, che non so qual fine il caso avesse,   205
Ch'allor co 'l gregge dilungato a paschi
(Ch'era ne la stagion che a Sirio giunto
Il sole, in terra di cocente arsura
Sembra ch'incenerisca e fere e piante),
Duo giorni pria che la novella acerba   210
Intendessi passaro, onde ogni speme

Alessi

As I said, rarely or never do the honest prayers we offer up to the gods on high remain unanswered. The heavens' mercy towards us is all too great. Now, shepherd, dry your tears and continue.

Tirsi

As I said, I had a son—oh, would that I had not!—and he had not yet reached his first year, when, as his happy mother was sitting with him by the river Ladon, holding her precious little burden close in her arms and gently playing with him, a band of passing villains suddenly happened upon them. She was hardly able to save her own life and (ah, cruel mother!) flung her dear son to the ground in escaping. Alas! Only to think of it almost kills me! So soft a prey, and so precious, for such rough hands to seize! Oh, my poor child! O wretched father!

Alessi

[*Aside*] Hark! What good fortune I am here discovering for Androgeo! [*To Tirsi*] So his mother, fleeing as a timorous woman well might—do not call her a cruel one!—from the hands of these brutes, left her son a prey to their ravenings?

Tirsi

Ah! I do not know how the story ended, for I was at that time away, leading my flocks to pasture (for it was the season when the sun arrives in Sirius and seems with its fierce heat to burn to ashes the beasts and plants of this earth). Two days, then, had passed, before the terrible news reached my ears, and by that time I had no hope of regaining my dear

Perdei di ricovrare il caro figlio;
Pur posi ogni arte per spiarne, e in vano.
Ahi, chi sa? Forse il mio tenero germe
(Debile acquisto a quell'ingorde voglie)   215
Stato fie vilipeso, e destinato/[45v]
A satollare (ahi lasso!)
Di crude fere e inumane il gusto.
Questo pensier più d'altra cosa grava
L'alma e d'acuto telo il cor trafigge.   220
O spoglia cara, o me dolente! Ahi, figlio,
Figlio: nome soave,
Ora acerbo, qual già bramato tanto.

Alessi

PIU' che 'l mal deve l'uomo creder il bene.
Non ti lagnar, pastor, cotanto, ch'io   225
Teco m'accingo a questa impresa, e forse
Averrà che d'avermi il tuo dolore
Aperto ancor non ti rincresca; quando
Se pur qua giunto sei per ricercarne,
Tal spero oprarmi in questo, ch'oggi udirne   230
Qualche cosa potremo. Hor stanne lieto,
Ma fa ch'io vegga quanto anco qui serbi.

Tirsi

Misero me, che rimembranza amara
È del mio caro figlio!
D'Amarilli gentil (che la mia moglie   235
Per cara figlia avea) questo fu dono;
Che proprio parto il mio figlio stimando,
Di comporlo leggiadro avea sol cura,
E fra molti altri di sua man trapunti
Pregiati doni e belli,   240
Questo drappo fec'ella, che qui serbo
In ogni parte a quel simile a punto
Che del mio dolce figlio
Entro accogliea le tenerelle membra,
Allor che orbo restai   245
Di lui, che luce a punto/[46r]
Era de gli occhi miei. Ma non han fine

son. Certainly, I did all I could to find out what had transpired, but in vain. Ah! Who knows whether my tender seed—such a fragile acquisition to slake such fierce greeds!—was scorned by them and cast aside as prey for ravening and inhuman beasts. Alas! That is the thought that preys most cruelly on my soul, and pierces my heart with the sharpest spear. Oh dearest creature! O what pain! Oh my son, my son! How sweet that word sounds—yet it is now as harsh to me as once it was precious.

Alessi

We should always incline to believe the good rather than the bad. Shepherd, do not lament so, for now I am here to share with you in your endeavors, and it may be that you will have cause to be glad that you opened your heart to me. And if you have come here to try to learn something further, I shall help you, and hope that before this day is out, you may hear some news. Let this gladden your heart; but meanwhile let me see what it is that you are clutching there.

Tirsi

Alas! It is a bitter keepsake of my dear son. This was a gift of fair Amarilli, the dear daughter of my wife, who loved my son as though he were her own child, and thought only of decking him as beautifully as she might. Among many other precious and lovely gifts she made for him was this shawl I am holding here. In every respect, it is identical to that in which my sweet child's little limbs were wrapped on that day when I remained blinded of his light—for, indeed, he was the light of my eyes.

Quivi le mie sciagure, altra anco il core
Aspra cagion mi affligge. Un anno ancora
Dopo tanto mio duol fornito a pena   250
Era, quando pietoso forse il cielo
Del mio gran danno un'altro figlio diemi,
Co 'l qual cercai disacerbare in parte
L'affanno mio. Ma in van, che qual nel core
La mia sciagura avea, fissa negli occhi   255
Anco tenea di lui l'imago cara
Ad ogn'ora; e confesso, ch'io dovea
Scemar (se non finire) il duolo almeno
A la beltate, al gran valore, al senno
Ch'in giovenile etate questo mio   260
Novo figlio mostrava, e gli Dei forse
Me ne diero sdegnati alto castigo.
E la malvagia mia futura sorte
(che in presaghirla il cor troppo era desto)
Forse tal mi rendeva   265
Lunge da ogni contento. Ancora giunto
A tre lustri non era il mio secondo
Figlio, quando da me, senza pur dire
A dio, se 'n gì, né d'Amor so se punto
(che non lo credo), o pur di cercar vago   270
Nove contrade,³¹ dove oggi due anni
Due mesi sono e un giorno, che, per quanto
Ne abbi cercato intorno, io non ho ancora
Giamai di lui novella alcuna udita.
Questa l'ultima fia possa ch'io tenti   275
Per addolcire il mio destin, scorgendo/[46v]
Che RARO uom fugge quanto già permesso
Al nascer suo gli fu dato del ciel in sorte.
Per ritrovarmi al sacrificio tardo
Giunsi, me'n duol, ch'avrei trovato forse   280
Almen qualche consiglio al mal che m'ange.
Or ch'altro più non spero
Per me di bene al mondo, riposato
Qui un poco, cercarò Melampo, e poscia
Salutatollo, il piè girar di novo   285
Intendo a la capanna mia, dov'io
Senza partir più mai, di speme in bando,

But my afflictions did not end there! Another cruel accident came to blight my happiness. A year had scarce passed after this my first sorrow, when the heavens, perhaps pitying of my misery, gave me another son. I tried, with this gift, to mitigate my sorrow in some part. But in vain, for just as the pain of my loss remained rooted in my heart, so the dear image of my first child remained fixed before my eyes at every moment. I confess that I should have tried, if not to forget him, at least to allow my sorrow to fade with time; I should have let myself enjoy the beauty and valor and wisdom that this new son of mine showed from his tenderest years. I did not, and perhaps it was because of this that the gods in their anger sent me another cruel punishment. Or perhaps it was a premonition of my future ill luck (for my heart was keen to scent it) that held me back from the happiness I might have felt at that time.

This second son of mine was not yet fifteen years old when he left me without saying farewell, whether spurred by Love (though I have no reason to think so) or by a curiosity to see the world. And it is now two years, two months, and a day that I have been searching for news of him, without hearing anything. My journey here shall be my last attempt to mitigate my suffering, for I now see that a man rarely escapes the destiny that has been decided for him at his birth. I am grieved that I arrived too late for the sacrifice, for I was hoping I might at least hear some news that might lighten the burden that I bear. Now that all hope is lost, I shall rest here awhile and then seek out Melampo and greet him; then I shall turn my weary feet back to my hut, there to eke out my days in sad despond.

Vo' finir questa vita in abbandono
(fuore che un duolo eterno, ogn'altra cosa
Lasciando). O figli cari, o padre, o morte!   290

Alessi

Chi non ti confessasse a pien meschino
Pastor, di senno e di pietate privo
Certo sarebbe in tutto. Or qui ti posa
Un pezzo, e a me questo fascel concedi
Che agli pastori (ancor uniti forse   295
Qui giù dal colle) mostrerollo, il caso
Tuo discoprendo loro, e buona o rea
Ch'io nova abbia dell'uno o dell'altro figlio
A te, Melampo ed io verremo insieme.

Tirsi

Deh sì, fa ch'io lo vegga, e pur di questo   300
Fascel fa quanto vuoi, pastor, ma poco
Che più sperar mi resta.

Alessi

     A dio.

Tirsi

       A dio.

Alessi

S'a le miserie altrui pietate abbiamo,
Raro avien che dal ciel con larga mano
Largito non ci sia l'istesso dono.   305
Sento al cor di costui l'acerbo caso/[47r]
Ah così ella ch'adoro dentro il seno
Sentisse il mio destin, spiacere avendo
Del mal che per lei sento.
Dov'or sei, cara ninfa? Quanto tardo   310
A rivederti, tante Amor ripiglia
Punte al mio petto, ed al cor fiamme ardenti.
Questo giorno sia spero (s'io non erro)
Per Androgeo felice. Or ecco (o quanto
Mi dispiace fermar), questo è Leggiadro.   315

No more shall the lure of hope tempt me to direct my steps elsewhere: I shall cleave alone to my eternal woe, leaving all else aside. O my dear sons! O poor father! O death!

Alessi

Anyone who failed to feel pity at your tale, wretched shepherd, would certainly be bereft of all reason and humanity. Now rest here a while, and let me take this bundle you have been carrying, so that I may show it to the shepherds and tell them your story. I think I shall find them at the foot of the hill. Then I shall return here with Melampo, bringing back with me any news I have managed to gather of your sons, whether good or ill.

Tirsi

Yes, pray do bring Melampo back here to me. As for this bundle—do what you will with it, shepherd, though I have little hope that any good will result.

Alessi

Farewell.

Tirsi

Farewell.

Alessi

If we show compassion to others' woes, it is rare that the heavens do not reward us with the same gift. This poor man's cruel fate has deeply touched my heart. Ah, would that my own misfortunes could awake the same feeling within the heart of her whom I adore, and that she might have mercy on me for the woes I suffer for her sake! Ah, dear nymph, where are you now? How long it seems until I can see you! Love is piercing my heart with new arrows and burning it with new flames. Today, if I do not err, is to be a happy one for Androgeo. Oh, but here is Leggiadro. How I regret all this delay!

SCENA SESTA

Leggiadro, Alessi, Tirsi

Leggiadro
Bramo Alessi da te favor, ma tosto   1
Ti conviene d'oprar.

Alessi
                        Né minor fretta
Or è la mia. Ma dimmi quanto fare
Ho per te, ch'ad un tempo insieme a duo
Potendo, io servirò.

Leggiadro
                        Lascio da parte   5
Le parole soverchie, Alessi, ch'io
Dir ti dovrei per usar teco troppo
(S'io non inganno) libertate, osando
Di commandarti, e ti conosco a pena.
S'ascriva il tutto a la bontà ch'io stimo   10
In te. Ma, convenendomi esser breve
In ragionarti, il mio bisogno è questo.
La sorella amo di Serrano, e bramo
In matrimonio averla, e seco a punto
Di questo a parlamento ho posto or ora/[47v]   15
Fronimo, conscio a pien del mio desire,
Il qual per agio aver di poter fare
Per me quanto conviensi, a ritrovarti
Mi pregò, e trattenerti. E qui soggiunse
L'istesso ancor il mio padron Serrano,   20
Che t'ama molto, e fa disegno, penso,
Pria che tu parta alcun solazzo darti,
E ambi cura m'hanno dato infine
D'intender poi di Flori il caso a pieno,
E di dirlo (potendo) al sacerdote.   25
Ora vorrei che colà giù n'andassi
Poco da dove n'incontraste lunge,
E a mio favor tu t'adoprasti ancora.

SCENE SIX

Alessi, Leggiadro

Leggiadro

Alessi, I need your help, and fast.

Alessi

I too am pressed for time. But tell what you need from me, and I shall do it if I can.

Leggiadro

I shall lay aside all ceremony, Alessi, even though it seems to me that I am taking a great liberty in asking you to help me in this way when I barely know you. It is the innate goodness I sense in you that is to blame. To be brief, though, this is my case. I love Serrano's sister and desire to ask her hand in marriage; and I have just now asked Fronimo—who is fully informed of my desires—to approach Serrano on my behalf. Fronimo asked me to seek you out and detain you while he conducted this business for me. And my master Serrano added his wishes to Fronimo, for he is greatly taken with you and wishes, I think, before you leave, to organize some diversion for you. Both, besides, asked me to find out in full what has happened to Flori and, if I discovered it, to tell the priest. Now, I wanted to ask whether you would go down to near where we first met and join with Fronimo in speaking for me with Serrano. You will find them not far from the place where we met.

Alessi

    Vie più ti mostri allor cortese quando
    Più di servirti occasion mi porgi,   30
    E io rimarrò pago allor ch'io possa
    Sodisfar (te servendo) ancor a me stesso.
    Vado, e pur spera ch'adoprar io m'abbia
    Per te senza più dire.

Leggiadro

                  Or odi ancora,
    E sarò breve.

Alessi

                Sì, di grazia.

Leggiadro

                    Quando   35
    Serrano pur negasse a la richiesta
    Di Fronimo di darmi la sorella,
    Allegando ch'io son (per sua ragione)
    Servo, e che altrove di rippor'ha in mente
    La sorella, soggiungi allor che Tirsi   40
    È il padre mio, qui tanto noto a ogn'uno,
    Benché lontano il nostro gregge pasca,
    Che non è alcun pastor che per bontate
    E per ricchezze non l'ammiri ed ami;
    E quando entro al suo cor di questo alcuno/[48r]   45
    Dubbio nascesse, m'offerisco trarre
    Mio padre in queste parti, d'anni grave
    Quanto di senno, ad ogni mia richiesta,
    Purch'ei di me sentir novella possa,
    Che stimar deve morto, poiché sono   50
    Più di due anni che da lui partimmi
    Senza commiato, sol per fama acceso
    De la costei bellezza, in cotal guisa
    Che meno è il foco ardente.
    Ma qual stupor t'ingombra sì che sembri   55
    Più ad imagin di marmo che ad uomo vivo?

Alessi

The best way you can show your courtesy to me is to give me further occasion to serve you; and I shall be all the happier in that, in serving you, I believe I can also help myself. I shall go where you ask and hope I can help you. I need no further instructions.

Leggiadro

No, listen! I shall be brief.

Alessi

Speak on.

Leggiadro

If Serrano should refuse Fronimo's request that he give me his sister in marriage, on the grounds that I am only a servant and that he has other plans for her, your part is to tell him that my father is Tirsi. He is known to everyone in these parts, even though he pastures his own flocks far away, for there is no shepherd who does not love and admire him for his goodness and his wealth. And if Serrano should still doubt, then I shall be happy to bring my father to these parts to confirm it, though he is as heavy with years as he is with wisdom. He would certainly come if he thought he could hear news of me, as he must by now think me dead— for it is now more than two years since I left him without taking my leave, lured away by Gelinda's beauty, which had inflamed my desire more keenly than any fire. But why do you stand so amazed at this news, more like a marble statue than a living man?

Alessi

    Tirsi è 'l tuo padre?
Dammi la man, ch'or or felice spero
Vederti, e prima che l'aurato crine
Ne l'onde Febo attuffi, di tua donna   60
Felice possessor. Ma ben diverso
Fu l'oprar tuo ver me da quanto fare
Ora intendo per te, già trattenuto
Il misero mio piè veloce e sciolto
Avendo oggi (oimè!) qui, c'ha reso Amore   65
Avinto e pigro sì, che non so quando
Partir potrò d'Arcadia.

Leggiadro

                Quando Amore
La colpa ave di ciò, che ne poss'io?
Ma dimmi la cagione.

Alessi

             Or non è il tempo.
Andiamo. Or vedi se costui conosci   70
Qui corcato tra l'erbe. Pian, che dorme!
Ei si deve sognando tra le braccia
Tener persona cara: mira come
Sembra che di piacer si strugga, e al seno/[48v]
L'aria si stringe in dolci larve involto.   75

Leggiadro

    O caro padre! O ciel! Deh, Amore, o come?
O Dei, me lo guidate al maggior uopo.
Io vo' destarlo. Padre caro, o padre!

Tirsi

    Ahi chi scortese il mio contento sturba,
E la mia pace? Chi l'amato figlio   80
Dal mio petto ha (crudel) levato, e desto
(Me destando) entro a l'alma un duolo eterno?

Alessi

    Non diss'io che sognava?

Alessi

Tirsi is your father? Give me your hand, for I hope to see you happy at once, and the happy possessor of your lady before Phoebus dips his golden head in the waves. But what you have done to me is very different from what I now hope to do for you. You detained my wretched footsteps here in Arcadia, and these steps, once swift and free, are now so tightly shackled that I despair of ever leaving. This is the work of Love.

Leggiadro

If the fault is of Love, then how can I be blamed for it? But explain what has happened.

Alessi

This is not the moment. Let us go. Now, see whether you recognize that man lying there in the grass. Hush! He is sleeping, and in his dreams he must be holding someone dear to him in his arms. Look how he seems to melt with pleasure, and how he clutches to his breast the empty air, as if surrounded by sweet strange shapes.

Leggiadro

O dearest father! O heavens! O Love, how can this be? Have the gods guided him to me in this my hour of need? I must wake him! Father, my dear father!

Tirsei

Who is it who so rudely breaks into my happy repose? Who is it who so cruelly tears my dear son from my breast? Who is it who in waking me has awakened an endless sorrow in my heart?

Alessi

Did I not tell you he was dreaming?

Leggiadro
> Amato padre, ecco ch'io sono a punto,
> Anzi che ve lo rendo.

Tirsi
> > Figlio!

Leggiadro
> > > Padre!   85

Tirsi
> Amato figlio!

Leggiadro
> > Padre caro!

Tirsi
> > > > Ahi, figlio!

Tirsi
> Da improviso piacer venuto è meno
> (Misero vecchio). Di soverchia gioia
> Ripieno ha il core, il qual cessato essendo
> Dal vital moto in guisa tale il rende.   89 90

Leggiadro
> M'avrà la sorte mia fatto ad un tempo
> Lieto e misero insieme?
> Padre!

Alessi
> > > La cinta sciogli, che lo stringe.
> Ecco che si risente.

Leggiadro
> > Padre caro!

Tirsi
> Oimè!

Leggiadro

Beloved father, it is I! Let me return your son to you.

Tirsi

My son!

Leggiadro

Father!

Tirsi

Beloved son!

Leggiadro

Dearest father!

Tirsi

Ah, son . . .

Alessi

This sudden pleasure has been too much for him. Poor old man, he has fainted from an excess of joy. His heart is quite full, and has ceased its vital motions. This is what has caused his collapse.

Leggiadro

But surely it cannot be that I am fated to be happy and wretched together? Father!

Alessi

Loosen his girdle, which constrains him. Look, he is moving.

Leggiadro

Dearest father!

Tirsi

Alas!

Alessi

    Tirsi, apri gli occhi. Ecco il tuo figlio.   95

Tirsi

    Ahi fi [. . .]

Alessi

                Di nuovo essangue torna. Quanto
    Ei si risente più, più segno porge
    D'interno gaudio, e se di vita l'uomo
    Più facilmente trae del duol la gioia,
    Temo ch'ei non si moia.   100

Leggiadro

    Almen le resti, o Dei, tanto di vita
    Ch'io le chieggia perdono, e ch'io l'impetri.

Alessi

    Lascia il pianto, o Leggiadro. Ecco di novo
    Egli ritorna, e già ti mira. Tirsi!/[49r]

Leggiadro

    Amato padre, io so ch'errai, volgendo   105
    Da te lontano il piè, che sol poggiare
    Dovea per l'orme tue paterne. Amore
    Ne fu cagion, che sino
    Gli Dei sforza del cielo. Quest'etate
    Mia giovenile, l'altrui colpa omai   110
    Da te perdon m'impetri, o caro padre.

Tirsi

    Lèvati, amato figlio, del mio core
    Unico speme, e cara, ch'ogni colpa
    T'è già rimessa. Troppo grande acquisto
    È stato questo mio. Tutt'altro ancora   115
    Per te da me s'ottenga, o figlio caro.
    Pur ti stringo ancor dentro a queste braccia,
    Pur ti veggo e pur t'odo.

Alessi

> Tirsi, open your eyes. Here is your son.

Tirsi

> Ah, son

Alessi

> Once again, he has turned quite white again—though each time he re-
> turns to consciousness, one can see his inner joy more clearly. But if it is
> true that it is joy, more than sorrow, that can cause our death, then in-
> deed I fear for his life.

Leggiadro

> O ye gods, let him at least live for long enough for me to ask his for-
> giveness, or beg it!

Alessi

> Leggiadro, do not weep. See, he is once more returning to his senses. He
> is looking at you. Tirsi!

Leggiadro

> Beloved father, I know that I was in error when I turned my steps away
> from you: those steps that should by rights always have followed in
> yours. Love was the cause—Love who is capable even of bending the
> gods to his will. Dear father, I beg you, forgive me my trespass. Consider
> my youthful age and the force that was working on me.

Tirsi

> Dear son, raise yourself up: All is forgiven. You are my heart's only dear
> hope. This gift is all too great. My wishes have been granted. O dearest
> son! I can still hold you in these old arms! Still look at you! Still hear you!

Leggiadro

    Da concedermi, o padre, ancor vi resta.

Alessi

    Parmi che 'l sole intepedisca i raggi,   120
    Piegandosi a l'occidente. Meglio fia
    Ch'andiamo insieme ad oprar quanto brami,
    Leggiadro, ch'altra gioia ancora forse
    L'alme v'ingombreran, sì come spero,
    Pria che del ciel quest'occhio eterno asconda   125
    A noi mortali il lume suo sì vago.

Tirsi

    Gentil pastore e saggio, ti riconosco
    Parte ancora da te del mio contento,
    Poiché s'altri m'avesse data nova
    Ch'era fornito il sacrificio, senza   130
    Altro da me cercar, indietro il passo
    Avrei tosto rivolto, con pensiero
    (Come ti dissi) di non procurare
    Pace a la disperata mia fortuna./[49v]
    Cortese, tu con dolci modi e saggi,   135
    Soavemente violentando il mio
    Voler a dirti, m'astringesti a pieno
    Tutta la sorte mia. Tu poscia ancora
    Con nobili maniere (oltre misura
    Benigno) alcuna speme m'additasti,   140
    Presago forse ch'in gran parte il cielo
    Oggi appagar doveva i miei desiri.

Alessi

    OGNI ben di qua giù si riconos[c]a
    Pur dagli Dei, che S'UOM mortale oprando
    Giova ad altrui, mercè del cielo è solo,   145
    Troppo sendo imperfetto per se stesso.

Leggiadro

    Andiamo, che tra via queste e molt'altre
    Parole potran dirsi, ch'anco troppo
    Temo che siamo stati.

Leggiadro

Father, there is one thing more I would ask of you.

Alessi

It seems to me that the sun's rays are dying, as it falls in the west. Leggiadro, we had best go now to do what you wished, for another joy may yet burden your souls, as I hope, before this eye of the heavens hides its lovely light from us mortals.

Tirsi

Noble and wise shepherd, I recognize my happiness as stemming in part from you. For if others had told me that I was too late for the sacrifice, without inquiring any further of my condition, I would surely have turned my steps back, thinking in my despair that I would find no solace for my cruel fate. But you, with your courtesy and the sweetness and wisdom of your words, gently violated my will and forced me to apprise you fully of my story. And then, in the most noble manner, and with surpassing kindness, you pressed me to retain some shred of hope—a presage, perhaps, that today the heavens would grant my wishes.

Alessi

All good things on this earth come from the gods, and if a mortal by chance does some good to his fellow man, the merit is not his, but heaven's, for of himself he is too weak.

Leggiadro

Let us go. We can speak of this and other things on the way. I fear we may already be late as it is.

Alessi

Andiam.

Tirsi

Andiamo.

Il fine del quarto atto

Alessi

    Let us go.

Tirsi

    Yes, let us go.

    End of act four

[50r] ATTO QUINTO

SCENA PRIMA

Flori, Licori

Flori

Poi chi m'assicura ch'io rivegga   1
Oimè, cara Licori,
Il mio straniero e fuggitivo amante?
Ma pur, lassa, si parta,
Che la memoria sua   5
Giamai fin ch'avrò vita
Non partirà dal cor, dove il bel foco
Primo giunse d'Amor, ch'a questo petto
L'ultimo fia che poco o assai lo scalde.
Il mio fatale e volontario affetto   10
Non avrà fin giamai: sì vuole Amore,
Tal di questo mio cor fido è 'l costume.

Licori

Non dubitar che noi 'l troviamo, e ch'egli
Non resti e non gradisca del tuo core
Un affetto sì grande, quando pure   15
Far lo potrai co 'l canto
Viver'eternamente. S'ami, spera,
Flori, ch'a FARSI amar, maggiore incanto
Non è, ch'amar, se da un pastor di nome/ [50v]
Chiaro intendeste il ver, ch'or Adria onora   20
Del bel Aufido e de le Muse in grembo
Nato, che SFORZA ad ammirarlo ancora
Suso nel ciel gli Dei. Anzi che in grado
Avrà forse da te l'esser amato,

ACT FIVE

SCENE ONE

Flori, Licori

Flori

Alas! Dearest Licori, how can I know whether I will see him again, my strange and elusive Lover? But even if he departs from this place, as long as I live the memory of him will always be etched on this heart of mine where first love's fires were kindled; for no other man will henceforth stir the least breath of desire in this breast. My fatal chosen passion shall see no end, for thus Love wills it—well do I know the habits of this faithful heart of mine.

Licori

Fear not, for we shall find him; nor should you fear that he will not remain here and return this heartfelt passion of yours, especially as you have the power to confer eternal life on him through your song. If you love truly, Flori, then hope, for there is no surer way to make oneself loved than to love, if one is to believe what one hears from a famous shepherd, now honoring Adria with his presence, but born in the lap of the lovely Aufidus and of the Muses: a man who forces *[SFORZA]*[84] the very gods of the heavens to admire him. So perhaps your shepherd will

Nè tali nozze mai credo ricusi   25
Il tuo fratel. Ma perché piangi? Lassa!
Lassa pianger a me, che nulla veggo
Di rimedio al mio male.

Flori

Piango, Licori, che dal tuo parlare
Poco restami (lassa) che sperare.   30
Tu sai ch'io servo Delia, e non mi lice
Al nodo d'Imeneo pur di pensare.
Ahi, che s'Alessi gradirà il mio affetto
(Questo mi duol), vorrà meco venire
A qualche fin di maritaggio, e [s']io   35
non vorrò consentirci, ei fuggerassi,
(Lassa) io morrò, che senza Alessi in vita
Pur un sol giorno oimè restar non posso.

Licori

Perché non vuoi legarti con Alessi
Col nodo d'Imeneo, se tanto l'ami?   40
Vorrai forse (vil ninfa) a lui piacere
Con brame irregolate
Di vietato commercio?

Flori

Tolga, Delia, da me tali pensieri.
Nè a l'un, nè a l'altro modo   45
Vogl'io piacerle mai
Col fin che par ch'ogni pastor sì agogni.

Licori

Ora t'intendo. Castamente amarlo
Vuoi, nè legarti in matrimonio seco?/ [51r]

Flori

Questo sol brama il cor, non potendo altro.   50

Licori

Ah, quai pensieri insoliti, qual['] brame
T'invogliano ancor, Flori? Io mi pensava

welcome your love—nor, I think, would your brother refuse such a marriage. But why do you weep? Poor creature, leave weeping to me, for—alas!—I can see no remedy for my sufferings.

Flori

I weep, Licori, because what you say leaves me—alas!—with little hope. You know that I serve Delia and that it is forbidden to me even to think of the knot of Hymen. It grieves me to think that, if Alessi returns my passion, he will wish our story to lead to marriage; and, when I do not consent to his wishes, he will abandon me. And then—alas!—what will remain to me but death, for without my Alessi, I shall not be able to live a single day.

Licori

And why do you not wish to bind yourself to Alessi with Hymen's knot if you so love him? Can it be, shameless creature, that you think of pleasing him with the irregular desires of forbidden concourse?

Flori

May Delia ever preserve me from such thoughts! Nor in the one, nor the other way, do I ever wish to grant him that pleasure for which it seems all shepherds long.

Licori

Now I understand you. You wish, then, to love him chastely, without binding yourself to him in marriage?

Flori

That is what my heart desires—for it can have no other wish.

Licori

Ah, what strange thoughts and desires are these that still entice you,

Ch'ormai fossi chiarita
Di correr dietro a l'impossibil sempre.
Qual havrem dagli Dei grazia ottenuta   55
Per te nel sacrificio, s'anco in guisa
Di pria ti struggi, e da te stessa a pena
Scieglier non sai lo stato tuo confuso?
Cotesti tuoi pensier troppo lontani
Fur mai sempre da quei d'ogni altra ninfa.   60

Flori

E di questo mi godo, che ben sai
Che A CONSEGUIR difficil cosa spirto
Nobil vie più s'accende, e sai che L'OPRE,
Quant'ardue più, tanto più illustri sono.
Ho dagli Dei pur troppo grazia avuta.   65
Non ti doler di questo. Ecco, pur veggio
D'Amaranta mia l'urna, e non vaneggio.
E che ti par? A l'uom dono maggiore
Far non può il ciel che d'intelletto ornarlo.
Dobbiam dolerci che benigno m'abbia   70
Aperto il lume, onde non sogno, od erro?

Licori

Come non erri, se ad un tempo amando
Sprezzi quanto sol bramano gli amanti?
E disiando fuggi d'ottenere
Quello che far sol ti potria felice?   75

Flori

Null'altro, sol ch'Alessi m'ami, io bramo,
E per tal grazia aver, torrei la morte.
Come fuggo tal don? Tu ben sai, ch'erri.

Licori

Se di legarti in matrimonio seco/ [51v]
Neghi, no 'l fuggi dunque?   80
Egli è riposo pure,
E desiato pregio degli amanti.

Flori? I thought you were now cured of your habit of ever chasing the impossible. What use was it for us to obtain such rare grace from the gods for you in the sacrifice, if just as before you still yearn vainly and seem intent on inflicting on yourself your wonted state of confusion? These thoughts of yours have always been quite remote from anything a nymph has thought before.

Flori

And I glory in that fact! For, as you know, noble spirits are most inspired by the most difficult tasks; you know well, too, that the more arduous a deed, the more apt it is to win fame. I have received from the gods almost too great a boon of grace; do not be sorry for that. See—I can gaze on my Amaranta's urn without my mind wandering. Does that seem nothing to you? What greater gift can the gods bestow on us than to endow us with reason? Should we be sorry that the heavens have so benignly illumined my mind that I no longer dream or rave vainly?

Licori

You think that you are not raving when you say that you are in love, and yet despise precisely what all lovers most desire? And when, afflicted with desire, you seek to flee that which alone could bring you satisfaction?

Flori

I desire nothing but that Alessi should love me; and to experience that grace, I would gladly sacrifice my life. What are you saying, that I flee what I seek? It is you, not I, who is raving!

Licori

But if you refuse to bind yourself to him in marriage, is this not to flee the grace you seek? Such union is pure contentment and the desired prize of all true lovers.

Flori

> Ahi, se non posso! A Delia servo. Ancora
> Esser posso felice senza il fine
> Che gli amanti del volgo invoglia e prende.   85

Licori

> Veder non so (quand'ami tanto) come
> Tu possa esser felice e non t'unire
> A la cagion che i tuoi desiri invoglie.
> Ch'altro è Amor, che desir di compiacersi
> In cosa bella? Pur cred'io che bello   90
> Costui ti sembri, e non vorrai goderlo
> Onestamente? O ancor sei sciocca, od erro.
> A Cinzia servo anch'io , ma di seguire
> Giovami il commun uso, con sua pace,
> Se degnerami il ciel di tanto dono.   95

Flori

> Avide luci di terreno amante
> Non mirar cosa mai con tal diletto
> Qual i miei lumi vagheggiaro il bello
> Idolo mio sovran con gaudio immenso.
> E non sì bello mai   100
> Parve a Delia Orione, come parve
> A me questi ch'adoro.
> Ma non già di beltate solamente
> (Licori) esterna il mio desir s'appaga,
> O di bearmi in lei sol cura pongo.   105
> Passo a cosa più degna, penetrando
> Di lui l'interno con la mente, ed indi
> L'ali impiumando al vago mio desire
> A' sommi giri salgo, ove m'è dato/ [52r]
> Poi d'acquetare a pieno i miei desiri.   110
> La sua bellezza esterna vo' che vaglia
> Solo a guidarmi (o dolci gradi!) al cielo
> Poiché a me stessa mille forme e mille
> Pingo celesti, in lui mirando fiso.
> Già da la sciocca plebe io m'allontano   115
> Che in cosa vil compiace il gusto, e frale
> Solo, sprezzando quel ch'a' saggi piace,

Flori

But I cannot marry, as a follower of Delia! Besides I do not doubt my ability to find contentment without that end to which the vulgar throng of lovers aspires.

Licori

If your love is as powerful as you say it is, I cannot see how you can be truly content without uniting yourself to the cause from which your desires derive. For what else is love than the desire to take pleasure in a beautiful object?[85] I am quite sure that this man seems a thing of beauty to you, and yet you do not wish for the chance to enjoy him in a manner compatible with honesty? You must indeed still be mad, if I am not much mistaken. I too serve Cynthia, but, with her grace, I shall be all too happy to follow common custom if the heavens grant me the opportunity.

Flori

The avid eyes of an earth-bound lover never gazed on anything with such delight as mine surveyed with eager rapture the beauties of my sovereign idol, and Orion never seemed as fair to Delia, as this man whom I so adore seemed to me.[86] But my desire, Licori, is not such as to be appeased merely by this external beauty; what I yearn for is not simply to revel in these fair forms. Rather, I wish to pursue a worthier object: to penetrate his inner substance with my mind, and thence, feathering the wings of my fine yearning, to fly on upwards to the highest spheres, where I may at last satisfy my desires in full. All I seek in his outward beauty is that it serve me as a guide to lead me—by what sweet steps!— to heaven. As I gaze on him, my searching eye pictures for me a thousand celestial forms, and, already, I feel that I am leaving far behind me the foolish, vulgar hordes who seek only what they can taste with their senses, cleaving to a vile and frail object and despising what most pleases

E del mio caro Alessi la bell'alma
Amo, degn'opra del gran Maestro eterno:
A quella ben disio d'unirmi, e posso   120
Farlo senz'atto indegno, e ovunque sia
Ella congiunta starmi a tutte l'ore.
Così di consacrarmi a Delia meco
Piacesse a lui, che ben sarei felice
E fortunata allora.   125

Licori

Perché dunque ti lagni, e se disposto
È di gradirti cerchi? S'ancor lungi
Dici poter unirti a quella parte
Di lui ch'ami? E poc'or poi mi dicesti
"S'ei partirà morrommi?" Ah, Flori, Flori,   130
giovane sei, ben me n'accorgo. Or dunque
Lasciam che parta, e, ritrovato Androgeo,
Tu per me (quanto promettesti) oprando
Nel caso mio t'impiega, al tuo fratello
Nova certa recando del tuo stato.   135

Flori

Mi struggo per timor, ch'altrove volti
Egli abbia i suoi pensieri, e che non possa
Quest'alma seggio avere entro al suo seno,
E ch'io trovar non possa in questa vita/ [52v]
Oggetto in cui, mirando,   140
A gustar venga il gaudio de' beati.
Ben allor potrà dirsi ch'io non aggia
Dal sacrificio alcuna grazia avuta
Quand'ei gradir mi neghi; anzi gli Dei
(S'esser può) m'abbian fatto immortal danno,   145
Ma se 'l mio affetto accoglie, e sua mi degna,
Chi mai di me fu più felice in terra?
Fien da me reiterati in cotal giorno
Agli alti Dei tutti i dovuti onori,
E parta pure il mio pastore amato   150
D'Arcadia allor, che lunge e presso lieta
L'alma mia seguirallo unita seco
In vita e 'n morte, e in ogn'evento fida.

the wise. I love the beautiful soul of my dear Alessi, as a worthy creation of our great eternal Master. With his soul, indeed, I yearn for union—a union that can be attained without any shameful act—and wherever that soul goes, I would have my own accompany it constantly. Oh, if he would only consent to consecrate himself to Delia alongside me—then, then, I should be happy, and fortunate!

Licori

Why, then, are you lamenting, and tormenting yourself over whether he will reciprocate your love, if, as you claim, you can be at one with that part of him that you desire even when you are physically distant from him? And, if that is so, why did you say just now, "If he leaves, I shall die?" Oh Flori, Flori! I realize as you speak quite how young you are. Well, let him leave! Meanwhile, let us find Androgeo, so that you may first try to further my chances with him, as you promised. And let us convey the news of your recovery to your brother.

Flori

I am consumed with dread that Alessi's thoughts may be turned else-where, for then this soul of mine will find no place within his breast. And I shall never find another object which can fill me, as I gaze on it, with some foretaste of the raptures of the blessed. Then truly will it be able to be said that I received no grace today from the sacrifice, when he re-fuses to respond to my love; rather, it will seem then that the gods—if this is possible—have inflicted eternal harm on me. But if he welcomes my passion and deigns to make me his, then who was ever happier on this earth than I shall be? That day shall see me returning again and again to heap new honors on the gods on high. Then let my beloved shepherd leave Arcadia if he must; for, far or near, my soul will happily accompany him, united with his in life or death and faithful come what may.

Licori

> Sol brami dunque di sapere s'ha sciolta
> L'alma? E se può riamarti?   155

Flori

> Questo solo e null'altro il cor disia,
> Ma per chiarirti a pieno
> Et a l'un modo ed a l'altro
> Eternamente mi conviene amarlo.

Licori

> Che dunque se 'l tuo affetto ei non gradisse   160
> Dispereresti tu poter altrove
> Volger i tuoi pensieri? e di tua sorte
> Far a te stessa legge?

Flori

>   Oimè, Licori,
> Non sai che dice un buon pastor? Ch'a un solo
> Dar si deve la fede, o insieme a mille.   165
> Già non son' io donna volgar. La morte
> Ben con sue leggi imporrà fine a questa/[53r]
> Vita, ma chi cessar le brame puote
> Se il mio destin gradisco? È a un tempo istesso
> Il mio voler e 'l ciel già mi condanna   170
> Amar un sol, com'altro far non deve
> Donna che del suo onor (saggia) abbi cura.

Licori

> Sì, quando l'alma ha in gentil petto albergo
> E ch'è di pari affetto ricambiata.

Flori

> I termini d'amar non sai, Licori: 175
> Poco val contra Amor forza od ingegno.
> Deve l'amante (quando di tal nome
> Non gode indegnamente) e pur non fia
> Di reciproco affetto ricambiato,
> Ma odiato ancora, amar non solo   180
> Ma l'idol suo adorar, ben mille morti

Licori

This alone then concerns you? To know whether his heart is free, and whether he can return your love?

Flori

This alone and naught else my heart desires. But I should make it clear to you that I must always love him, whether or not he returns my love.

Licori

You are saying that, even if your love is not welcome to him, you despair of being able ever to turn your desires elsewhere? Will you set such self-drawn limits on your future destiny?

Flori

Alas, Licori! Do you not know what one good shepherd says?[87] That we must give our love to one, or else to all. I am no common woman. Death will certainly put an end to this life of mine, but who can still my yearnings, if I have chosen this to be my fate? My will and my heaven-sent destiny coincide in this: I can love only one. But what woman wise enough to have due care of her honor can do otherwise?

Licori

Indeed—when her soul has found its resting-place within a noble breast, and when her love is returned as it deserves.

Flori

Licori, you know not how far true love extends. Neither force nor reason can prevail against it. The lover (if he is worthy of such a name) must persist in his love, not only when his love is not reciprocated, but even when he is hated. He must not merely love but worship his idol; he must

Passando, e poi dir "nulla cosa ho fatto,"
Poi ch'alta ricompensa esser le deve
Di quanto ei fa del suo gradito amato
Una dolce parola, un guardo, un atto.   185

Licori

Dura condizione a cui sopponi
Questa sorte d'amanti e crude leggi.
Ecco ch'a noi se 'n viene il tuo diletto.
Penso ch'amor qua ce lo guidi. Ancora
Non s'è accorto di noi: parmi che aspetti.   190
Vogliamo salutarlo? Ei sta pensoso.

Flori

Lascia questi occhi compiacersi alquanto
De la sua amata vista. O caro, caro
Beato lume e santo! Temo, temo
Struggermi fral obietto a la chiarezza   195
Del mio bel sol, che sol nel mondo adoro./[53v]
Ecco ch'a noi si volge.

Licori

                    Ei ne saluta.

SCENA SECONDA

Alessi, Licori, Flori

Alessi

Ninfe, s'aggia di voi cura Diana,   1
Se cortesi vi sieno e fonti e linfe,
E se da gli archi vostri uccisa resti
Ogni fera, e io parta
Vivo da le saette de' vostri occhi,   5
Ditemi dove andate? S'usa forse
A straniero pastor qual'io mi sono,
I saluti negar? Ah, mi si renda
Cosa maggiore almeno ch'appo voi
Forse men val! Pur vi tacete ancora?   10

suffer a thousand deaths, and dismiss his suffering as nothing. And the highest reward he aspires to, for all he does, must be no more than one sweet word, one glance, one gesture from the one he loves.

Licori

Well! You certainly impose harsh conditions on your preferred type of lover, and cruel laws. But look! Here comes your heart's delight. It must be love that guides him hither. He still has not seen us and seems to linger. Shall we greet him? He looks pensive.

Flori

O, let these eyes feast a while on the beloved sight of him. O dearest, dearest, most blessed, holy light! O, I fear to melt, fragile creature that I am, before the beams of my fair sun [*sol*], whom alone [*sol*] I love. Look, he is turning towards us.

Licori

Indeed, he is greeting us.

SCENE TWO

Alessi, Flori, Licori

Alessi

Nymphs, may Diana watch over you, and may the streams and springs of these woods ever salute you with their murmuring waters; may every beast fall beneath your arrows, and may I succeed in taking my leave from you without being equally wounded by the sweet arrows of your eyes! Tell me, where are you going? Is it the custom in this place to deny a greeting to a stranger-shepherd such as myself? Although in truth I am hoping for rather more than a greeting, though it may seem less to you: the return of something once mine. Nymphs, are you still silent?

Licori

> Ben venuto, pastor. Noi tardavamo
> Sì perché par che tu ci chieggia alcuna
> Tua cosa, e non l'abbiam. Tu Flori forse
> Alcuna hai cosa sua, che così taci?

Flori

> Cosa non ho d'altrui ch'io sappia certo.   15
> Il mio d'aver sarei contenta! Ah, ch'anzi,
> Più no 'l voglio; il donai, e 'l dono eterno
> Sarà, com'anco la mia fè, l'affetto.

Alessi

> Misero, temo, temo!
> A cui, Ninfa gentil, facesti il dono?   20
> Era tuo forse, o di ragione altrui?
> S'ALTRI donando esser cortese intende
> Del suo convien che doni,/[54r]
> E SE di lode è vago, mentr'ei dona,
> Non speri il guiderdon di quanto ei porge.   25

Flori

> Cortese dunque io son, ch'allor donai
> Cosa libera mia, ma non so come
> Degna ben sia di lode, quando pure
> (A dirne il ver) del dono ricompensa
> Tale bramai, che sopra ogni tesoro   30
> È preziosa e cara.

Alessi

> Ahi, che odo? Amarò dunque solo? O Ninfa,
> Ben è colui beato a cui donasti
> Ed altretanto ingrato, s'ei non rese
> A un picciol tuo favor, quanto bramasti.   35

Flori

> Misera, io non donai: fu chi mi tolse
> (Quando ben dritto miro)
> E chi non sa d'averlo, ora il possede.

Licori

> Shepherd, greetings! If we were slow in responding to you, it is because you seem to be asking for us to return something to you, when we have nothing of yours. Unless, Flori, you have something of this man's that you have not mentioned?

Flori

> I have nothing that belongs to another, to the best of my knowledge. Would that I were as sure that no one had anything of mine! Ah, but no! For I no longer want what I have given away—I gave it for all eternity, along with my faith and my love.

Alessi

> Ah, what do I hear! I am smitten with fear. Gentle nymph, to whom did you make this gift of which you speak? And was what you gave yours to give, or did it belong to another? For a gift to be a true gift, one must give of one's own, and for it to be praiseworthy, one must give with no hope of return.

Flori

> Then my gift was a true one, for I gave something that lay freely within my possession; but whether it was praiseworthy I know not. For, to tell the truth, I long for something in return—and something dearer and more precious than any treasure.

Alessi

> Alas, what do I hear! My love shall be in vain. O nymph, happy that man to whom your gift was given! Happy—and unworthy, if he does not deign to return in full the smallest favor on your part.

Flori

> Alas! I did not give freely; rather, now I think well on it, what was mine was cruelly stolen from me and now lies in the possession of one who does not know himself to possess it.

Alessi

Felice possessor! Deh foss'io quello.

Licori

Se vuoi rimedio, fa 'l tuo male aperto.   40

Alessi

Del mio foco gentil tu sola in parte,
Bella Ninfa, potrai scemar la fiamma
Ch'arde non sol, ma incenerisce il core,
Per me cortese oprando. Io amo Flori,
Ma che mi valerà se, com'intendo,   45
Ha d'alpe il cor duro e di scoglio in guisa
Contro a' colpi d'Amore. Ecco ch'asconde
A gli avidi occhi miei l'avorio e l'ostro.

Licori

Invola forse il viso a gli occhi tuoi
Flori acciò tu non veda   50
Al variar del volto il core espresso.
Ma quando a le sue voglie oneste e saggie
Fosse il disio conforme/[54v]
Che tu dì che sì t'arde, e ti piacesse
Seguir Diana seco in caste voglie,   55
Allor ben spererei
Ch'ella gradisse il tuo cotanto affetto.
Ma se a nodo giugal pensi, lasciamo
(Od a vano altro amor) di più parlarne,
Poich'ella ha già disposto   60
Viver di Delia serva.

Alessi

Altro non bramo o spero
Che 'l sol de gli occhi, e l'armonia soave
De l'accorte parole, ch'or m'hanno
Sì raddoppiate al cor saette e fiamme.   65

Alessi

Happy possessor, then! Would that I were that man!

Licori

If you seek some remedy to your suffering, it were well to speak plainly of it.

Alessi

[To Licori] Lovely nymph, you alone, through your courteous assistance, can help me in part to relieve the flame of that noble ardor that burns my heart, and has reduced it already to ashes. I love Flori! But what can this avail me when, as I am told, she has a heart as hard as stone and stands steadfast as a rock against all the assaults of Love? Look, even as I speak, she hides from me the ivory and roses of her sweet visage.

Licori

It may be that Flori conceals her face from you that you may not see her heart revealed in its changing colors. If the desire that you say so consumes you is compatible with her honest and decent wishes—if you are prepared to serve Diana alongside her and to observe chastity in love— then I have good hope that she would accede to your great passion. But if you aspire to marriage (or to some vainer end of love), then all further discussion is idle, as Flori has resolved to live a true follower of Delia.

Alessi

All that I long for and desire in her is the sweet sunlight of her eyes and the soft harmonies of her sage words, which even now, as we spoke, pierced my heart and stoked its flames to new heights. I shall follow Cynthia alongside her if this is what she wishes, and shall be a faithful

Seguirò seco Cinzia, s'a lei piace,
E ne le pugne di feroci belve
Fedel Mimmaleon sarolle sempre,
In solitarie selve onesto amante
E pronto servo a' cenni,   70
Con pur cor rendendo a Cinzia seco
Di profonda umiltate altero censo.

Licori

Non più celare, o Flori, al tuo pastore
De l'onesto tuo cor la pura fiamma.
Volgi le luci in quelle luci amate,   75
Che dianzi mi dicevi
Che in disusato modo ardèanti l'alma,
Non più teme o rispetti,
Ch'è troppo gran Signore
L'alato invitto amore.   80

Alessi

O me beato sovra ogni pastore!

Flori

Che mi gioverebbe di celare
L'ardor ch'ho dentro al petto, se nel viso
Omai la fiamma appare?/[55r]
T'amo, Alessi, no 'l nego,   85
In disusato modo.
De' tuoi begli occhi il pianto
Ch'estinguir dovea 'l foco
Esca fu a le mie fiamme.
Ma tali son queste mie fiamme pure   90
Ch'ardendo non consumano, sì tempra
L'ardor di pudicizia umor soave.

Alessi

O cara ninfa, o mia regina, o Dea!

Licori

Ecco Flori, il pastore a cui dovresti
De la tua crudeltà chieder perdono.   95

Mimallon[88] at her side in all her fierce struggles against the beasts, and an honest companion in the most solitary and remote places, ever ready to obey her every sign and, with a pure heart, to render to Cynthia alongside her the humble tribute of my most profound reverence.

Licori

Flori, seek no longer to conceal the pure flames of your honest heart from this your shepherd. Let your eyes once more meet those eyes that you so love, and which, as you said, so strangely and mysteriously burned their way into your heart. Let all fears and all caution be banished, for that dauntless winged god, Love, is too great a power to withstand.

Alessi

O I am the happiest of all shepherds!

Flori

What would it avail me further to conceal the burning love I feel within my breast, now that those same flames are alight in my cheeks? Alessi, I love you, and love you extraordinarily. I shall not deny it. Those tears that fell from your fair eyes, that could have extinguished flames with their dampness, instead kindled the fire within me. But it is a fire that burns me without consuming me, for it is tempered with the sweet dew of modesty.

Alessi

O dearest nymph! My queen, my goddess!

Licori

Flori, see, here comes that shepherd to whom you should ask pardon for your past cruelties.

Alessi

Ahi, quanto il suo venir m'annoia! Vezzi
Però le debbo far, ch'ei merta. Androgeo,
Donde ritorni sì affannato? Forse
Da qualche zuffa di selvaggia fera?
Cosa ho da dirti di rilievo, e appunto   100
Perciò molti pastori ti cercan anco.

SCENA TERZA[32]

Androgeo, Licori, Flori ed Alessi

Androgeo

Alessi, amico caro, il ciel lodato   1
Ch'ancor non sei partito: per trovarti
Fatt'ho gran strada in fretta. Ecco la cara
E cruda ninfa mia, ma non più mia
Conviemmi di chiamarla: io suo, piuttosto   5
Mai sempre potrò dirmi, poiché ancora
Che per lei non mi strugga e non vaneggi/[55v]
(Mercè del ciel), non però intendo mai
Dal suo voler partirmi, e quell'impero
Ch'Amor le diede in me, vo' che ritenga.   10
Flori, del sacrificio la cagione
Ben so che saper dei, che per null'altra
Fu che sol per dare fine al tuo cordoglio
E 'l mio scemar per te cocente ardore.
Or (de gli Dei mercè) te veggio lieta.   15
Io non incenerisco, ma sì bene
Ardo ancor per disio di poter fare
Cosa che ti sia grata, e or venivo
Per confermarti sopra me l'impero
Che già sprezzasti. Eccomi tuo qual pria,   20
Di caduco disio non già ripieno
Più, ma di voglie regolate e caste.
Troppo ardì, certo, e troppo
Di farti sua sperando il tuo fedele.
Or non più si vaneggi, e non più s'erri.   25
Amo le tue virtuti e vo' servirle,
Impazzar non già più, non più adorarti

Alessi

Ah, how his coming here at this moment irks me! And yet I must treat him courteously, for he is a worthy man. Androgeo, whence are you coming so weary in aspect? Perhaps from some battle with wild beasts? I have something of importance to tell you, and many other shepherds seek you likewise.

SCENE THREE

Androgeo, Licori, Flori, Alessi

Androgeo

Alessi, my dear friend, may the heavens be praised that you have not yet departed: I have hastened here from far off in the hope of seeing you. Ah, there is my dear and cruel nymph—though I should no longer say "mine." Rather, I am hers and shall be ever after. For although (by the grace of heaven) I no longer consume myself and rave madly for love of her, that does not signify that I shall ever cease to honor and obey her wishes. May that power over my will which Love consigned to her remain hers through my free choice. Flori, I well know that you must know the reason for the sacrifice: its motives were at once to bring an end to your grief and to temper my burning love for you. Now (may the gods be praised), I see you happy once more, and I no longer feel myself reduced to cinders by your presence; but I do still burn with desire to do anything that I may do to please you. Indeed, one reason for my coming here now was to confirm my past offers of servitude, which once you despised and rejected. I am yours, as before—but now filled no longer with a fierce sensual passion, but with a more temperate and chaste affection. Certainly, your faithful servant was too bold and hoped too keenly to make you his, but now he has put such madness behind him and errs no longer. I still revere your virtues and seek to serve them, but I shall no longer pursue my love to the point of madness or worship you as a god-

Voglio, qual fea di Dea celeste, in guisa
Che forse il cielo e gli Dei nostri santi,
Mentre il dovuto onore a lor levai,   30
Me punir' cieco amante e idolatra.

Licori

Or ti convien, se m'ami, qui mostrarlo.
Flori, rispondi al tuo pastor cortese.

Flori

Non sprezzo, Androgeo, il dono: anzi, l'accetto,
Ed ora vo' far prova se disporre   35
Posso di quell'impero
Del quale or (tuo mercè) m'hai rinvestita./[56r]
So che tu sai ch'a me non lice in modo
Coniugal di legarmi, avendo offerto
A Cinzia gli anni miei, e or che scerni   40
Il dritto, meno penso che tu speri
A cosa tal, benché il tuo gran valore,
Il chiaro ingegno, la virtù pregiata,
Di maggior ninfa ancor degno ti renda;
Ond'ho pensato, che se di Melampo   45
(Di questa mia compagna il vecchio padre)
Le voglie al mio desir piegar potessi,
E che pronta ella fossi a compiacermi,
Vorrei che in questo poi mi compiacesti
Tu, di farla tua donna e sposa tua.   50
Allor ben crederei poter disporre
Di te con sicurtate in ogni evento,
Poiché Licori a punto è lo mio core,
La più parte del tempo i' starei seco,
E ben dir si potrebbe   55
Tre cori uniti una sol voglia regge.

Androgeo

Par ben che il cielo, o Flori, mi facesse
Con gran ragion tuo servo, se nel fine
Per te mi si dovea far tanto bene.
Resta sol che Licori non si sdegni   60
Ch'io le sia amante e sposo, che un sol cenno

dess; for it may be because I conferred on you the tribute that should have been theirs that the gods were pleased to punish me with madness as a blind and idolatrous lover.

Licori

[*Aside*] Now, if you love me, Flori, this is the moment to show it. [*To Flori*] Flori, reply to this your courteous shepherd.

Flori

Androgeo, I do not despise your gift; on the contrary, I accept it willingly. Indeed, I am resolved to put to the test this power to command your services with which you have so graciously now reinvested me. I know you know that I may never bind myself in a conjugal tie, having vowed my life to Cynthia. And now that you have come to your senses, I am quite sure that you no longer have any thought of aspiring to such a thing, although your great worth and fine intellect and estimable virtue would make you deserving of the hand of a far worthier nymph than I. And so the thought has come to me that, if Melampo, the aged father of this my companion Licori, could be persuaded to accept you as suitor to his daughter, and if she herself were willing to accede to this desire of mine, then you could give me no greater pleasure than to ask her hand in marriage. Then, indeed, would I feel that I could ever depend on your services—for Licori is, as you know, the companion of my heart, and I cannot envisage ever being long parted from her. Thus, through your marriage, we may become three hearts united in a single desire.

Androgeo

Flori, it seems that the heavens did not make me your servant without reason, if such a great boon was destined to come to me through your good offices. If it does not displease Licori, I shall readily declare myself her

De' tuoi m'è legge espressa, oltra che sempre
Dopo te non vidi io ninfa veruna
Che più di lei piacesse a gli occhi miei.

Flori

Che sospiri, Licori? Non vuoi forse   65
Tu compiacermi in questo.

Licori

Io sospirai, volgendo fra me stessa/[56v]
Le ragion che pur oggi mi dicesti
E quelle insieme ancora
Che tu m'hai detto mille volte e mille.   70

Flori

Quai son queste ragioni?

Licori

                    Io mi ricordo
Che spesse volte intente al mormorio
Del sacro fonte degli allori, u' cade
L'onda ch'a ber co 'l suon mill'alme invita
(Benché a poche si dia porvi le labbia),   75
Di là passando molte ninfe e 'n braccio
Tenendo accolti i pargoletti figli
Co i cari sposi[33] a lato, io ti dicea:
"Flori, beata copia, mira, mira;
Soavi frutti han colto   80
De le loro speranze quelle ninfe
(O dolci appoggi e cari!).
E noi, ch'al fin corremmo
Per alleggiar il pondo
Di quell'età che per se stessa è grave,   85
Altro che pentimento?
E per scoscese rupi, spini e bronchi
Dietro correndo inutilmente a fere?'
E sorridendo allor tu rispondevi
'Sian nostri figli le cose create   90
dal divino nostro pelegrino ingegno,
Nè serva ad uomo angelica fattura."

lover and her husband, for your every wish is my command; besides
which, I never saw a nymph besides yourself so pleasing to my eyes as her.

Flori

Licori, why are you sighing? Are you reluctant to accede to my wishes
in this?

Licori

I was sighing as I thought back on what you were saying to me earlier today, and to other things you used to say a thousand times over.

Flori

What things are you speaking of?

Licori

I remember how often as we dallied by the sacred spring by the laurel
grove—that spring whose murmuring draws a thousand souls eager to
drink from it (though to few it is given to taste its waters)[89]—we would
see many nymphs pass by, cradling their little ones in their arms, with
their loving spouses beside them; and I would say "Flori, what happy
abundance—look, look! Sweet are the fruits that those nymphs have
gathered from their hopes: what dear little helpmates they have gar-
nered for themselves! But we? What will we have to lighten the burden
of wearisome old age, other than regret? What will it avail us when we
are old and gray, all this useless chasing of beasts over hills and rocks and
thickets?" And you would reply, with a smile: "May our offspring be the
products of our divine and rare intellects. Lord forbid that a creation of
the angels should ever become a servant to man!"

Alessi

Sol di mia donna alta risposta degna!

Flori

Deh, lasciamo, Licori: or non è il tempo
Di replicar passati detti. È vero   100
Ch'io lodai, lodo, e loderò mai sempre/[57r]
Il non servire ad uomo, che d'uomo ha solo
La sembianza, onde copre insane voglie
Spesso, e di mostro e fera ingegno e mente.
Non sai che veste quasi d'uom la forma   105
Anco la simia e 'l pardo, ed altri tali,
E son però animali?
Questi son da fuggirsi! Ma si lasci,
Dico, di ragionar or di tal cosa:
Ad altro tempo di mostrarti spero   110
Quale sia la cagion che l'uom distingue
Dal bruto. Ora pur dì, vuoi di me in vece
Sodisfar ad Androgeo? A me rispondi?

Licori

D'uopo non credo sia l'ir raccontando
Quanto a paro di me sempre t'amassi.   115
Pur che 'l vecchio mio padre a ciò consenta
A compiacer tue voglie eccomi pronta.

Androgeo

Saggia risposta!

Licori

                    Pria saper dovevi
Parmi d'Androgeo il cor. Fors'altra ninfa
Ama, e per compiacerti or dice il tutto: 120
E pur tu sai che DUO voler discordi
Di nodo tal non mai devrian legarsi.

Androgeo

Ninfa gentil, null'altra donna, ho detto,
Dopo Flori mai piacque a gli occhi miei.

Alessi

A lofty response which could only have come from my lady!

Flori

Come, Licori, let us lay aside such memories: this is no time to repeat past sayings. It is true that I have praised (and do praise and shall ever praise) the choice to serve no man—no man, that is, who is a man only in appearance, for very often beneath such appearances lurk inhuman desires and a mind worthier of a beast or a monster. Did you not know that apes and pards can similarly assume a form that looks almost human, and yet they are no less beasts? This is the sort of man we should flee at all costs—but, as I say, this is no time for a conversation of this kind. Some other time, I shall gladly tell you how a man—a true man—differs from the beasts. For the moment, only tell me: will you consent to take my place in satisfying Androgeo's wishes? What is your reply?

Licori

I think there is no need for me to tell you that I have always loved you as myself. If my aged father gives his consent, then I shall be quite willing to second your desire in this.

Androgeo

A sage reply!

Licori

But first, it seems to me, you should discover the secrets of Androgeo's heart. Perchance he loves some other nymph, and consents to this marriage only to please you; and yet, as you know, no marriage should ever be joined in which both partners' wills are not united.

Androgeo

Gentle nymph, as I said, no other woman, except for Flori, has ever pleased my eyes as much as you.

Stanne sicura, e se null'altra cosa 125
In me degna di te non troverai,
So che di fede almeno passerò inanzi
A ogni marito e amante.

Licori

Tanto sperar debb'io dal tuo sembiante.
Eccomi pronta (Flori), a quanto vuoi./[57v] 130

Flori

Benedetta sia tu, Licori saggia,
Androgeo, s'a te par, dalle la mano.

Androgeo

Così faccio. Licori, or che ad Amore,
Al mio nume terreno, e piace al cielo
Di farmi tuo, a te non spiaccia ancora 135
D'accettarmi per tale,
Che sopra ogn'altro mi terrò beato.

Licori

Ecco il pegno di fè, se 'l vecchio padre
Con le paterne sue posse non sturba
De' nostri accesi cor l'oneste voglie. 140

Alessi

Novelli amanti e lieti, or non temete
Che aspireravvi, anzi che 'l sol si corchi
Co 'l carro³⁴ aurato in grembo a Teti, il cielo
Propizio sì, che in doppia gioia immersi
Già vi veggo felici; ed or venivo 145
Per rapportarti, Androgeo, nova tale
Che di candida pietra fia ben degno
Che un giorno tal tu segni.
Ma serbo a dirti a miglior tempo il resto
In stato aventuroso: or fia ben dritto 150
Che alcun, per me, prego tu porga a questa
Che di gradir pur segno ha poc'or dato
L'affetto, e la mia fè, che non ha pari.

Be quite assured; for if you find in me no other thing that is worthy of you, I can swear that in fidelity at least I shall outstrip all other husbands and lovers.

Licori

Indeed, your countenance promises well for your honesty. Flori, I am entirely at your disposal.

Flori

Wise Licori, may you be blessed for that decision! Androgeo, if it please you, give her your hand.

Androgeo

I shall indeed. Licori, since it has pleased Love and this my terrestrial goddess, and the heavens to make me yours, let it not displease you either to accept me as such, for, if you will, I shall consider myself the happiest of men.

Licori

Here is my hand on it—if my aged father does not choose to pit his paternal might against the honest desires of our loving hearts.

Alessi

New and happy lovers, have no fear, for the heavens will look kindly on you, and envelop you in a double joy before the sun sinks with his golden chariot to rest in the lap of Thetis.[90] I already picture you filled with joy, and I was coming here now to bring a piece of news to you, Androgeo, that would be worthy of being graven on gleaming marble. But I shall save this to tell you later, when the time is more propitious. For the moment, I must beg you to put in a good word for me with this nymph, who, just before you arrived, was showing herself inclined to accept the unequalled love and devotion I bear her.

Androgeo

    Indarno sieno i preghi: ad altro spera,

    Ch'altera sprezza questa ninfa il calle   155

    Da 'l comun piè donnesco impresso, e poggia

    Per solitaria strada a mercar lode.

Flori

    Ahi, ch'ora avien ch'altri mi leva in tutto

    Di poter di me stessa più disporre.

    Questo pastore, Androgeo, questo, questo/[58r]   160

    M'ha furato dal petto l'alma e 'l core,

    E in disusato modo or tutta m'arde.

    Il vago pianto, che da' suoi begli occhi

    Vidi cader sì[35] molle in guisa il diaspro

    Di che armata portai buon tempo l'alma,   165

    Ch'ella a' colpi d'Amore inerme langue,

    Piegata sì che nullo scampo veggo

    Per lei, fuor de la mano

    Del mio gradito Alessi, anzi mio Rege.

Alessi

    Con quai, Regina mia, fregi d'onore   170

    Il mio stato aggrandir cerchi, s'io sono

    Tuo servo? Ah, che m'offendi!

Flori

    Idolo caro, ah non più s'usi meco

    Tali parole: tu mio Duce amato,

    Solo hai sovra di me libero impero,   175

    E gioverammi sol (gloria stimando

    questa) de' servi tuoi, serva chiamarmi.

Androgeo

    Son desto, o sogno? Il dritto scorgo od erro?

    Temo finti mirar di larve effetti.

Licori

    Veraci son di questa ninfa i detti,   180

    Pastor: sicuro pur stanne ch'ella ama

    Sovra l'uso mortal sì lealmente

Androgeo

All words would be in vain. Direct your hopes elsewhere, for this nymph loftily despises the accustomed paths trodden by her sex, and instead seeks her own solitary route to fame and honor.

Flori

Ah, is another now seeking to deprive me of the power to dispose of myself as I wish?[91] This shepherd, Androgeo—the man you see before you—has stolen my heart and soul, and I find myself burning with an unaccustomed flame. The precious tears I saw falling from his lovely eyes melted the impenetrable jasper that had long girded my soul, and it now languishes defenseless before Love's onslaught, so stricken that I can see no hope for a cure other than from the hand of my beloved Alessi—my king!

Alessi

What fine trophies are these with which, my queen, you are seeking to elevate my state? You are quite wrong to call me your king. Call me rather your servant!

Flori

Idol of my heart, speak not so! You alone, my beloved Prince, reign freely over me: I should account it the greatest of honors to be a servant to your servants.

Androgeo

Am I dreaming? Can I be seeing this aright? I fear I must be suffering some delusion of the senses.

Licori

This nymph's words are true. Shepherd, be assured that she is indeed in love; and she loves with a faith that passes all human understanding,

Ch'ella sola può dirsi
Saper amare in eccellenza al mondo.

Flori

Amo, non star dubbioso: ah, ch'anzi adoro,   185
Adoro, e così grande
È 'l amor mio che tutti gli altri passa.
Questo solo mi spiace, che vorrei
Più amar, né più si può, che lo so certo.

Androgeo

Omai contento son di quanto al cielo/[58v]   190
Piacque di me dispor, felice a pieno,
Che da le voglie tue cortesi avuta
Abbia sì cara e sì gentil compagna.
Mi stupisco a ragion sol di due cose:
Che sia di già fatto il tuo cor prigione   195
D'Amor, che sì biasmavi,
E ch'altre volte Alessi t'abbia chiesta
Pietà co' preghi e pianti, oggi pur finto
Avendo meco non sapere il nome
Tuo, dimandando a me minuto conto   200
De l'esser tuo, che forastier bramare
Dicea conto d'Arcadia e de le ninfe.
Sai ben fingere, Alessi!
Addio, fratel, perché da me celarti?

Alessi

Hai preso error, Androgeo. Io non sapea   205
L'amato nome, e sol da te l'intesi.

Androgeo

Hai ben ragione, Alessi, di scherzare,
Poi ch'Amor ti diè quello
Per cui tolse a me il senno.

Alessi

Deh, fosse pur! Tu scherzi; io dico il vero.   210

such that she alone of all mortals can truly say that she knows what it is to love.

Flori

Do not doubt that I love—nay, rather, I adore, and my love is such that it towers above all others. My only regret is that I cannot love more— but it would be impossible to do so, as I can say with certainty.

Androgeo

[*To Flori*] Well, I am fully content with all that the heavens have disposed as my fate, since with your own hands you have given me such a dear and sweet companion. But two things continue to puzzle me. First, I am perplexed that your heart should now be a prisoner of Love, when once you spoke so harshly of that god. And secondly, if Alessi has been courting you with his prayers and tears, I do not understand why he feigned today not to know even your name, and interrogated me long on all that concerned you, saying that, as a stranger to Arcadia, he wished to know more about this land and its nymphs. Alessi, you are a master of disguise! But why all this feigning, dear brother?

Alessi

Androgeo, you are mistaken. I did not even know her beloved name until you informed me of it.

Androgeo

Alessi, you jest—as well you might, since Love granted you that thing for which I lost my wits.

Alessi

How can you think such a thing! It is you who are jesting: I am speaking the sober truth.

Androgeo

    Come non dici il falso?
    Poc'or non disse Flori
    Che le lagrime tue
    Entro al sen le destaro
    Con disusato modo il foco ond'arde?   215

Flori

    Ti svellerò i miei detti, Androgeo (hai torto)
    Con raccontarti a pien l'istoria. Or odi.
    Nel sacrificio stando (e non so come)
    Volsi le luci ne' begli occhi amati
    Del mio pastore, e un pianto scorsi (ahi lassa!/[59r]   220
    Dio sa perch'ei piangeva)
    Che mi destò pietà, madre d'amore
    Nel petto, e indi amor. Così pur dianzi
    Lo raccontai contra Licori, ed ella
    Ch'amava te mi disse; e l'una a l'altra   225
    Domandavamo negli amori nostri
    Consiglio, e insieme aita.

Androgeo

    Dunque pria che t'amasse
    Alessi, tu l'amavi?

Flori

    L'amava, e destin fu che me gli avinse,   230
    E l'amerò in eterno, né so[n] ancora
    Certo però s'ei m'ami.

Alessi

    Ah, che posso operar, mia Dea, per farti
    Certa, che t'aggio al par de l'alma cara?

Androgeo

    E la mia Dea, la mia Licori, dunque   235
    Anco m'amava pria?

Flori

    È così a punto.

Androgeo

But how can it be true? Did not Flori say just now that your tears unexpectedly awakened in her the flames in which she now burns?

Flori

Androgeo, you are mistaken. I shall discover the mystery of my words by recounting the whole story. Now listen. While the sacrifice was taking place—I know not how—my eyes met the sweet eyes of my own beloved shepherd, and I saw that those eyes were full of tears. Ah, the Lord only knows why it was that he was weeping! And his tears awoke in my heart a pity that was the mother of love, and my love for him was born soon afterwards. I told Licori of this just now, and she told me that she loved you, and the two of us shared counsel on our love and vowed to help one another.

Androgeo

So you loved Alessi before he loved you?

Flori

I loved him, and shall love him for ever; and it was fated that I should win him to me. Though I am still not entirely sure that he really does love me in return.

Alessi

Ah, my goddess, what must I do to assure you that I love you as dearly as my own soul?

Androgeo

And *my* goddess, my Licori—is it true that she was already in love with me?

Flori

Indeed it was.

Licori

           Resta, poi ch'abbiamo
Fatti palesi i nostri amori, ch'anco
D'Alessi udiamo il caso ond'ei piangea,
Con le lagrime sue destando al core   240
(Misera) di costei fiamma e ardore.

Androgeo

Ben sarebbe il dovere. Alessi, or via!

Alessi

Volentier dirò il tutto.
Mentre ancor giovanetto, né capace
D'amor, pasceva il gregge in ripa al . . .   245
Mi venne udito il grido
D'immortal Ninfa, anzi di Dea celeste,
Ond'io lasciando a' miei bifolchi cura
De' greggi miei, ne venni a servir questa
De l' . . . Dea, tra noi mortali/[59v]   250
Certo Cinzia novella.
Quivi inalzati i miei pensieri, godeva
Ben sovente la vista
Di real ninfa, in caste voglie ardendo,
Ma (lasso), che a ridirlo io mi distruggo,   255
De la sua vera gloria spogliò il mondo
Morte, e me d'ogni bene.
Così, dal duol traffitto, molte piagge
Allor cercai compagne, e boschi; e infine
Volgeami il piede a le paterne rive,   260
Ove sola ho lasciata una sorella,
Che in modo avinsi a pastor degno, e tale
Ch'in valor già stimato è un novo Marte.
Così passando oggidì qua, Leggiadro
Al sacrificio mi trattenne, ed io,   265
Che 'l vostro stato in parte udito avea,
E d'Amaranata morta il caso ancora,
Piansi la fiamma mia sublime estinta.
Allor pietoso Amor forse le luci
Guidò de la mia Flori a rimirare   270
Il mio dolore, ove pietà n'ebbe ella.

Licori

Now that we have all revealed our loves, it remains only for Alessi to reveal the reason why he was weeping those tears that were destined to stir such flames and ardor in our poor Flori.

Androgeo

Indeed, it is only right that he should tell us. Come, Alessi!

Alessi

I shall happily tell all. When I was still a boy, and not yet of an age for love, I was grazing my flocks on the banks of the . . . ,[92] when the fame reached my ears of a famous nymph—nay, an immortal goddess! And, leaving my flocks to the care of my men, I went to . . . to serve this divine being, who seemed a second Diana to us mortals. My thoughts were inspired to new heights by her presence, and I would gaze with delight on this royal nymph, burning with chaste desire. But, alas!—the very thought of it still fills me with anguish—Death stripped the world of her true glory and me of my every happiness. Then, pierced by a keen grief, I long wandered disconsolate among lonely desert wastes and forests, until at last I decided to turn my steps toward the shores of my fatherland, where a sister still dwells, whom I married to a valorous shepherd, worthy to be esteemed a second Mars. As I was passing through these parts today Leggiadro bid me stay to watch the sacrifice, and since I had heard your story in part, and knew of the sad fate of dead Amaranta, I was reminded of my own sublime lost love and wept for her. Then Love, perhaps taking pity on me, guided the sweet eyes of my Flori to gaze

Quinci perché gl'è vero
Ch'AMORE a nullo amato amar perdona,
Mi volsi a ricambiar essa pietate,
E 'l pensier ch'avea già di non amare   275
Cangiando, di costei m'accesi in guisa
Di scosso foco, dal focil del grido
De le virtute sue percosso il core,
Già di marmo, che tutto ora converso
In esca, avampò in dilettevol fiamme,/[60r]   280
Oneste sì, che fin a[ll]ora,³⁶ a Delia
Ho il mio corso vital già dedicato.
Or di novo gradirmi t'apparecchia
Pur cara ninfa mia con più pietate
Come a cosa già tua, che ben sia onesto.   285

Flori

Ahi, che l'aver d'altrui troppo pietate
A me stessa nemica omai m'ha resa.
Pur che serbi, o mio Alessi, i desir casti
Contra il mio puro affetto e la mia fede,
Sua rota volga pur l'instabil Dea,   290
E m'aggiri a sua voglia or basso or alto,
E varchi pur l'empio de l'uom nemico
Avaro tempo, e sorga Apollo, e pure
L'inargentata suora, e rieda e parta
E l'uno e l'altro, e rieda e parta, e morte   295
Anco squarci il mio velo umano e frale,
Che poi sorta la spoglia, ai lochi bassi
Scenda, o sagli nel cielo a far dimora,
L'alma fia, dopo Dio, ch'un sol adore.

Androgeo

Nova coppia d'amanti, e novo modo   300
D'amar! Or non è meglio
Per dar principio a far perfetto il nodo
Ch'a la mia cara ninfa
(Per grazia del mio nume) or m'ha legato,
Che ci partiamo insieme?   305
Ma mentre che n'andian, cosa racconta,
Tu ch'hai scorso del mondo, Alessi, degna
D'esser udita, che faremo intanto
Breve il camino e lieve.

pityingly on my sorrow, and since, as it is true that Love allows no love to go unanswered,[93] I turned my own eyes toward her and returned her pity. And then the resolve I had been nurturing never to love again was dissolved, and I burned like a fire newly stoked, my flames fanned by the fame of her virtues, which smote my heart. Once impenetrable as marble, it is now all ablaze and burning with flames of exquisite bliss, and flames so honest and chaste that from now on I wish for nothing more than to devote the whole course of my life to Diana. Now, my lovely nymph, fill my heart with still more pleasure by looking on me still more kindly, for I am entirely yours, and the thing is honest.

Flori

Ah! By looking too kindly on another, I have become cruel to myself! But, my Alessi, if you will only consent to return my pure love and faith with your chaste desires, then let the volatile Goddess turn her wheel any way she will, now lifting me on high and now casting me low.[94] And let miser Time, man's cruelest foe, do his worst: let Apollo rise, followed by his silvery sister, and let them set again, and then rise, and set and rise; and let Death, even, rend apart my fragile mortal veil! For when my soul departs its shell, whether it descends to the depths or soars up to make its home in the heavens, it will continue to adore you, second only to my God.

Androgeo

O new and wondrous pair of lovers, and new and wondrous love! But is it not time for us to go now? I am eager to tie the knot that is to bind me to my dear nymph, thanks to the good offices of my goddess. But as we go, Alessi, to speed us on our way, tell us something of interest, you who have traveled the world.

Alessi

Già di donna immortal or ben conviene/[60v]   310
Ch'io vi racconti, e che cantiamo andando
Le sue lodi ch'appresi: Or questa impera
Nova PALLA, VICINA a le contrade
Ch'iriga intorno il Trebbia, ivi adorata
Da satiri, silvani e de' pastori.   315
Sola siede maggior, bella egualmente.
Or le sue lodi incise
Entro a questa corteccia
Cantiamo andando.

Androgeo

             Via, cantian'!

Licori

                   Cantiamo!

Flori

Che dir volessi io pensai per cosa   320
Rara e divina oggi nel mondo, quale
È di REGIO PASTOR l'immortal grido,
Che dolce il canto in cotal guisa forma
Che al suon divin de le sue altere noti
Ferma rapido il corso il MINCIO, e Febo   325
Di generosa invidia punto frena
Etoo e Piroo (mal grado suo), fermando
Le sfere a l'armonia soave in cielo,
D'alta dolcezza ingombre il moto anch'esse.
(ORSA FELICE che co 'l mondo a paro   330
Vivrà chiaro il tuo nome in degne carte!)
Ecco, da rozza man d'abietta ninfa
Che il suo valor celeste ammira, impresse
Di lui le lodi a punto in questa scorza
Di verdeggiante faggio. Ma che? Puote   335
Uom terreno del cielo angelo lodare?

Alessi

It is fitting that I should tell you of an immortal lady, and we can sing her praises as we go. This new PALLAS rules in the VICINITY of those lands that are watered by the Trebbia, and she is worshiped by all the shepherds and satyrs and fauns of that place.⁹⁵ She reigns alone, constantly resplendent in her beauty. Come, let us sing these praises inscribed in the bark of this tree as we go!

Androgeo

Yes, let us sing!

Licori

Let us sing!

Flori

Wait, Alessi, I have thought of another rare and divine subject for praise: the immortal fame of a ROYAL SHEPHERD, whose song is so sweet that, at the sound of his lofty notes, the swift-flowing course of the Mincio halts in wonder, and Phoebus, pierced by a noble envy, reins back Aethon and Pyrois in spite of himself, and the spheres of the heavens stay their motion to listen to his rapturous harmonies.⁹⁶ O Fortunate She-Bear [ORSA FELICE], your name will live eternal, immortalized by the noble pages that bear it!⁹⁷ Here, see his praises on the trunk of this verdant beech tree. Though they are carved by the clumsy hand of the lowliest of nymphs, what matter? Can a mere mortal ever hope to praise an angel as he deserves?

Androgeo
> L'una e l'altra si canti, degna lode
> Agevolando intanto il camin nostro.

Licori
>   Faccian come vi par.

Alessi
> Or via, si canti./[61r]

I	l Re de l'universo	340
S	celse, tra mille, una sovrana e chiara	
A	lma, e qui la ripose, ove di rara	
B	eltà l'essempio scorto, uom sia converso,	
E	con la mente al cielo, e con l'affetto.	
L	e gratie ha seco tutte, e come obietto	345
L	ucido i cori alluma, e 'l TREBBIA impara	
A	risuonar con la pura onda alterna	
P	ALLAVICINA nostra gloria eterna.	

C	hiunque de l'Esperia in un soggetto	
V	eder disia l'alte eccellenze tutte,	350
R	imiri ove'ha ricetto,	
T	ra semidei, terreno Dio, ridutte	
I	vi in soggiorno eletto	
O	drà le Muse con soave canto	
G	ONZAGA reiterare, onor di MANTO.	355

SCENA QUARTA

Serrano solo

Serrano
> Che m'ha giovato, Amor, l'usar inganno   1
> Per posseder la grazia al fin di Flori?
> Nel tuo regno adoprar non so che vaglia
> Più fede o frode. Ahi, che ben cieco il volgo
> Con ragion ti dipinge   5
> Dandoti l'ali e di fanciullo forma,
> Perché ferisci a caso,
> Fuggi quel, che ti segue, e mal discerni/[61v]

Alessi

Let us sing the well-deserved praises of both as we go, and the journey will seem as nothing.

Licori

Let us do as you wish.

Alessi

Then let us sing! [*They sing together*] The divine ruler of the universe chose from among thousands a noble and precious soul and placed it here in our midst in order to offer to the world a thing of rare beauty, that men's minds and hearts might be drawn by this means to the heavens.[98] All the graces are in her, and she illuminates our hearts like a beacon, while the Trebbia learns to hymn with its rippling waters the eternal glories of our ISABELLA PALLAVICINA.[99]

Whoever desires to see all the glories of Hesperia[100] gathered in a single person, let him look within the exquisite dwelling where this terrestrial god resides, surrounded by semi-deities; there he will hear the muses with their sweet tones praising CURZIO GONZAGA, the honor of MANTO.[101]

SCENE FOUR

Serrano alone

Serrano

So, then, Love, what has all my plotting to gain Flori's good graces finally availed me? I do not know what is more successful within your realm: strategy or sincerity. Oh, that popular view of you is certainly right, that pictures you as a whimsical winged boy! It is quite true that you choose your victims arbitrarily, and flee those who seek you, and reward or pun-

L'altrui merto o la colpa.
Di trattener a bada io mi pensai   10
I pastorelli in giochi, acciò seguendo
Il sacrificio intanto, e lor lontani
Essendo, riguardato io sol tra pochi
Prima fossi d'ogn'altro; e pur fu in vano.
Toccato è in sorte a forastier pastore   15
Di Flori il dolce sguardo insieme e crudo.
Egli ora gode lieto di quel core
Sì altero, il non ancora
Ad altro possessore compartito
Ben perfetto possesso.   20
E com'intesi anco Licori, ingrata
Falsa e crudel, che si fingea d'amarmi,
È scoperta d'Androgeo calda amante.
Tal rifferta m'ha fatto or ora Filli,
A cui scoperte l'una e l'altra s'hanno.   25
Deh, Amore, Amor! Quanto poc'anzi errai
Chiamandoti fanciullo cieco alato.
Or rivocando quel parer primiero,
Ti confesso su in ciel tra gli altri Dei
Il più antico, il più giusto, e al veder Argo.   30
Ho meritato da Licori infine
Per inganno aver frodi. Io mi ricordo
Che fintamente le diceva: "io amo,
Amo, Licori, tanto," altra intendendo,
Ma mi sovien ben anco la risposta: 35
"Et io", ella diceva, "amo, Serrano:
Ah così non amassi! Io amo tanto,"
Io di Flori intendendo, ella d'Androgeo./[62r]
Ma che? Più giusto Amore esser non puotte,
Ancora che più d'ogn'altra amassi Flori,   40
A mill'altre facea buon viso a un tempo.
Amor dunque a ragion m'ha castigato.
M'ha castigato or come? se mi porge
Nova ventura? Fronimo richiesta
M'ave pietà per la più bella ninfa   45
Di queste selve, Urania. Vo' gradirla,
Poiché sogliamo noi dire in ogni modo
Ch'al fine, al fine, elle son tutte donne.

ish without regard to desert. My plan was to detain the shepherds in games for the duration of the sacrifice, so that I stood a better chance of being the first to catch Flori's eye. But it was all in vain: a stranger-shepherd was destined to be the object of Flori's sweet and cruel gaze, and he now basks in the ownership of that haughty heart, which has always before resisted all attempts to possess it. A prize indeed! And now I hear that Licori too, who had feigned to love me, has now been revealed as desperately in love with Androgeo. False, cruel, ungrateful creature! Filli just told me all about the loves of both of these nymphs, having heard the details from their own mouths.

But ah, Love, I erred just now when I called you a wanton, blind, winged boy. I take all that back: I now see, on reflection that you are, of all the gods in heaven, the most ancient, the most just, and keen-sighted. After all, what did I deserve from Licori but deceit in return for my own deceptions? I well remember how I used to court her, telling her, "Licori, I am madly in love." And indeed I was, but with another! She would reply: "Serrano, I too burn with love—would that I did not!" As I now see, where I was referring to Flori, she must have been referring to Androgeo. In fact, all in all, it must be confessed that Love has dealt with me as I deserved. For, even though it is true that I loved Flori more than any other nymph, that did not stop me from courting every other that crossed my path. So, I am deservedly punished by Love. But the punishment can hardly be called a harsh one, if the god now seems to be offering me a new opportunity. Fronimo has asked whether I might be persuaded to look kindly on the love of Urania, the fairest nymph of all these woods. I may indeed be disposed to do so—for, as we men like to say, when it comes down to it, one woman is very like another!

SCENA QUINTA

Fronimo, [Serrano] [37]

Fronimo

Non può l'uman pensier giunger in parte   1
A penetrare insomma degli Dei
Gli alti secreti immensi.
Or di repente alta letizia ingombra
Omai d'ogni pastore il core e l'alma,   5
Cui dianzi fu da turbo
D'alta procella in strana guisa afflitto.
Resta sol ch'io ritrovi
Serrano, che pur or lasciai, per dirgli
Quanto è di ben successo in breve spazio.   10
Eccolo a tempo.

Serrano

                    Fronimo, cercato
Ho 'l sacerdote assai per far l'ufficio
Ch'io devo seco, un sì felice fine
Avuto avendo il sacrificio. E anco
Se da alcun straniero avessi/[62v]   15
Potuto de lo stato aver certezza
Di Leggiadro, per l'opra che poc'anzi
Tu mi chiedesti in suo servigio, e quando
Alcun'altra contezza
Anco non possa aver, la sua fè sola   20
Vo' che vaglia, e disposto son di darli
Per consorte Gelinda mia sorella.

Fronimo

Serrano, il sacerdote, a cui tenuto
Son come tu del beneficio avuto,
Ora è giunto, ov'accolti insieme stanno   25
A la capanna tua ninfe e pastori,
Di doppia gioia e nova ingombro ogn'uno.
Di Leggiadro gentile il vecchio padre
Già s'è trovato: più temer non dei
Che non sia vero quanto ei disse. Tirsi,   30

SCENE FIVE

Fronimo, Serrano

Fronimo

[*Aside*] It is true that the power of human thought can never fathom the vast and mysterious secret reaches of divine providence. Suddenly today an unlooked-for happiness has engulfed the hearts and souls of all dwellers of Arcadia, where before we were afflicted by strange turbulences, like ships tossed on a stormy sea. All that remains is for me to find Serrano, with whom I spoke not long ago, to tell him all the good news the last few hours have brought. Ah, there he is!

Serrano

Fronimo, I have been looking for the priest, to give him my heart-felt thanks, now that the sacrifice has had such a successful outcome. I also wished to ask him whether he had managed to discover anything from some foreign visiting shepherd that might confirm Leggiadro's identity, in connection with the request that you addressed to me just now on his behalf. Though if it proves impossible to find any such confirmation, I am inclined simply to take his word for it and to give him my sister Gelinda as a wife.

Fronimo

I am as indebted to the priest as you are, Serrano, for the great boon we have both received from the sacrifice. Know, then, that he is back, and is with the nymphs and shepherds who have gathered at your hut, all filled with a new and strange and double joy. Doubt no further the truth of noble Leggiadro's words, for his aged father Tirsi has already been

Del sacrificio al grido tratto, giunse
Qua per trovare il figlio, e fu d'Alessi
Opra che 'l conoscesse.

Serrano

O mio caro Leggiadro, un punto, un anno
Mi sembrerà poter gli amplessi teco   35
Iterare amichevoli. Ben dissi
Sempre ch'eri di stato
Nobil, qual di costumi.

Fronimo

Altre, altre ci restano a godere
Gioie maggior, Serrano.   40
Tu manchi sol di tanta gioia a parte,
Al giunger tuo saran compite in tutto
(Mi dà 'l cor) l'allegrezze in ogni parte.

Serrano

So che vuoi dir. Melampo de' mostrarsi
A contentar (difficile) i desiri/[63r]   45
Di Licori, che, accesa
D'Androgeo, il deve aver richiesto al padre,
Perché strano parrà di darla dove
Di Fortuna non è pur picciol bene.
Ma si rimedia a questo   50
Or or per me, che compartirgli intendo
Quanto al mondo possedo.

Fronimo

Gran liberalità d'animo è certo
Il compartire altrui quelle sostanze
Che le fè proprie il ciel, tanto più ch'OGGI   55
Par che null'altra cosa prezzi l'uomo
Fuor che l'or, d'ogni mal sola cagione.
Ma non sarà d'uopo, Serrano, in questo
Che tu dimostri del tuo degno core
La liberalitate; or t'apparecchia   60
Di bella ninfa di gradir l'affetto,
Che a questo fin sol ti cercava a punto,

found: He had come here on hearing of the sacrifice, hoping to find his son, and they were reunited through the good offices of Alessi.

Serrano

O my dearest Leggiadro! I can hardly wait to see you and once again dearly to embrace you. I always thought that the nobility of your bearing must betoken nobility of birth!

Fronimo

And there are yet further and greater joys in prospect, Serrano! The others are all eagerly awaiting you, to share in their delight. Something tells me that, by the time you arrive, their happiness will be complete.

Serrano

I know you are talking about the prospect of Melampo's agreeing to accede to the desire of Licori, who is in love with Androgeo and must by now have asked her father for his consent to their marriage. It is hard to think that he will agree, for it will seem strange to him to let her wed a penniless shepherd. But I have already thought out a remedy for this and shall propose it forthwith: I intend to endow Androgeo with half of my fortune.

Fronimo

It is certainly an act of great liberality to distribute so freely those worldly goods with which the heavens have endowed us—especially in the present day, when it sometimes seems that no one cares for anything other than amassing gold, which is the root of all evil. But there is no need on this occasion, Serrano, to display the liberality of your noble heart; rather, prepare yourself to return the affections of a lovely nymph! It was to tell you this that I came here, and to inform you, as well, that

E per dirti ch'Androgeo più ricchezze
Non de' bramar. Or dimmi pure, alcuno
Sapea d'Androgeo il caso?   65

Serrano

Oggi ad Alessi, che pastor mi parse
Saggio e gentile, sol lo raccontai,
E fuorché tu in Arcadia altri no 'l sanno.

Fronimo

Tu non avrai cagion di compartirgli
Le tue ricchezze. Egli ha trovato padre,   70
E padre tal, ch'ei potrà darne altrui.

Serrano

Dunque trovato s'è di cui sia figlio
Il mio fratello Androgeo?

Fronimo

     S'ha trovato,
E tal che stupirai.

Serrano

     Chi fu cagione/[63v]
Di tanta sua ventura?

Fronimo

     Credo Alessi.   75
Giunsi ch'or l'uno or l'altro figlio Tirsi
(E Androgeo e Leggiadro, che di questi
Egli è scoperto padre) al sen stringeva
Colmo (per gaudio tal) di pianto gli occhi,
E parole diceva a l'uno e a l'altro   80
Quasi fuori di senso, che dettando
Confuse gli venian gaudio soverchio
Per la pietate in un, per la dolcezza
Avrebbon (credo) insino i sassi pianto.
Felice ambasciatore allor fui scelto   85
Tra tutti gli altri a rapportarti questa
Nova felice e cara.

Androgeo has no further need for riches. But tell me, did anyone know the story about how Androgeo was found?

Serrano

I told it today to Alessi, who seemed a wise and noble shepherd. Otherwise, in the whole of Arcadia, no one knows but you.

Fronimo

As I say, there is now no call for you to share your riches with him. He has found a father, and a father who is of such means that he can afford to be liberal himself.

Serrano

Then the true parentage of my brother Androgeo has been discovered?

Fronimo

It has indeed, and you will be amazed.

Serrano

Who is responsible for this great discovery?

Fronimo

I think it is Alessi's doing. When I arrived, Tirsi—for he is the father!—was already clasping first Leggiadro and then Androgeo to his breast, with his eyes brimming over with tears of joy, and babbling incoherently to both of them the words dictated by his surpassing joy. The pity of the sight and the sweetness would, I think, have moved the very stones to tears! I was fortunate enough to be chosen for the happy task of conveying these glad and welcome tidings to you.

Serrano

Felice nova e cara, caro giorno,
Giorno beato a pieno! Tirsi, dunque,
È del mio caro Androgeo padre?

Fronimo

                    È vero,   90
E di Leggiadro ancora. Resta solo
Che della bella Urania il degno affetto
A te piaccia gradire,
Come in suo nome ti pregai pur dianzi.

Serrano

Qual per me cosa a te negar si puote,   95
Caro amico e fratel? Purché di Flori
Sien contente le voglie, altro mai giorno
(Da che gira il tuo cerchio il gran pianeta)
Non è di questo ancora
Stato il più aventuroso.   100
Purché Urania contenti, ecco di fede
Il pegno, la mano porgi. Altra mai ninfa
Non mi sia donna o sposa.

Fronimo

Lodato sia il ciel. Licori a pien contenta/[64r]
Gode, già conseguito   105
Dal vecchio padre il caro amante, e quello
Che in fascie già le destinaro i cieli;
Ed è stupore a rimirar quei vecchi,
Tirsi e Melampo, raddoppiar gli amplessi,
Che mille rimembranze rinovando   110
Ebri nuotano in mar ampio di gioia.
Darello, anch'ei, come che intorno egli abbia
Mille accuse e rinfaci,
E che da l'aria insino oda sgridarsi
Da la sua propria conscienza immonda,   115
Già condannato, va da gli altri scevro,
Languente, e qual chi in rimembrar sue colpe
Suol pien di tema e di dolor, che ad imago
Simile è d'uom ch'apeso sia per voto.

Serrano

Glad and welcome indeed! O happy day! Thrice-blessed day! Tirsi, then, is the father of my dear Androgeo?

Fronimo

He is, and of Leggiadro. Now all that remains is that you consent to return the love of the fair Urania, as I begged you earlier in her name.

Serrano

Dearest friend and brother, I can deny you nothing. As long as Flori is happy with this outcome, let it be. Oh, was there ever a more fortunate day, as long as the sun has been spinning in its orbit! If it please Urania, here is my hand on it as a pledge of faith: she alone shall be my lady and my wife.

Fronimo

The heavens be praised! Licori, too, is in ecstasy, now that her father has consented to her marriage with her dear beloved. Indeed, it is just the outcome that their fathers had destined for them almost from the moment of their birth.[102] It was quite a marvel to watch the aged Tirsi and Melampo wrapped in each other's embrace and reviving a thousand shared memories, as they wallowed in the great ocean of joy, intoxicated with happiness. As for Darello, he is plagued by a throng of recriminations and accusing voices, so that it seems to him that the very air is thick with reproach; even his own filthy conscience condemns him, and he shuns all other human company, the very image of a man racked by guilt and fear. If you saw him, you would think him the picture of the hanged

I pensieri (conformi 120
Al voler degli Dei) di Flori in vita
L'han trattenuto. Ella recise il laccio
Ch'avvolto egli s'aveva intorno al collo,
E disse, "vivi, che maggior castigo
Non saprei darti, quando pure è vero 125
Ch'uom di maligna mente in vita purga
Anco gli errori, seco stesso irato,
E pien di mal talento ogn'or pugnando."

Serrano

Non parlian di costui. Viva, se Flori
Pur così vuol, ma egli è di vita indegno. 130
O DEL cielo infallibili ed eterni
Decreti, cui non puote
Distornar qua giù l'uom con forz'umana,
Intesi che già data/[64v]
S'avean Melampo e Tirsi fè d'unire 135
In matrimonio i figli. O (torno a dire)
Mirabili del ciel secreti eterni!

Fronimo

Anco Flori beata in ampio mare
Di soverchio contento gode, nulla
Più sperando che avere unico impero 140
Sopra il suo amato Alessi, e l'uno e l'altro
S'han data fè d'eternamente amarsi,
E seguir l'orme ambo di Cinzia insieme.
E in caste voglie ardendo
Sperano incomparabil paragone 145
Scoprirsi al mondo, e vero,
Di continenza e fede essempio degno.

Serrano

A copia sì fedel arrida il cielo,
Onde riescan paghe le lor brame!
Ma che tardiam? Colà n'andiam ov'io 150
Spero gioia gustar maggior d'ogn'altra.

man he chose to be. It was Flori who saved him, following the dictates of the gods. She cut the noose with which he had encircled his neck, saying "Live, rather, for I can think of no greater punishment for you! Indeed, for an ill-intentioned man life itself is a scourge as he is constantly at war with himself."

Serrano

Bah! That is quite enough about him. Let him live if it should please Flori—but he certainly does not deserve to. But, oh, how infallible and eternal are the decrees of the heavens! No mortal power can sway them! Did I hear aright, that Tirsi and Melampo had already long ago pledged to unite their son and daughter? I can only repeat: how wondrous are the eternal mysteries of the heavens!

Fronimo

Flori, too, is bathed in a endless ocean of delight. Her only desire now is to reign in the heart of her beloved Alessi, and the two have pledged to love one another eternally, while following together in the footsteps of Diana; they burn in chaste flames and hope in this way to show a shining example to the world, as paragons of continence and fidelity.

Serrano

May the heavens smile on so faithful a pair, and satisfy their every desire. But what are we waiting for? Let us go! I hope that the joy that surpasses all others awaits me.

Fronimo

Andiam, ch'è ben ragion gioire a tante
E sì fatte dal ciel grazie ottenute,
De le quali dobbiam lode immortali
Dar solo agli alti Dei, fatti pietosi   155
Nel sacrificio, per cui resi a pieno
Sono contenti i preghi e desir nostri.

Il fine

Fronimo

Yes, let us go. Who would not be delighted at all these great boons that the heavens have showered upon us? For all these gifts, we must eternally praise the immortal gods on high, who turned their pitying gaze on our sacrifice and deigned to satisfy in full our prayers and our desires.

The end

MADDALENA CAMPIGLIA ALLA
SUA FLORI

Poggia, o mia Flori, al volo dietro, ardita,
Di raro stuol di Cigni, e mostra quanto
L'altrui lagrime belle, un vago pianto
Sovente ha in gentil virtù infinita.
La santa, e del tuo petto alta ferita
Aperta mostra fuor, che averrà intanto
Ch'appaghi il mondo d'un eterno vanto
La candidezza tua, se sia gradita.
E mentre di tua fiamma al puro ardore
Si scalda ogn'alma più d'amor rubella,
E divien molle ogni saldo petto
Dica il tuo caro *ALESSI,* il tuo diletto:
"O me felice sovra ogni Pastore,
Se m'unì a tanta fè benigna stella."

[sig. i, 1v] Per ben'amar, mia *FLORI,*
Odi quai lode intorno a te si danno!
I disusati ardori
Che t'apportano al cor gradito affanno
Tempra, ch'alta mercede
Dal tuo *ALESSI* s'aspetta a la tua fede.
Ma par che dirmi io t'oda: "I miei tesori,
Il vanto ch'ogn'or bramo,
D'esser'amata è sol, da cui sol'amo."

MADDALENA CAMPIGLIA TO
HER FLORI

Boldly take flight, my Flori, following the select flock of swans![103] Show how the sweet tears and graceful weeping of another can work untold marvels on a noble heart; show forth the lofty, sacred wound in your breast, that your purity, if it please the world, may be rewarded by eternal fame. Even those souls most averse to love will thaw before the flame of your pure ardor, and the most obdurate hearts will melt; and meanwhile, let your darling *ALESSI,* your only joy, utter these words: "O most fortunate of shepherds, in that some kindly star has linked my fate with such an exemplar of faith."

Listen, my Flori, to all these praises that are echoing around you as a reward for your noble love! Temper that unwonted ardor that brings such pleasing pain to your heart, for your faith will receive a noble recompense from your *ALESSI.* But I seem to hear you saying, "My dearest wishes, and most constant aspiration is only to be loved by that man who is the only object of my love."

APPENDIX A:
NOTE ON THE ITALIAN TEXT

Since no manuscript exists for *Flori*, the present transcription follows the text contained in the sole sixteenth-century edition of the play, published in Vicenza in 1588 by the heirs of Perin Libraro and Tomaso Brunelli. The edition exists in two variant issues, distinguished solely by the printer's mark on the title-page. Where one bears the usual mark of the heirs of Perin (an anchor with a dolphin), the other carries instead an emblem of the god Pan previously used by the printer Giorgio Angelieri, especially in his publications of dialect works by the Vicentine poet Giambattista Maganza. This may suggest that Angelieri was involved to some degree in the publication, even though his name does not appear on the title-page: a hypothesis supported by the fact that, although based in Venice, he is known to have collaborated in this period with Vicentine publishers, especially Giorgio Greco, who was involved in the publication of Campiglia's *Discourse on the Annunciation* in 1585 and was to publish her *Calisa* in 1589.[1]

The 1588 edition of *Flori* is in octavo format. It contains three separately numbered sequences: the dedicatory letter and prologue (numbered fols. 1r–8v), the text of the play (numbered fols. 1r–64r), and an appendix (not found in all copies) containing poems in praise of the work by Campiglia and others (numbered sig. i, 1r–sig. k, 8v). The text on the title page of the two variant issues reads as follows:

FLORI / FAVOLA / BOSCARECCIA / Di Maddalena Campiglia. / [Woodcut illustration of Pan playing his pipes, with the motto ET NOBIS HUIUS PLACUERUNT CARMINA CANNÆ] / In Vicenza, Appresso

---

1.   For illustration of the two printers' marks, see Zappella, *Le marche dei tipografi e degli editori italiani del Cinquecento*, 2: figs. 55 and 930; and see 1: 285–86 for discussion of the Pan motif. See also Vaccaro, *Le marche dei tipografi ed editori italiani*, 43; and Zironda 1997, "Giorgio Angelieri," 1: 30–32,

gl'heredi di Perin Libraro, & Tomaso / Brunelli compagni. 1588. / Con
Licentia de' Superiori.

FLORI / FAVOLA / BOSCARECCIA / Di Maddalena Campiglia. /
[Woodcut of an anchor with a dolphin wound around it] / IN VICENZA/
Presso gl'heredi di Perin Libaro, / & Tomaso Brunelli compagni. / 1588. /

Con Licentia de' Superiori.

As noted, some printed copies of *Flori* contain a separately paginated appendix with verse relating to the play. This appendix opens with two poems by
Campiglia herself (sig. i, 1r–v, at pp. 302–3 of this volume), followed by a woodcut of Campiglia's emblem, a phoenix, with the motto "Tempore sic duro" (sig.
i, 2r).[2] There follows a sequence of poems in praise of the work, headed "Diversi
componimenti in lode dell'opera" (sigs. i, 3r–k, 8v), which contains compositions by Angelo Grillo, Antonio Frizzimellega, Antonmaria Angiolello, Camillo
Camilli, Claudio Forzatè, Cortese Cortesi, Diomede Borghesi, Fabio Pace,
Francesco Melchiori, Francesco Sarcinelli, Gregorio Ducchi, Gerardo Bellinzona, Giovanni Battista Titoni, Giuseppe Gagliardia, Giovanni Battista da
Velo, Orazio d'Este, Lodovico Ronconi, Lucillo Martinenghi, Marco Stecchini,
Muzio Manfredi, Muzio Sforza, Paolo Chiappino, Pietro Paolo Volpe, Prospero
Cattaneo, Quintio Saracino, Regio Melchiori, and Vicenzo Tassello.[3]

METHOD OF TRANSCRIPTION

The transcription follows the original as closely as possible, preserving, for
example, its often nonstandard usage with regard to the use of single/double

---

esp. 31–32. The hypothesis put forward by Vaccaro and Zironda that the Pan motif was used for
editions of dialect poetry on account of its thematic appropriateness (given Pan's status as a rural deity, associated with "rustic" song) receives support from its appearance on the title-page of
Campiglia's pastoral, also theoretically "rustic" in genre. On Angelieri's collaborations with
Giorgio Greco, see Zironda, "Giorgio Angelieri," 30; also, more generally, on collaborations between publishers in this period, see Costabile, "Forme di collaborazione." For examples of the issue with the anchor motif, see London British Library 1071.1.16; Venice, Biblioteca Marciana,
Dramm. 3804. For examples of the issue with the Pan frontispiece, see Cambridge, U.K., Cam-
bridge University Library, Bute 130 (4); Vatican City, Biblioteca Apostolica Vaticana, Ferraioli,
V.4317; Biblioteca Marciana, Dramm. 255 and Dramm. 1595.4

2. See appendix B.

3. See the introduction, pp. 31–32. Of the copies listed in note 1 above, the following contain
the appendix described here: British Library, 1071.1.6; Vatican Library, Ferraioli V. 4317; Biblioteca Marciana, Dramm. 3804 and Dramm. 255.

consonants. The following minor changes have, however, been made for the convenience of the modern reader:

- The letters *u* and *v* have been distinguished according to modern usage.
- The letter *h* has been removed when used only for (pseudo-) etymological purposes, though it is retained where it serves a diacritic function.
- The letter *j* in intervocalic or initial position has been altered to *i*.
- In final position, both in nouns and verbs, *j* has been rendered by *î* if it indicates *-ii*; or *i* if it is purely a graphic feature.
- The sequence *-(t)ti* followed by a vowel has been changed to *–zi* (e.g., *negotio* becomes *negozio*; *attione* becomes *azione*).
- *Et* has been changed to *e*, except when it precedes words that begin with an *e*, when it has been changed to *ed*.
- Word boundaries have in some cases been changed: conjunctions, and prepositions + definite article not requiring *raddoppiamento sintattico* have been joined together (e.g., *perché, benché, fuorché, poiché, nei, degli*), as have expressions such as *intanto, invero, insomma, purtroppo*, and *talvolta*. Variant spellings of *allor(a)* and *talor(a)* (e.g., *alhora, al'hora, a l'hor, tal'hor*) have been standardized to follow modern usage.
- Abbreviations (and symbols) have been given in full, and accents follow standard usage.
- Capitalization generally follows standard modern usage, except where it fulfills an important rhetorical function (as where full capitals are used to mark the opening of the moral *sententiae* that are such a notable feature of the text).
- Punctuation follows the original as far as possible, although some changes have been necessitated by omissions and inaccuracies in the original.
- Additional editorial interventions are indicated by square brackets. These include the page numbers of the original edition.

The copy used for the transcription here was that in the Cambridge University Library, Bute 130 (4). The present text was checked against the text of the British Library copy (1076.1.16).

APPENDIX B:
MADDALENA CAMPIGLIA'S EMBLEM
AND PORTRAIT

THE EMBLEM

An important element in Campiglia's authorial self-presentation in her later published works is her personal emblem (fig. 1): an image of a phoenix rising from the flames with the motto "Tempore sic duro" (In this manner I endure through time). A woodcut reproduction of this is found in the 1589 edition of *Calisa* (see Perrone, "*So che donna ama donna*," cit., 91), and in an appendix containing commendatory poetry which is found in some copies of the *Flori* (see appendix A). In the *Calisa*, the emblem is accompanied by an explanatory sonnet by Campiglia, whose text reads as follows:

> De i miei desiri accesi il rogo ascendo
> E l'ali sparte del pensier diletto
> Provo, che tal non cape in uman petto,
> Mentre nel sol ch'adoro il guardo intendo.
> In puro foco indi felice ardendo
> Sgombrar sento da l'alma l'imperfetto,
> E in dolci fiamme (opposta à chiaro obietto)
> Sola Fenice nova forma io prendo.
> Sola Fenice in ben'amar, del core
> In sì soave ardor le voglie affino,
> Nè vil pensiero entro al mio seno albergo,
> Ove dal NUME mio, che umile inchino,
> Qualità presa, ancor lasciarmi a tergo,
> Spero qual arse in più perfetto amore.

As I ascend the pyre of my ardent desires, I can feel the spreading wings of my cherished dream, far transcending the capacity of any mortal breast. Fixing my eyes on the sun that I adore, I joyfully burn in the purest fire and feel my soul purged of human dross, while, enveloped in sweet flames and gazing on my bright object, I find my-

Campiglia's emblem from *Flori* (1588). Engraving from *Calisa, ecloga* (1589). By permission of the British Library (1071.1.16)

self strangely transfigured, taking on the form of the sole phoenix. Like a sole phoenix in the purity of my love,[1] *I refine my heart's desires in this gentlest of furnaces, nor can any base thought find shelter within my breast. And having absorbed the qualities of the divinity at whose feet I humbly worship, I can hope now to outshine even those who have loved most perfectly in the past.*

The image of the phoenix, a mythological bird supposed miraculously to renew its youth by bathing in flames, was widely used in the Renaissance to signify uniqueness and the aspiration to immortality, whether spiritual immortality or the temporal immortality of enduring fame. More rarely, since the phoenix was sole of its kind, it could also signify a commitment to celibacy, and it is used in this sense on two occasions in Moderata Fonte's dialogue, *Il*

1.   The phrase translated here echoes the opening line of a madrigal appended to the text of *Flori* in a manner that underlines Campiglia's identification with the protagonist of her drama.

merito delle donne (1600).[2] Campiglia's use of the image may be seen as drawing
on all these possible meanings, although the text of her explanatory sonnet
privileges the Neoplatonic theme of love as a means of spiritual ascent.[3] A
particularly striking feature of the poem is the very overt parallel it draws between Campiglia and her protagonist Flori, similarly possessed of a "unique"
love characterized by its miraculous transcendence of any base sensual component.

THE PORTRAIT

The portrait of Maddalena Campiglia reproduced as a frontispiece to the
present volume is part of the collection of the Museo Civico of Vicenza,
though it currently hangs in the nearby Teatro Olimpico. It can be dated to
around the time of her composition of *Flori*, the late 1580s or early 1590s.
Recent studies have attributed the work with increasing confidence to the
Vicentine painter Alessandro Maganza (1548–1632), an attribution that is
made all the more plausible by Campiglia's friendship with Alessandro's father, the poet Giambattista Maganza.[4] The portrait shows Campiglia dressed
with unusual austerity for a woman of her social background, conforming
with Vespasiano Giuliani's description of her devout and unworldly lifestyle
in his prefatory letter to her *Discourse on the Annunciation* (1586). Her stance and
the prominence given to the book she is holding foreground her status as an
author, in a manner reminiscent of contemporary portraits of male intellectuals. Together with Agnolo Bronzino's famous portrait of the poet Laura Bat-
tiferri degli Ammanati (Florence: Palazzo Vecchio) and the self-portraits
of Sofonisba Anguissola—similarly austere in their rejection of feminine
adornments—Maganza's portrait of Campiglia deserves to be recognized as
one of the most compelling of Italian Renaissance representations of a female
creative artist.

2.   Fonte, *The Worth of Women*, 54 and n. 16, 230.

3.   Similar Neoplatonic themes of a bird's flight toward a beloved sun and of spiritual transcendence through love are evident in the emblem of Curzio Gonzaga, the second dedicatee of
Flori, composed by 1582 with the motto "Et sole altro non aggio" (see Camilli, *Imprese illustri di diversi*, 40–42).

4.   Milani, "Quattro donne tra i pavani," 389–93. For discussions of the portrait, see the cata-
logue entries by A. Ballarin and G. Barioli in *Il gusto e la moda nel Cinquecento vicentino e veneto*, 108–9;
and by Vittorio Sgarbi in *Museo ritrovato*, 131 (no. B25). I should like to thank Professor Adriano
Mariuz for his kindness in procuring for me an advance copy of the entry on this portrait by
Francesca Lodi, which will be published in the forthcoming catalog of paintings in the Museo
Civico.

NOTES

NOTES TO ITALIAN TEXT

1. "Duchi" in original.

2. "Vene" in original.

3. Here, as often in the text, full capitals are used to mark the beginning of a *sententia*, or moral axiom.

4. "Sonno" in original.

5. "Stessa" in original.

6. "Comsuma" in original.

7. "Melle" in original; it also appears as "mele" below.

8. This is "è" in original.

9. The slightly unclear sense suggests some typographical error at this point.

10. This address to Silvano is clearly an error, in that he is the speaker here.

11. "Discoprise" in original.

12. "Mo" in original.

13. As in several other instances, the second "Damone" is not capitalized in the original.

14. "Fole" in original.

15. "Forsi" in original.

16. "Leggiadro" is not capitalized in the original (see note 13).

17. "Ridette" in original.

18. "Salga" in original.

19. "Fole" in original.

20. "Questi" in standard Italian.

21. In the original, the parenthesis closes at this point.

22. "Sonn" in original.

23. "Fole" in original.

24. "Sne" in original.

25. "Pinte" in original.

26. "Redo" in original.

27. "Eranno" in original, as below.

28. "Savra" in original.

29. Alternatively, this could be rendered "E sempre viva / La terrò" ("I shall keep it ever alive").

30. "Natto" in original.

31. "Contrate" in original.

32. "Quinta" in original.

33. "Spesi" in original.

34. "Carco" in original.

35. "Se" in original.

36. "Adhora" in original.

37. The original has "Leggiadro" instead of "Serrano."

NOTES TO ENGLISH TEXT

1. On Isabella Pallavicino Lupi (in the Italian the family name appears in the feminized form, Pallavicina) and Campiglia's relations with her, see the introduction, pp. 4, 6, 9 and 27–28. On Gregorio Ducchi, mentioned below in the letter, see pp. 6, 8, and 33 in the introduction.

2. On Curzio Gonzaga and Campiglia's relations with him, see the introduction, pp. 4, 11, 13, 14, and 32. On Angelo Ingegneri, mentioned below in the letter, see p. 6, 7n18 in the introduction.

3. The reference is to Gonzaga's moralizing chivalric romance, *Il fido amante*, or *Il fidamante*, which was published for the first time in Mantua in 1582. A revised edition, with verse summaries of each canto provided by Campiglia, appeared in Venice in 1591. For discussion, see Pignatti, *Un principe letterato del secolo XVI*, 50–108; also Ridolfi, "Gonzaga, Curzio," 706; Grandi, "Di Curzio Gonzaga e delle sue opere," 543 and n. 39. The poem narrates the eponymous protagonist's love for the warrior maiden Ippolita, or Vittoria, against the background of a conflict between pagan and Christian forces. Aspects of its representation of female characters are of interest in connection with *Flori:* see especially Pignatti, 102–3, on Gonzaga's description of Ippolita's early life as a votary of Diana, and ibid., 84–85, on his narrative of the exemplary friendship of Virginia and Costanza, modeled on a classic and much-cited exemplum of heroic male friendship in Virgil's *Aeneid.*

4. See Morsolin, *Maddalena Campiglia*, 25; Mantese, "Per un profilo storico della poetessa vicentina Maddalena Campiglia," 97.

5. The reference here is to Campiglia's first published work, the *Discourse on the Annunciation* (see pp. 7–8, 31).

6. This idea was commonly presented in moralizing and literary works of the period, and proposed by academies and the *imprese* [emblems] of literati. One of the main goals of the Accademia Olimpica, for example, was to encourage members and, through their example, the citizens of Vicenza to pursue virtuous activity, drawing youth away from the moral corruption associated with idleness. For an attempt to identify the passage in Augustine alluded to here, see Perrone, *"So che donna ama donna"*: *La* Calisa *di Maddalena Campiglia*, 45–46.

7. This remark reflects the concerns of contemporary neo-Aristotelian literary theory, which insisted on unity of plot as a key aesthetic criterion. *Episodi* (digressive interludes) were permitted only if used sparingly, especially in drama, which was required to be structured more tightly than more expansive narrative forms such as epic. For the general context of this passage, see p. 14.

8. Some theorists of drama, attentive to practical demands, recommended the use of dialogue over monologues, and that soliloquies be kept as short and plausible as possible to maintain audience interest (Ingegneri, *Della poesia rappresentativa e del modo di rappresentare le favole sceniche*, 13–14, 16; and see Guarini's annotations to his *Pastor fido*, 65v. For a general overview, see Molinari, "Scenografia e spettacolo nelle poetiche del '500").

9. The Vicentine nobleman and notary Paolo Chiappino (1538?–1593) played a major role in the literary and dramatic activities of the Accademia Olimpica, of which he was a member from 1557. He was voted to the permanent position of secretary in 1582, and a statue representing him still stands in the theater of the academy (Teatro Olimpico). His literary works include various verse compositions, orations, and translations (see Calvi, *Biblioteca e storia*, 5: 234–35; Chiappini di Sorio, "Un letterato di Vicenza: Paolo Chiappino").

10. The prologue to *Flori* is the part in which the influence of Tasso's *Aminta* (first published in 1580/81) is most evident. Tasso's prologue also features Love, who has left the cities and courts to exercise his influence in humble pastoral parts. As in *Aminta*, Campiglia depicts Love boasting of his powers over other gods, and outlining his part in the action by overcoming a nymph's resistance to love, while he remains disguised among a chorus of shepherds. She departs from the earlier model, however, by omitting the frame-story (in which Love hides from his mother Venus), with its anticourtly polemic, and subversively sensual and libertarian suggestions. Her god instead emphasizes how, unusually, he will inspire an eternal, chaste, and holy love.

11. The reference is to the accounts in classical Greek and Roman mythology to the loves of Zeus, or Jove, king of the gods, for a sequence of beautiful mortals, male and female. In his pursuance of these loves, Jove typically adopted a disguise, abducting Ganymede, for example, in the guise of a swan or Europa in the form of a bull; hence the phrase in the text "in a thousand guises."

12. Pluto, god of the underworld in classical mythology, fell in love with, and abducted, Proserpina, daughter of the earth-goddess Ceres.

13. As is clear from what follows, the figure referred to here is the ancient Greek philosopher Aristotle (384–322 B.C.E.). Campiglia's phrasing in the text ("'l gran

maestro de' piu saggi") perhaps consciously echoes Dante's famous allusion to Aristotle in canto 4 of the *Inferno* as "il maestro di color che sanno" ("the master of those who know" [4.131]). The details of Hercules's, Achilles's, and Aristotle's shameful passions are referred to in more detail slightly later in the text. Hercules, after gaining the status of a god by completing a series of superhuman "labors," later stained his reputation through his infatuation with Omphale, queen of Lydia, who enjoyed humiliating him by dressing him in female attire and setting him to spin along with her hand-maidens. Similarly, a legend was told of Aristotle's being reduced by love to demeaning servitude to a woman, in this case the courtesan Phyllis. Both were popular cautionary examples in the Renaissance. The reference to Achilles is to the episode recounted by Homer in the *Iliad*, when the Greek hero refused to participate in the siege of Troy after a dispute with King Agamemnon over the "ownership" of the lovely girl captive Briseis.

14. Love was traditionally depicted as wounding people with arrows, which if made of gold would make the victim fall in love, or if made of lead would engender hatred. The "fatal waters" referred to are the sweet and bitter springs typical of romances (and found in some pastorals), which caused the person who drank from them to fall in love or to hate.

15. The device of a foreign shepherd arriving in Arcadia was commonplace in late-sixteenth-century pastoral drama, usually providing an opportunity for "recognition" and surprising plot reversals. A second "foreign" shepherd, Tirsi, appears later in *Flori* (4.4), closely modeled on similar returning older shepherds, for example in Alberto Lollio's *Aretusa* (1564), Ingegneri's *La danza di Venere* (The dance of Venus [1584]), and, notably, Carino in Guarini's *Il Pastor fido.* Alessi is more unusual, since his origins and identity remain deliberately obscured (see below, 5.3).

16. While the goddess Flora, associated with flowers, was sometimes evoked in mythological pastoral literature, the name is uncommon in pastoral drama, which typically repeats a fairly restricted range of names. (A nymph called Flora does however appear among the chorus in Bernardino Percivallo's *L'Orsilia,* 1589). Flori vaguely recalls names found in romance epic (Fiordiligi and Floridante) and reflects the tendency to use hellenizing pastoral names among the circle of Isabella Pallavicino Lupi—herself known as "Calisa." Campiglia adopted the name Flori as a pseudonym also in her pastoral dialogue *Calisa,* and it was used by contemporaries to allude to her (see the introduction, pp. 9, 27, 33–34).

17. Androgeo, an unusual name in pastoral drama, probably derives from Jacopo Sannazaro's immensely popular pastoral romance, *Arcadia* (1502), which features a venerated dead shepherd by this name. The name is also used by the Tuscan poet Chiara Matraini (1515–1604) to refer to her dead love. Etymologically, it means "man of the earth": an allusion, perhaps, to Androgeo's relatively sensual, and thus "earthbound," love for Flori, which is contrasted in the play with Flori's sublimated and thus nobler and more "divine" passion for Alessi.

18. The name Alessi (from the Greek Alexis) has been associated with pastoral verse since Virgil used it in his second *Eclogue.* The name recurs in Campiglia's eclogue, *Calisa,* referring to an accomplished poet-singer. On a possible identification of this figure in the *Flori* with Torquato Tasso, see note 92 below.

19. Amaranta is a recognized name in pastoral drama, and in fact forms the title of a play by a Mantuan contemporary of Campiglia's, Cesare Simonetti (*Amaranta, favola boscareccia* [Padua, 1588]), as well as of later ones by Bartolomeo Tacchello (Verona, 1611) and Giovanni Villifranchi (posthum., Venice, 1639). In Sannazaro's *Arcadia* (*Eclogue* 3, *Prosa* 4) a nymph is praised under the disguised name of Amaranta, which has suggestions of immortality and incorruptibility.

20. On the unusual practice of representing the protagonists of pastoral drama being finally consumed by Neoplatonic love, rather than by reciprocated sensual passion resulting in marriage, see the introduction, p. 21.

21. In the phrase "fidi Amanti" (the capitalization is found in the original), a tribute may be intended by Campiglia to Curzio Gonzaga's chivalric romance, *Il fidamante* (The faithful lover), which she praises in her dedicatory letter (p. 47).

22. These lines recall similar ones in the prologue to Tasso's *Aminta* (lines 76–88) ("Queste selve oggi ragionar d'Amore / s'udranno in nuova guisa: . . . / Spirerò nobil sensi a' rozzi petti, / raddolcirò de le lor lingue il suono; . . . / render simili a le piú dotte cetre / le rustiche sampogne; . . .": "Today these woods will be heard speaking of Love in a new fashion: . . . I will inspire noble feelings in their simple hearts and sweeten the sound of their voices . . . and make their rustic pipes sound like the most exalted lyres"). In both texts, Love's traditional power to ennoble his subjects serves to explain the stylistic incongruity of shepherds speaking and behaving in such a refined manner, with the result that the conventionally humble and unadorned style of pastoral can be raised to a "middle"—essentially lyric—style without any sacrifice of verisimilitude.

23. Ovid tells in his *Metamorphoses* the story of the nymph Byblis, whose incestuous love for her brother Caunus drove him into exile; having long sought him in vain, Byblis collapsed, bathed in tears, and was transformed into a fountain.

24. Campiglia's representation of Flori's lament at Amaranta's urn might have been inspired by Barbara Torelli's recent *Partenia* (1587) which featured the offstage tomb of a dead nymph, mourned over by the shepherd Lice (3.1). Other important vernacular precedents may include Tasso's lament of Tancredi at the tomb of Clorinda (*Gerusalemme liberata*, canto 12, stanzas 96–99), and Jacopo Sannazaro's elegiac laments and descriptions of funeral rites and games in *Arcadia*, especially 5 (pp. 99–105), 10 (*Prose*, pp. 177–78), and 11 (pp. 195–211). By the end of the century, a more tragic bias is detectable in "neo-classical" pastoral drama (see for example Guidobaldo Bonarelli's *Filli di Sciro*, 1607). The practice of using pastoral verse for funeral poems, often honoring and lamenting the loss of close friends, dates back to classical times (see Virgil, *Eclogue* 5, Bion, *Idyll* 1, Moschus, *Idyll* 3).

25. Scenes of madness, staged or natural, frequently occur in pastoral drama, mainly caused by unrequited love which drives a shepherd (or sometimes nymph) to suicidal frenzy (as in Tasso's *Aminta*) or to a debilitating melancholia (as in Sannazaro's *Arcadia*, 8 [pp. 134–46]). Important precedents for depicting love-madness in a pastoral setting were also to be found in classical pastoral verse (Virgil, Theocritus), lyric poetry (Petrarch), and romance (most famously in the sixteenth century, Ariosto's *Orlando furioso*, where the eponymous protagonist is driven to lunacy by his love for Angelica). In purely dramatic terms, such scenes could provide opportunities for bravura solo

performances, a notable example being the famous "mad" soliloquy of the actress, Is-abella Andreini (*La pazzia di Isabella*) performed in Florence in 1589. Campiglia may have drawn on the recent examples of mad characters in Angelo Ingegneri's *La danza di Venere* (1584), 1.2, and Giovanni Donato Cucchetti's *La Pazzia* (The madness [1581, acts 3–4]). *Flori* is unusual, however, in having two mad characters who need to be cured.

26. Flori's transition into "raving" is marked in the text by an initial speech in rhymed verse, contrasting with the usual blank verse of the original.

27. The reference is to the course of the sun, figured in classical mythology as the fiery chariot of the sun-god Phoebus (or Apollo); the phrase thus means "darkness would not fall."

28. Sacred oracles, originally characteristic of classical tragedies, became incorpo-rated into pastoral drama especially as a result of Guarini's *Pastor fido*, a development which attracted some critical condemnation. Campiglia may also have drawn on the example of Sophocles's *Oedipus Rex*, translated by Orsatto Giustinian (1585). *Flori* marks one of the first instances of this device in a pastoral play; previously, predictions were more commonly made by a magician or enchantress figure.

29. Alcides is an alternative name for Hercules. Rather than to his birth, the refer-ence is in fact to the night of Hercules's conception, when his father, Jupiter, ordained that the hours of darkness be extended to the length of three normal nights in order to prolong the pleasures of his illicit tryst with Hercules's mother, Alcmena, whom he had tricked by disguising himself as her husband.

30. Religious ceremonies to honor the gods or to cure love-madness, such as the sac-rifice to which Licori refers here, were a familiar feature of Renaissance pastoral liter-ature (see Sannazaro, *Arcadia*, 3 [pp. 75, 78–80], 10 [pp. 165–77]), and could provide striking visual display in pastoral drama. While the rites are ostensibly pagan (in-spired, for example, by Ovid's *Fasti* and *Metamorphoses*), they could also present a lightly veiled classicizing transcription of modern Christianity.

31. The nymphs of pastoral drama were traditionally presented as votaries of Diana, goddess of the hunt.

32. As the capitalization of the word *vittoriosa* in the original makes clear, the refer-ence is to Vittoria Colonna (1492–1547), the most celebrated Italian female writer of the sixteenth century. The reference to the river Tiber that follows in the text is ex-plicable in the light of Colonna's long residence in Rome. That to the Mincio (the river running through Mantua) is more perplexing, and may refer more to Colonna's contacts with the ruling Gonzaga dynasty there than with the city itself. The men-tion here of two Italian rivers may seem incongruous, given the Arcadian setting of the *Flori*, but this mingling of Arcadian and contemporary topographical references is a well-established tendency within the Renaissance tradition of pastoral literature, with Tasso's *Aminta*, for example, containing veiled references to the court of Ferrara.

33. Damone is an archetypal pastoral name, found for example in Virgil's *Eclogue* 8, and among the cast of Bernardino Baldi's epithalamium written to celebrate the mar-riage of Isabella Pallavicino Lupi's son (see the introduction, p. 33). Campiglia's priest diverges from most such figures in pastoral drama before Guarini's *Il Pastor fido* (apart from in Beccari's *Il Sacrificio* [The sacrifice], first printed 1555), since his reli-

gious powers make no use of magic and are given unquestioned authority. This marks an important change in pastoral drama in the later part of the century.

34. Pan is the most powerful woodland god in Arcadia; half-man half-goat, he represents wild, instinctual nature, watching over shepherds and their flocks.

35. The following exchange between Licori and the priest Damone briefly raises the problematic doctrine of free will central to Catholicism (in contrast to the Calvinist belief in predestination), which holds that God leaves humans free to choose between good and evil actions. At the same time, a benign divine Providence was believed to determine the outcome of all events (see Nolan, "Free Will," and the introduction, p. 18).

36. The "icy goddess" is Diana, who insisted on chastity among her followers. Hymen was the classical god of marriage. The tension between chastity and love or marriage alluded to here was a *topos* in pastoral drama, often highlighted by contrasting groups of characters (for example of nymphs and shepherds, or of younger nymphs and older female characters). The polemic was often framed in terms of a rivalry between the deities of Cupid/Venus and Diana (though Diana herself was not immune from love, see n. 43).

37. The reference is to the moon, whose tutelary goddess, Diana, was sister to the sun-god Apollo.

38. Of the moral *sententiae* that punctuate Melampo's speech, this is perhaps the one with the most obvious literary ascendancy, recalling a famous speech of Francesca da Rimini in Dante's *Inferno* (5.121–23) itself echoing a passage in Virgil.

39. Pales was the Roman goddess of sheepfolds and pastures, who was celebrated in an annual festival on 21 April (see Sannazaro, *Arcadia, Prosa* 3).

40. This form of manneristic word-patterning was a feature of Venetian lyric poetry in this period, associated especially with the school of Domenico Venier (1517–82).

41. This and subsequent stage directions in brackets have been added for the sake of clarity. As with other printed dramatic texts of the period with literary pretensions, no stage-directions are given in the original. Neo-Aristotelian critics believed that the text alone should provide enough indications to allow a reader to visualize the action (as in classical drama). This practice contrasted with that of the *commedia dell'arte* and evidently sometimes resulted in some practical misjudgments (see Andrews, *Scripts and Scenarios,* 43–45, 73–74).

42. In fact, Damone (in 1.2) only specified that Flori would "be cured, but then set afire by a man's sudden gaze"; Serrano comments on this additional clause.

43. The reference is to the handsome shepherd Endymion, in Greek mythology, who attracted the amorous attentions of Diana after she admired him sleeping naked on Mount Latmos. Caria was an ancient kingdom in Asia Minor.

44. Satyrs, fauns, and silvans are all among the original mythological inhabitants of the wild reaches of Arcadia, and followers of Pan. Their "semi-divine" status is generally discredited in pastoral drama (Giraldi Cinthio's *Egle* is an exception); rather, their display of bestial lust and violence makes them a foil for the civilized and noble-minded shepherds. The classical "Silvanus" (god of fertile lands and gardens) has been rendered in translation by the more common and closely related English term "wild

man" (see Husband, *The Wildman: Medieval Myth and Symbolism,* 11; Garraffo, "Il satiro nella pastorale ferrarese del Cinquecento"; Tylus, "Colonizing Peasants."

45. Delia and Cynthia (slightly later in the text) were alternative names for Diana, both derived from her birthplace, on the island of Delos, also known in antiquity as Cynthus.

46. This classical rhetorical figure (*adynaton*) is commonly found in Renaissance pastoral writings of all genres; see, for example, Tasso's *Aminta,* 1.1, lines 43–46: "torneranno i fiumi / a le lor fonti, e i lupi fuggiranno /dagli agni . . ." ("the rivers will flow back to their source, the wolves will flee from sheep . . ."); and Sannazaro's *Arcadia,* 5 (Prose, p. 102): "i velenosi tassi sudaranno mele dolcissimo e i dolci fiori il faranno amaro. . ." ("The poisonous yews will ooze sweetest honey and the sweetest flowers will make it bitter. . .").

47. The reference to a tigress may be unexpected here, but is consistent with the traditions of pastoral drama, whose semi-mythical Arcadian setting allowed for a less strict observance of verisimilitude than was prescribed in comedy or tragedy (see Ingegneri, *Della poesia rappresentativa,* 26). Among the exotic beasts featured in sixteenth-century Italian pastorals are bears, lions, and, in the backdrop to Beccari's *Sacrificio* (performed 1587), even elephants (see Ivaldi, *Le Nozze Pio-Farnese e gli apparati teatrali di Sassuolo del 1587,* 9), as well as mythical creatures such as a Triton (Ongaro, *Alceo,* 1582). On more standard animals, see Clubb, *Italian Drama in Shakespeare's Time,* 142–51.

48. The repeated references in this scene to the "dance" into which Love leads his subjects may be meant as an allusion by Campiglia to certain recent pastoral plays in which staged dances mark the turning point for the lovers or the moment of initiation: Ingegneri's *La danza di Venere* (3.3–4), and especially Guarini's *Il Pastor fido,* in which the *Giuoco della cieca* (3.1) takes the form of a choreographed blind man's buff.

49. The following narrated episode, which lacks structural function, sheds further light on Flori's character. It recalls a similar, though gender-reversed one in Tasso's *Aminta* (1.1, lines 181–231), in which a woman's false coquettishness is used to explain Tirsi's resistance to love. It is unclear whether the episode in *Flori* serves a similarly allusive, autobiographical function.

50. The motif of a lovesick shepherd writing on trees is associated with pastoral verse since its classical origins (see Virgil, *Eclogues,* 5, lines 13–14, and 10, lines 53–54). Besides being a common *topos* in early modern pastoral drama, it is also found in pastoral episodes in romances and epics, notably Ariosto's *Orlando furioso* (canto 23, stanzas 102–9; canto 19, stanza 36), and Sannazaro's *Arcadia,* 5, (Prose, p. 97), 11 (*Eclogue* l.15, p. 206). In Tasso's *Gerusalemme liberata* (canto 7, stanzas 19–20), unusually, it is a woman—the lovesick princess Erminia—who engraves her lover's name on the trees, making her perhaps a precursor for Flori in this play. Another precursor for Flori in this respect may be Torelli's nymph Talia (*Partenia,* 3.1). The motif recurs in Campiglia's eclogue *Calisa* (Perrone, *La Calisa di Maddalena Campiglia,* lines 2–4, p. 75).

51. Competitive games between groups of shepherds or nymphs play a significant part in pastoral drama, where they can take the form of sporting events, singing contests, and even kissing competitions (in Guarini's *Il Pastor fido,* 2.1). Serrano seems to envisage sporting games of the kind described at length in Sannazaro's *Arcadia* (*Prosa* 11), modeled on those in classical epics.

52. This scene, in which Flori is accused to the priest of blasphemy, introduces the possibility that the sacrifice may not be performed, and provides the necessary "obstacle" to the plot, as required in dramatic theory (see the introduction, pp. 17–18).

53. The original contains an untranslatable pun here, on "Amore" (Love) and "amaro" (bitter). The conceit was frequent in the tradition of Petrarchan love-lyric and is followed here by a near-quotation of a famous line of Petrarch's ("Amor non è già quel ch'io sento," "It is not love that I feel"; cf. l.1 of Petrarch's Sonnet 134: "S'amor non è, che dunque è quel ch'io sento" [If it is not love, what is it then that I feel?]).

54. Elaborate, pseudo-rustic artifacts such as carved bowls and crooks are a common feature of pastoral literature, where they often serve as a pretext for the type of detailed self-reflexive description known as *ekphrasis*, particularly associated with epic poetry. A famous classical example is Virgil's third *Eclogue*, 36–42, 43–47. For sixteenth-century examples, see Sannazaro, *Arcadia* (*Prose* 9 and 11); Beccari, *Il Sacrificio* (3.2); and Lollio, *Aretusa* (3.4).

55. Actaeon, in classical mythology, was a huntsman who died torn apart by his hounds after having been turned into a deer by Diana. Apollo, god of the sun and of poetry and music, was also often depicted with a bow.

56. The husband of the dawn goddess Aurora, or Eos, was Astraeus. The reference to old age, however, makes it likely that Campiglia is thinking here rather of Tithonus, a lover of Eos's, to whom the goddess gave the gift of eternal life while neglecting to grant him perpetual youth, and who as a result withered so pitiably with the years that Eos eventually converted him into a cicada.

57. This is the huntsman Adonis, beloved of Venus (who had an important shrine on Cyprus, near her birthplace). Like Narcissus, mentioned earlier, Adonis was famed for his beauty.

58. See above, p. 53 and n. 13.

59. Arcadian shepherds have been depicted as singers since their earliest classical origins; consequently, musical interludes are an integral part of pastoral drama (see the introduction, under "*Flori*: 'Closet Drama' or Performance Text?")

60. The Parcae, or Fates, in classical mythology, were three goddesses who controlled the life and death of humankind. The reference here is specifically to the third Parca, Atropos, who cut the thread of human life at the moment of death.

61. This is addressed to Amaranta, in whose burial place the sacrifice is to take place.

62. Tantalus, in classical mythology, was punished for a transgression against the gods by being tormented by an eternal thirst and hunger, exacerbated by the sight of water and fruit which he is unable to reach.

63. The river Lampeus, like the Ladon and Erymanthus, mentioned below, were established features of Arcadian topography, mentioned by classical writers such as Pausanias and Polybius.

64. The text appears corrupt at this point, but the omission of the name of the river may be intentional, as similar omissions are found in a later speech of Alessi's (see p. 281 and note 92 below).

65. This cry suggests the words used by the tragic hero of Tasso's *Gerusalemme liberata* (canto 13, stanza 49; canto I, stanza 7), Tancredi, after being vanquished by an apparition of his dead beloved: "più non potrei [vinto mi chiamo]"; "I can do no more, I acknowledge my defeat."

66. Aeolus was the classical god of storms and winds. The reference to his "prisoners" below in the text is probably an allusion to the myth that, during Ulysses's return to Ithaca, Aelous consigned him all the winds that might blow adversely to his voyage, confined in a bag.

67. This additional clause attributed to the priest's oracular prediction is mentioned here for the first time; see note 42 above.

68. The reference is again to Diana, the goddess of the moon; see note 37.

69. The passage that follows, quite gratuitous from the point of view of the plot, is constructed as a tribute to a series of Campiglia's literary acquaintances, whose names are picked out in a series of puns, in a manneristic literary game very characteristic of the period. The first, here, is the Genoese poet Angelo Grillo (1550–1629), who contributed a prefatory sonnet to Campiglia's *Calisa*. The "animals" referred to below are Torquato Tasso (1544–1595), the most famous poet of the age, and the Venetian *literato* Orsatto Giustinian (1538–c. 1603). The reference to a lion (*LEONE*) probably alludes to Giustinian's devotion to Venice, symbolized by the lion of St. Mark.

70. The translation here is conjectural, as the object of the verb is unclear.

71. As the mention of the river Bacchiglione indicates, the text is referring here to Campiglia's home town of Vicenza. As what follows makes clear, the "glorious shepherds who follow Alcides" (or Hercules) must be the members of Vicenza's prime literary academy, the Accademia Olimpica (on which see the introduction, pp. 6–7). Hercules featured prominently in the iconography of the academy, which took its name from the Olympic games, said to have been initiated by the hero (see Mazzoni, *L'Olimpico di Vicenza*, 101; and Niccolini, "Le accademie," 95).

72. The "rich and mighty hut" referred to in this rather strained pastoral reference is the Teatro Olimpico in Vicenza, which was inaugurated in March 1585 with a performance of Sophocles's *Oedipus Rex*, in a translation by Orsatto Giustinian. The actors' costumes, designed by Giambattista Maganza, a friend of Campiglia's, were exceptionally sumptuous for this occasion (Mazzoni, *L'Olimpico di Vicenza*, 132–33, 149).

73. The pastoral name Leucippo refers to the dramatist Angelo Ingegneri, who directed the Vicentine performance of *Oedipus*. He adopted this name in the *canzone* that prefaces his *La danza di Venere* of 1584, singing the praises of "Calisa" or Isabella Pallavicino Lupi, one of the dedicatees of the present play. Ingegneri's play also features a shepherd character of the same name, as do works by other writers in this circle, such as Barbara Torelli and Muzio Manfredi (*Contrasto amoroso*).

74. The figures referred to here are the musicians, Isabetta (Isabella) and Lucietta (Lucia) Pellizzari, sisters of Antonio, a musician and caretaker for the Accademia Olimpica. Noted especially for their performances on cornetto and trombone, the sisters were employed permanently by the academy from 1582 and won much acclaim for their part in the 1585 performance of *Oedipus Rex* (see note 72 above). They

moved to Mantua in 1587. See Fenlon, *Music and Patronage in Sixteenth-Century Mantua*, 1: 127–281.

75. Echo was a mythological nymph who was silenced by divine intervention and only able to repeat others' last syllables. She died for love of the vain shepherd Narcissus, in love with his own image, but her plaintive voice lingered on after her death. The device of an echo responding, usually prophetically, to the laments and anguished questions of shepherds and nymphs was common in later sixteenth-century pastoral drama, following precedents in classical and humanistic literature (see Imbriani, "L'Eco responsiva nelle pastorali italiane"; Cian, "Ancora di Giovanni Muzzarelli, la 'Fabula di Narciso' e le 'Canzoni e Sestine amorose,'" 85–88; and Ingegneri, *Della poesia rappresentativa*, 18–19). Probably the most famous example is found in Guarini's *Pastor fido* (4.8), but the same device occurs in the pastoral plays of Barbara Torelli and Angelo Ingegneri as well. Pastoral lyric verse, musical interludes (*intermezzi*), and early opera also make use of this device.

76. As recommended by Guarini in his annotations to *Il Pastor fido* (177v), the echo-responses in these lines are integrated within the hendecasyllable meter of the line, rather than being appended. The translation of these lines inevitably sacrifices word-for-word accuracy in the interest of preserving the rhyme.

77. The motif of the *amour de loin*—where a character falls in love with someone purely through repute—was common in medieval and Renaissance literature, though not especially so in pastoral drama.

78. The phrase in the original, "solo e pensoso," echoes the opening of a famous sonnet of Petrarch's (35), which portrays the love-struck poet wandering alone and avoiding human company.

79. Leggiadro's attack on avarice and its power to corrupt natural impulses, and especially love, mirrors similar speeches by the Satyr in Tasso's *Aminta* (2.1 lines 59–71), and especially in Barbara Torelli's *Partenia* (1.2, 2.6, 3.2). This theme draws on classical sources, though, surprisingly, Campiglia omits any reference to the correlative pastoral *topos* of the Golden Age.

80. Midas, king of Phrygia, was granted a wish by Bacchus and rashly asked that all he touched should be turned to gold. He was subsequently forced to beg the god to retract his gift when he realized that the effects extended even to the food he attempted to eat.

81. The following display of innocent vanity by a young nymph newly awakened to love, observed by hidden onlookers, recalls a similar episode in *Aminta* (3.2, lines 34–65), though the latter is notably more sensual.

82. The line echoes a famous line of Dante's (*Inferno*, 5.100); see n. 93.

83. This sacred mountain, a familiar part of the landscape of Arcadia, could appear (together with others) in the backdrop to pastoral scenes (for example, see the prologue to Agostino Beccari's *Sacrificio* [The sacrifice], printed in 1555).

84. This is presumably the poet Muzio Sforza (1542–1597), a literary acquaintance of Campiglia's, associated with the Olympic academy of Vicenza since at least 1563, and present at the inaugural performance of the theater in 1585 (MS Biblioteca Bertoliana, Vicenza, *Atti dell'Accademia Olimpica*, 2 (fasc. 10 "L"), fols. 9r, 33v). Sonnets by him

appear appended to all three of Campiglia's published works. Adria is the Adriatic Sea (here standing for Venice), Aufidus, the Latin name of the river Ofranto, in southern Italy.

85. Licori's arguments here echo contemporary Aristotelian thinking on love, which is counterposed, as so often in Renaissance treatises, with the Platonic position represented by Flori.

86. Orion was a giant renowned for his hunting skills, like Diana. Many mythological tales refer to his pride and his rape of nymphs (including the goddess herself), which finally led to his divine punishment; but the present allusion must follow the version in which Diana so loved Orion that she even considering marrying him. Her brother Apollo, alarmed by this proposal, consequently tricked her into killing him, after which he was transformed into a constellation of stars.

87. The vagueness of this allusion, presumably to a contemporary writer or authority on love, makes identification difficult.

88. The Mimallones were followers of the god Bacchus, distinguished by the horns they wore on their heads when celebrating his rites. Other than this faint connection with hunting, the basis of Alessi's analogy here is unclear.

89. The spring, arising by a grove of laurels—the tree sacred to Apollo, god of poetry—is obviously symbolic of poetic inspiration.

90. The mention of the sea nymph Thetis, mother of Achilles, is perplexing here, unless she is intended generically to symbolize the sea.

91. Flori's insistence on her freedom to determine her destiny without reference to external authority figures is an unusual feature of her characterization; see the introduction, p.26 n. 68.

92. The pseudo-autobiographical section that follows has occasioned the identification of Alessi with the Sorrento-born Torquato Tasso by various critics (Chiodo, De Marco, and Perrone, though not Daniele), following Bernardo Morsolin (*Maddalena Campiglia*, 42–43). In particular, the "immortal goddess" has been viewed as referring to Princess Leonora d'Este of Ferrara (d. 1580), who was the subject of many poems by Tasso, while the "valorous shepherd" is identified with Marzio Sersale, married to Tasso's sister, Cornelia. This reading is, however, complicated by the unusual omission of the name of the river, and of later locations mentioned in Alessi's speech, while elsewhere in the play, such features are included for encomiastic purposes (see nn. 32, 71, 95). Tasso's very strained relations with the Ferrarese court at the time, which he had recently left following his long imprisonment there on the grounds of insanity (1579–86), may provide some explanation for the ellipses. If this identification is correct, it is notable that Alessi bears no traces of madness.

93. The original closely echoes a line from canto 5 of Dante's *Inferno* (5.103), from a famous speech by the tragic heroine Francesca da Rimini, already alluded to earlier in the play (see notes 38 and 82).

94. The "volatile goddess" is Fortune, conventionally represented with a wheel.

95. This is, of course, one of the dedicatees of the play, Isabella Pallavicino Lupi, Marchioness of Soragna, introduced by a pun on her name picked out in the text by capitalization (for other examples of this device see pp. 64, 180, and 286). Pallas is an

alternative name for Minerva, goddess of wisdom; this association was often made in encomiastic verse dedicated to the Marchioness. The river Trebbia, which flows north of the Appennines, near Piacenza by Pallavicino's lands, provides a further means of identification.

96. The figure referred to under this guise is Curzio Gonzaga, the other dedicatee of the *Flori* and one of Campiglia's closest literary acquaintances. Aethon and Pyrois were the horses that drew the chariot of the sun god Apollo, or Phoebus, who was also the god of poetry.

97. The "fortunate she-bear" (*ORSA FELICE*) puns on the name Felice Orsini Colonna, the duchess of Paliano, and literary *amour* of Curzio Gonzaga. Various sonnets and other verse of his are dedicated to her, including his *Il fidamante* (1582), which begins with an invocation to the Orsa. Her name appears among the list of illustrious women in canto 14 of the 1591 edition (fols 77r–v) alongside Isabella [Pallavicino] Lupi and Elena Campiglia. She also appears in the form of a she-bear in Gonzaga's personal *impresa* (emblem), as pictured in the frontispiece to his epic poem (1582): see Camilli, *Imprese illustri di diversi*, 40–42; Perrone, "'So che donna ama donna,'" n. 15, 310.

98. The reference here is to the Neoplatonic theory of love, in which desire for mortal beauty is seen as potentially the first step towards spiritual union with God.

99. In the original, where the song is set out as a two-stanza poem, the Marchioness's first name is spelt out as an acrostic in the first letters of each line of the first stanza, as is Gonzaga's in the second.

100. Hesperia was the Greek name for Italy (its literal meaning is "land of the setting sun").

101. Manto is here being used synechdochically to indicate the city of Mantua, alluding to the legend that the city's mythical founder, Ocnus, named the city after his mother, the Theban prophetess Manto.

102. See above, pp. 73–75, and the introduction, p. 19.

103. This reference to swans may well be an allusion to an episode in Ariosto's *Orlando Furioso* (canto 35, stanzas 14–16, 22–23), in which swans symbolize those rare, true poets capable of immortalizing their subjects. The image is taken up by many of the authors of the laudatory sonnets addressed to Campiglia, which follow these two poems in the original 1588 edition.

SERIES EDITORS'
BIBLIOGRAPHY

Note: Items listed in the volume editors' bibliography are not repeated here.

PRIMARY SOURCES

Alberti, Leon Battista (1404–72). *The Family in Renaissance Florence.* Trans. Renée Neu Watkins. Columbia: University of South Carolina Press, 1969.

Arenal, Electa and Stacey Schlau, eds. *Untold Sisters: Hispanic Nuns in Their Own Works.* Trans. Amanda Powell. Albuquerque: University of New Mexico Press, 1989.

Astell, Mary (1666–1731). *The First English Feminist: Reflections on Marriage and Other Writings.* Edited and with an introduction by Bridget Hill. New York: St. Martin's Press, 1986.

Atherton, Margaret, ed. *Women Philosophers of the Early Modern Period.* Indianapolis, IN: Hackett, 1994.

Aughterson, Kate, ed. *Renaissance Woman: Constructions of Femininity in England: A Source Book.* London and New York: Routledge, 1995.

Barbaro, Francesco (1390–1454). *On Wifely Duties.* Trans. Benjamin Kohl. In *The Earthly Republic,* ed. Benjamin Kohl and R. G. Witt, 179–228. Philadelphia: University of Pennsylvania Press, 1978.

Behn, Aphra. *The Works of Aphra Behn.* 7 vols. Ed. Janet Todd. Columbus: Ohio State University Press, 1992–96.

Boccaccio, Giovanni (1313–75). *Famous Women.* Ed. and trans. Virginia Brown. The I Tatti Renaissance Library. Cambridge, MA: Harvard University Press, 2001.

———. *Corbaccio, or the Labyrinth of Love.* Trans. Anthony K. Cassell. 2d rev. ed. Binghamton, NY: Medieval and Renaissance Texts and Studies, 1993.

Brown, Sylvia. *Women's Writing in Stuart England: The Mother's Legacies of Dorothy Leigh, Elizabeth Joscelin, and Elizabeth Richardson.* Stroud: Sutton, 1999.

Bruni, Leonardo (1370–1444). "On the Study of Literature (1405) to Lady Battista Malatesta of Montefeltro." In *The Humanism of Leonardo Bruni: Selected Texts,* trans. and introd. Gordon Griffiths, James Hankins, and David Thompson, 240–51. Binghamton, NY: Medieval and Renaissance Studies and Texts, 1987.

Castiglione, Baldassare (1478–1529). *The Book of the Courtier.* Trans. George Bull. New York: Penguin, 1967.

Christine de Pizan (1365–1431). *The Book of the City of Ladies*. Trans. Earl Jeffrey Richards. Foreword by Marina Warner. New York: Persea Books, 1982.

———. *The Treasure of the City of Ladies*. Trans. Sarah Lawson. New York: Viking Penguin, 1985. Reprint, trans. and introd. Charity Cannon Willard; ed. and introd. Madeleine P. Cosman. New York: Persea Books, 1989.

Clarke, Danielle, ed. *Isabella Whitney, Mary Sidney, and Aemilia Lanyer: Renaissance Women Poets*. New York: Penguin Books, 2000.

Crawford, Patricia, and Laura Gowing, eds. *Women's Worlds in Seventeenth-Century England: A Source Book*. London and New York: Routledge, 2000.

Daybell, James, ed. *Early Modern Women's Letter Writing, 1450–1700*. Houndmills, England, and New York: Palgrave, 2001.

Elizabeth I: Collected Works. Ed. Leah S. Marcus, Janel Mueller, and Mary Beth Rose. Chicago: University of Chicago Press, 2000.

Elyot, Thomas (1490–1546). *Defence of Good Women: The Feminist Controversy of the Renaissance*. Ed. Diane Bornstein. Facsimile Reproductions. New York: Delmar, 1980.

Erasmus, Desiderius (1467–1536). *Erasmus on Women*. Ed. Erika Rummel. Toronto: University of Toronto Press, 1996.

Female and Male Voices in Early Modern England: An Anthology of Renaissance Writing. Ed. Betty S. Travitsky and Anne Lake Prescott. New York: Columbia University Press, 2000.

Ferguson, Moira, ed. *First Feminists: British Women Writers 1578–1799*. Bloomington: Indiana University Press, 1985.

Galilei, Maria Celeste. *Sister Maria Celeste's Letters to Her Father, Galileo*. Ed. and trans. Rinaldina Russell. San Jose : Writers Club Press, 2000.

Gethner, Perry, ed. *The Lunatic Lover and Other Plays by French Women of the Seventeenth and Eighteenth Centuries*. Portsmouth, NH: Heinemann, 1994.

Glückel of Hameln (1646–1724). *The Memoirs of Glückel of Hameln*. Trans. Marvin Lowenthal. New Introd. Robert Rosen. New York: Schocken Books, 1977.

Henderson, Katherine Usher, and Barbara F. McManus, eds. *Half Humankind: Contexts and Texts of the Controversy about Women in England, 1540–1640*. Urbana, IL: University of Illinois Press, 1985.

Humanist Educational Treatises. Ed. and trans. Craig W. Kallendorf. The I Tatti Renaissance Library. Cambridge, MA: Harvard University Press, 2002.

Joscelin, Elizabeth. *The Mothers Legacy to Her Unborn Childe*. Ed. Jean LeDrew Metcalfe. Toronto: University of Toronto Press, 2000.

Kaminsky, Amy Katz, ed. *Water Lilies, Flores del agua: An Anthology of Spanish Women Writers from the Fifteenth through the Nineteenth Century*. Minneapolis: University of Minnesota Press, 1996.

Kempe, Margery (1373–1439). *The Book of Margery Kempe*. Trans. and ed. Lynn Staley. A Norton Critical Edition. New York: W. W. Norton, 2001.

King, Margaret L., and Albert Rabil Jr., eds. *Her Immaculate Hand: Selected Works by and about the Women Humanists of Quattrocento Italy*. Binghamton, NY: 1983. Reprint, 2d. rev. ed., Medieval and Renaissance Texts and Studies, 1991.

Klein, Joan Larsen, ed. *Daughters, Wives, and Widows: Writings by Men about Women and Marriage in England, 1500–1640*. Urbana: University of Illinois Press, 1992.

Knox, John (1505–72). *The Political Writings of John Knox: The First Blast of the Trumpet against the Monstrous Regiment of Women and Other Selected Works*. Ed. Marvin A. Breslow. Washington: Folger Shakespeare Library, 1985.

Kors, Alan C., and Edward Peters, eds. *Witchcraft in Europe, 400–1700: A Documentary History.* Philadelphia: University of Pennsylvania Press, 2000.

Krämer, Heinrich, and Jacob Sprenger. *Malleus Maleficarum* (ca. 1487). Trans. Montague Summers. London: Pushkin Press, 1928. Reprint, New York: Dover, 1971.

Larsen, Anne R., and Colette H. Winn, eds. *Writings by Pre-Revolutionary French Women: From Marie de France to Elizabeth Vigée-Le Brun.* New York and London: Garland, 2000.

de Lorris, William, and Jean de Meun. *The Romance of the Rose.* Trans. Charles Dahlbert. Princeton, NJ: Princeton University Press, 1971. Reprint, Hanover: University Press of New England, 1983.

Marguerite d'Angoulême, Queen of Navarre (1492–1549). *The Heptameron.* Trans. P. A. Chilton. New York: Viking Penguin, 1984.

Mary of Agreda. *The Divine Life of the Most Holy Virgin.* Abridgment of *The Mystical City of God.* Abr. by Fr. Bonaventure Amedeo de Caesarea, M.C. Trans. from French by Abbé Joseph A. Boullan. Rockford, IL: Tan Books, 1997.

Myers, Kathleen A., and Amanda Powell, eds. *A Wild Country out in the Garden: The Spiritual Journals of a Colonial Mexican Nun.* Bloomington: Indiana University Press, 1999.

Russell, Rinaldina, ed. *Sister Maria Celeste's Letters to Her Father, Galileo.* San Jose and New York: Writers Club Press, 2000.

Teresa of Avila, Saint (1515–82). *The Life of Saint Teresa of Avila by Herself.* Trans. J. M. Cohen. New York: Viking Penguin, 1957.

Weyer, Johann (1515–88). *Witches, Devils, and Doctors in the Renaissance: Johann Weyer, De praestigiis daemonum.* Ed. George Mora with Benjamin G. Kohl, Erik Midelfort, and Helen Bacon. Trans. John Shea. Binghamton, NY: Medieval and Renaissance Texts and Studies, 1991.

Wilson, Katharina M., ed. *Medieval Women Writers.* Athens: University of Georgia Press, 1984.

———, ed. *Women Writers of the Renaissance and Reformation.* Athens: University of Georgia Press, 1987.

———, and Frank J. Warnke, eds. *Women Writers of the Seventeenth Century.* Athens: University of Georgia Press, 1989.

Wollstonecraft, Mary. *A Vindication of the Rights of Men and a Vindication of the Rights of Women.* Ed. Sylvana Tomaselli. Cambridge: Cambridge University Press, 1995. Also *The Vindications of the Rights of Men, the Rights of Women.* Ed. D. L. Macdonald and Kathleen Scherf. Peterborough, Ontario, Canada: Broadview Press, 1997.

Women Critics 1660–1820: An Anthology. Edited by the Folger Collective on Early Women Critics. Bloomington: Indiana University Press, 1995.

Women Writers in English, 1350–1850. Fifteen volumes published through 1999 (projected thirty-volume series suspended). New York and Oxford: Oxford University Press.

Wroth, Lady Mary. *The Countess of Montgomery's Urania.* 2 parts. Ed. Josephine A. Roberts. Tempe, AZ: MRTS, 1995, 1999.

———. *Lady Mary Wroth's "Love's Victory": The Penshurst Manuscript.* Ed. Michael G. Brennan. London: The Roxburghe Club, 1988.

———. *The Poems of Lady Mary Wroth.* Ed. Josephine A. Roberts. Baton Rouge: Louisiana State University Press, 1983.

Zayas, Maria de. *The Disenchantments of Love.* Trans. H. Patsy Boyer. Albany: State University of New York Press, 1997.

———. *The Enchantments of Love: Amorous and Exemplary Novels.* Trans. H. Patsy Boyer. Berkeley and Los Angeles: University of California Press, 1990.

SECONDARY SOURCES

Ahlgren, Gillian. *Teresa of Avila and the Politics of Sanctity.* Ithaca, NY: Cornell University Press, 1996.

Akkerman, Tjitske, and Siep Sturman, eds. *Feminist Thought in European History, 1400–2000.* London and New York: Routledge, 1997.

Allen, Sister Prudence, R.S.M. *The Concept of Woman: The Aristotelian Revolution, 750 B.C.–A.D. 1250.* Grand Rapids, MI: William B. Eerdmans, 1997.

———. *The Concept of Woman.* Vol. 2. *The Early Humanist Reformation, 1250–1500.* Grand Rapids, MI: William B. Eerdmans, 2002.

Andreadis, Harriette. *Sappho in Early Modern England: Female Same-Sex Literary Erotics, 1550–1714.* Chicago: University of Chicago Press, 2001.

Armon, Shifra. *Picking Wedlock: Women and the Courtship Novel in Spain.* New York: Rowman & Littlefield, 2002.

Backer, Anne Liot. *Precious Women.* New York: Basic Books, 1974.

Ballaster, Ros. *Seductive Forms.* New York: Oxford University Press, 1992.

Barash, Carol. *English Women's Poetry, 1649–1714: Politics, Community, and Linguistic Authority.* New York and Oxford: Oxford University Press, 1996.

Battigelli, Anna. *Margaret Cavendish and the Exiles of the Mind.* Lexington: University of Kentucky Press, 1998.

Beasley, Faith. *Revising Memory: Women's Fiction and Memoirs in Seventeenth-Century France.* New Brunswick, NJ: Rutgers University Press, 1990.

Beilin, Elaine V. *Redeeming Eve: Women Writers of the English Renaissance.* Princeton, NJ: Princeton University Press, 1987.

Benson, Pamela Joseph. *The Invention of Renaissance Woman: The Challenge of Female Independence in the Literature and Thought of Italy and England.* University Park: Pennsylvania State University Press, 1992.

———, and Victoria Kirkham, eds. *Strong Voices, Weak History? Medieval and Renaissance Women in their Literary Canons: England, France, Italy.* Ann Arbor: University of Michigan Press, 2003.

Bilinkoff, Jodi. *The Avila of Saint Teresa: Religious Reform in a Sixteenth-Century City.* Ithaca, NY: Cornell University Press, 1989.

Bissell, R. Ward. *Artemisia Gentileschi and the Authority of Art.* University Park: Pennsylvania State University Press, 2000.

Blain, Virginia, Isobel Grundy, and Patricia Clements, eds. *The Feminist Companion to Literature in English: Women Writers from the Middle Ages to the Present.* New Haven, CT: Yale University Press, 1990.

Bloch, R. Howard. *Medieval Misogyny and the Invention of Western Romantic Love.* Chicago: University of Chicago Press, 1991.

Bornstein, Daniel, and Roberto Rusconi, eds. *Women and Religion in Medieval and Renaissance Italy.* Trans. Margery J. Schneider. Chicago: University of Chicago Press, 1996.

Brant, Clare, and Diane Purkiss, eds. *Women, Texts, and Histories, 1575–1760.* London and New York: Routledge, 1992.

Briggs, Robin. *Witches and Neighbours: The Social and Cultural Context of European Witchcraft.* New York: HarperCollins, 1995. Reprint, New York: Viking Penguin, 1996.

Brink, Jean R., ed. *Female Scholars: A Tradition of Learned Women before 1800.* Montréal: Eden Press Women's Publications, 1980.

Brown, Judith C. *Immodest Acts: The Life of a Lesbian Nun in Renaissance Italy.* New York: Oxford University Press, 1986.

———, and Robert C. Davis, eds. *Gender and Society in Renaisance Italy.* London: Addison-Wesley/Longman, 1998.

Bynum, Carolyn Walker. *Fragmentation and Redemption: Essays on Gender and the Human Body in Medieval Religion.* New York: Zone Books, 1992.

———. *Holy Feast and Holy Fast: The Religious Significance of Food to Medieval Women.* Berkeley and Los Angeles: University of California Press, 1987.

Cervigni, Dino S., ed. *Women Mystic Writers. Annali d'Italianistica* 13 (1995). Special issue.

———, and Rebecca West, eds. *Women's Voices in Italian Literature. Annali d'Italianistica* 7 (1989). Special issue.

Charlton, Kenneth. *Women, Religion, and Education in Early Modern England.* London and New York: Routledge, 1999.

Chojnacka, Monica. *Working Women in Early Modern Venice.* Baltimore, MD: Johns Hopkins University Press, 2001.

Chojnacki, Stanley. *Women and Men in Renaissance Venice: Twelve Essays on Patrician Society.* Baltimore, MD: Johns Hopkins University Press, 2000.

Cholakian, Patricia Francis. *Rape and Writing in the* Heptameron *of Marguerite de Navarre.* Carbondale and Edwardsville: Southern Illinois University Press, 1991.

———. *Women and the Politics of Self-Representation in Seventeenth-Century France.* Newark: University of Delaware Press, 2000.

Clogan, Paul Maruice, ed. *Medievali et Humanistica: Literacy and the Lay Reader.* Lanham, MD: Rowman & Littlefield, 2000.

Conley, John J., S.J. *The Suspicion of Virtue: Women Philosophers in Neoclassical France.* Ithaca, NY: Cornell University Press, 2002.

Crabb, Ann. *The Strozzi of Florence: Widowhood and Family Solidarity in the Renaissance.* Ann Arbor: University of Michigan Press, 2000.

Cruz, Anne J., and Mary Elizabeth Perry, eds. *Culture and Control in Counter-Reformation Spain.* Minneapolis: University of Minnesota Press, 1992.

Davis, Natalie Zemon. *Society and Culture in Early Modern France.* Stanford, CA: Stanford University Press, 1975. See especially chapters 3 and 5.

———. *Women on the Margins: Three Seventeenth-Century Lives.* Cambridge, MA: Harvard University Press, 1995.

DeJean, Joan. *Ancients against Moderns: Culture Wars and the Making of a Fin de Siècle.* Chicago: University of Chicago Press, 1997.

———. *Fictions of Sappho, 1546–1937.* Chicago: University of Chicago Press, 1989.

———. *Tender Geographies: Women and the Origins of the Novel in France.* New York: Columbia University Press, 1991.

———. *The Reinvention of Obscenity: Sex, Lies, and Tabloids in Early Modern France.* Chicago: University of Chicago Press, 2002.

Dictionary of Russian Women Writers. Ed. Marina Ledkovsky, Charlotte Rosenthal, and Mary Zirin. Westport, CT: Greenwood Press, 1994.

Dixon, Laurinda S. *Perilous Chastity: Women and Illness in Pre-Enlightenment Art and Medicine.* Ithaca, NY: Cornell University Press, 1995.

Dolan, Frances, E. *Whores of Babylon: Catholicism, Gender, and Seventeenth-Century Print Culture.* Ithaca, NY: Cornell University Press, 1999.

Donovan, Josephine. *Women and the Rise of the Novel, 1405–1726.* New York: St. Martin's Press, 1999.

Erauso, Catalina De. *Lieutenant Nun: Memoir of a Basque Transvestite in the New World.* Trans. Michele Stepto and Gabriel Stepto with a foreword by Marjorie Garber. Boston: Beacon Press, 1999.

Erdmann, Axel. *My Gracious Silence: Women in the Mirror of Sixteenth-Century Printing in Western Europe.* Luzern: Gilhofer and Rauschberg, 1999.

Erickson, Amy Louise. *Women and Property in Early Modern England.* London and New York: Routledge, 1993.

Ezell, Margaret J. M. *The Patriarch's Wife: Literary Evidence and the History of the Family.* Chapel Hill: University of North Carolina Press, 1987.

———. *Social Authorship and the Advent of Print.* Baltimore, MD: Johns Hopkins University Press, 1999.

———. *Writing Women's Literary History.* Baltimore, MD: Johns Hopkins University Press, 1993.

The Feminist Encyclopedia of German Literature. Ed. Friederike Eigler and Susanne Kord. Westport, CT: Greenwood Press, 1997.

Ferguson, Margaret W., Maureen Quilligan, and Nancy J. Vickers, eds. *Rewriting the Renaissance: The Discourses of Sexual Difference in Early Modern Europe.* Chicago: University of Chicago Press, 1987.

Ferraro, Joanne M. *Marriage Wars in Late Renaissance Venice.* Oxford: Oxford University Press, 2001.

Fletcher, Anthony. *Gender, Sex, and Subordination in England 1500–1800.* New Haven, CT: Yale University Press, 1995.

Frye, Susan, and Karen Robertson, eds. *Maids and Mistresses, Cousins and Queens: Women's Alliances in Early Modern England.* Oxford: Oxford University Press, 1999.

Gallagher, Catherine. *Nobody's Story: The Vanishing Acts of Women Writers in the Marketplace, 1670–1820.* Berkeley and Los Angeles: University of California Press, 1994.

Garrard, Mary D. *Artemisia Gentileschi: The Image of the Female Hero in Italian Baroque Art.* Princeton, NJ: Princeton University Press, 1989.

Gelbart, Nina Rattner. *The King's Midwife: A History and Mystery of Madame du Coudray.* Berkeley and Los Angeles: University of California Press, 1998.

Glenn, Cheryl. *Rhetoric Retold: Regendering the Tradition from Antiquity through the Renaissance.* Carbondale and Edwardsville: Southern Illinois University Press, 1997.

Goffen, Rona. *Titian's Women.* New Haven, CT: Yale University Press, 1997.

Goldberg, Jonathan. *Desiring Women Writing: English Renaissance Examples.* Stanford, CA: Stanford University Press, 1997.

Goldsmith, Elizabeth C. *Exclusive Conversations: The Art of Interaction in Seventeenth-Century France.* Philadelphia: University of Pennsylvania Press, 1988.

———, ed. *Writing the Female Voice.* Boston: Northeastern University Press, 1989.

————, and Dena Goodman, eds. *Going Public: Women and Publishing in Early Modern France.* Ithaca, NY: Cornell University Press, 1995.

Grafton, Anthony, and Lisa Jardine. *From Humanism to the Humanities: Education and the Liberal Arts in Fifteenth- and Sixteenth-Century Europe.* London: Duckworth, 1986.

Greer, Margaret Rich. *Maria de Zayas Tells Baroque Tales of Love and the Cruelty of Men.* University Park: Pennsylvania State University Press, 2000.

Hackett, Helen. *Women and Romance Fiction in the English Renaissance.* Cambridge: Cambridge University Press, 2000.

Hall, Kim F. *Things of Darkness: Economies of Race and Gender in Early Modern England.* Ithaca, NY: Cornell University Press, 1995.

Hampton, Timothy. *Literature and the Nation in the Sixteenth Century: Inventing Renaissance France.* Ithaca, NY: Cornell University Press, 2001.

Hannay, Margaret, ed. *Silent but for the Word.* Kent: Kent State University Press, 1985.

Hardwick, Julie. *The Practice of Patriarchy: Gender and the Politics of Household Authority in Early Modern France.* University Park: Pennsylvania State University Press, 1998.

Harris, Barbara J. *English Aristocratic Women, 1450–1550: Marriage and Family, Property and Careers.* New York: Oxford University Press, 2002.

Harth, Erica. *Ideology and Culture in Seventeenth-Century France.* Ithaca, NY: Cornell University Press, 1983.

————. *Cartesian Women: Versions and Subversions of Rational Discourse in the Old Regime.* Ithaca, NY: Cornell University Press, 1992.

Harvey, Elizabeth D. *Ventriloquized Voices: Feminist Theory and English Renaissance Texts.* London and New York: Routledge, 1992.

Haselkorn, Anne M., and Betty Travitsky, eds. *The Renaissance Englishwoman in Print: Counterbalancing the Canon.* Amherst: University of Massachusetts Press, 1990.

Herlihy, David. "Did Women Have a Renaissance? A Reconsideration." *Medievalia et Humanistica,* n.s., 13 (1985): 1–22.

Hill, Bridget. *The Republican Virago: The Life and Times of Catharine Macaulay, Historian.* New York: Oxford University Press, 1992.

A History of Central European Women's Writing. Edited by Celia Hawkesworth. New York: Palgrave Press, 2001.

A History of Women in the West. Vol. 1. *From Ancient Goddesses to Christian Saints.* Ed. Pauline Schmitt Pantel. Vol. 2. *Silences of the Middle Ages.* Ed. Christiane Klapisch-Zuber. Vol. 3. *Renaissance and Enlightenment Paradoxes.* Ed. Natalie Zemon Davis and Arlette Farge. Cambridge, MA: Harvard University Press, 1992–93.

A History of Women's Writing in Russia. Ed. Alele Marie Barker and Jehanne M. Gheith. Cambridge: Cambridge University Press, 2002.

Hobby, Elaine. *Virtue of Necessity: English Women's Writing, 1646–1688.* London: Virago Press, 1988.

Horowitz, Maryanne Cline. "Aristotle and Women." *Journal of the History of Biology* 9 (1976): 183–213.

Howell, Martha. *The Marriage Exchange: Property, Social Place, and Gender in Cities of the Low Countries, 1300–1550.* Chicago: University of Chicago Press, 1998.

Hufton, Olwen H. *The Prospect before Her: A History of Women in Western Europe, 1: 1500–1800.* New York: HarperCollins, 1996.

Hull, Suzanne W. *Chaste, Silent, and Obedient: English Books for Women, 1475–1640.* San Marino, CA: Huntington Library, 1982.

Hunt, Lynn, ed. *The Invention of Pornography: Obscenity and the Origins of Modernity, 1500–1800.* New York: Zone Books, 1996.

Hutner, Heidi, ed. *Rereading Aphra Behn: History, Theory, and Criticism.* Charlottesville: University Press of Virginia, 1993.

Hutson, Lorna, ed. *Feminism and Renaissance Studies.* New York: Oxford University Press, 1999.

Jaffe, Irma B., with Gernando Colombardo. *Shining Eyes, Cruel Fortune: The Lives and Loves of Italian Renaissance Women Poets.* New York: Fordham University Press, 2002.

James, Susan E. *Kateryn Parr: The Making of a Queen.* Aldershot and Brookfield: Ashgate, 1999.

Jankowski, Theodora A. *Women in Power in the Early Modern Drama.* Urbana: University of Illinois Press, 1992.

Jansen, Katherine Ludwig. *The Making of the Magdalen: Preaching and Popular Devotion in the Later Middle Ages.* Princeton, NJ: Princeton University Press, 2000.

Jed, Stephanie H. *Chaste Thinking: The Rape of Lucretia and the Birth of Humanism.* Bloomington: Indiana University Press, 1989.

Jordan, Constance. *Renaissance Feminism: Literary Texts and Political Models.* Ithaca, NY: Cornell University Press, 1990.

Kagan, Richard L. *Lucrecia's Dreams: Politics and Prophecy in Sixteenth-Century Spain.* Berkeley and Los Angeles: University of California Press, 1990.

Kehler, Dorothea, and Laurel Amtower, eds. *The Single Woman in Medieval and Early Modern England: Her Life and Representation.* Tempe, AZ: MRTS, 2002.

Kelly, Joan. "Did Women Have a Renaissance?" In *Women, History, and Theory,* by Joan Kelly. Chicago: University of Chicago Press, 1984. Reprinted in Renate Bridenthal, Claudia Koonz, and Susan M. Stuard, eds., *Becoming Visible: Women in European History.* 3d ed. Boston: Houghton Mifflin, 1998.

———. "Early Feminist Theory and the *Querelle des Femmes.*" In *Women, History, and Theory.*

Kelso, Ruth. *Doctrine for the Lady of the Renaissance.* Foreword by Katharine M. Rogers. Urbana: University of Illinois Press, 1956, 1978.

King, Carole. *Renaissance Women Patrons: Wives and Widows in Italy, c. 1300–1550.* New York and Manchester: Manchester University Press (distributed in the United States by St. Martin's Press), 1998.

King, Margaret L. *Women of the Renaissance.* Foreword by Catharine R. Stimpson. Chicago: University of Chicago Press, 1991.

Krontiris, Tina. *Oppositional Voices: Women as Writers and Translators of Literature in the English Renaissance.* London and New York: Routledge, 1992.

Kuehn, Thomas. *Law, Family, and Women: Toward a Legal Anthropology of Renaissance Italy.* Chicago: University of Chicago Press, 1991.

Kunze, Bonnelyn Young. *Margaret Fell and the Rise of Quakerism.* Stanford, CA: Stanford University Press, 1994.

Labalme, Patricia A., ed. *Beyond Their Sex: Learned Women of the European Past.* New York: New York University Press, 1980.

Laqueur, Thomas. *Making Sex: Body and Gender from the Greeks to Freud.* Cambridge, MA: Harvard University Press, 1990.

Larsen, Anne R., and Colette H. Winn, eds. *Renaissance Women Writers: French Texts/American Contexts.* Detroit, MI: Wayne State University Press, 1994.

Lerner, Gerda. *The Creation of Patriarchy.* New York: Oxford University Press, 1986.

————. *Creation of Feminist Consciousness, 1000–1870.* New York: Oxford University Press, 1994.

Levin, Carole, and Jeanie Watson, eds. *Ambiguous Realities: Women in the Middle Ages and Renaissance.* Detroit: Wayne State University Press, 1987.

————, et al. *Extraordinary Women of the Medieval and Renaissance World: A Biographical Dictionary.* Westport, CT: Greenwood Press, 2000.

Lewalsky, Barbara Kiefer. *Writing Women in Jacobean England.* Cambridge, MA: Harvard University Press, 1993.

Lewis, Jayne Elizabeth. *Mary Queen of Scots: Romance and Nation.* London: Routledge, 1998.

Lindsey, Karen. *Divorced, Beheaded, Survived: A Feminist Reinterpretation of the Wives of Henry VIII.* Reading, MA: Addison-Wesley, 1995.

Lochrie, Karma. *Margery Kempe and Translations of the Flesh.* Philadelphia: University of Pennsylvania Press, 1992.

Lougee, Carolyn C. *Le Paradis des Femmes: Women, Salons, and Social Stratification in Seventeenth-Century France.* Princeton, NJ: Princeton University Press, 1976.

Love, Harold. *The Culture and Commerce of Texts: Scribal Publication in Seventeenth-Century England.* Amherst: University of Massachusetts Press, 1993.

MacCarthy, Bridget G. *The Female Pen: Women Writers and Novelists 1621–1818.* Preface by Janet Todd. 1946–47. Reprint, New York: New York University Press, 1994.

Maclean, Ian. *Woman Triumphant: Feminism in French Literature, 1610–1652.* Oxford: Clarendon Press, 1977.

————. *The Renaissance Notion of Woman: A Study of the Fortunes of Scholasticism and Medical Science in European Intellectual Life.* Cambridge: Cambridge University Press, 1980.

Maggi, Armando. *Uttering the Word: The Mystical Performances of Maria Maddalena de' Pazzi, a Renaissance Visionary.* Albany: State University of New York Press, 1998.

Marshall, Sherrin. *Women in Reformation and Counter-Reformation Europe: Public and Private Worlds.* Bloomington: Indiana University Press, 1989.

Matter, E. Ann, and John Coakley, eds. *Creative Women in Medieval and Early Modern Italy.* Philadelphia: University of Pennsylvania Press, 1994. (This is a sequel to the Monson collection; see below.)

McLeod, Glenda. *Virtue and Venom: Catalogs of Women from Antiquity to the Renaissance.* Ann Arbor: University of Michigan Press, 1991.

Medwick, Cathleen. *Teresa of Avila: The Progress of a Soul.* New York: Alfred A. Knopf, 2000.

Meek, Christine, ed. *Women in Renaissance and Early Modern Europe.* Dublin and Portland: Four Courts Press, 2000.

Mendelson, Sara, and Patricia Crawford. *Women in Early Modern England, 1550–1720.* Oxford: Clarendon Press, 1998.

Merrim, Stephanie. *Early Modern Women's Writing and Sor Juana Inés de la Cruz.* Nashville, TN: Vanderbilt University Press, 1999.

Messbarger, Rebecca. *The Century of Women: The Representations of Women in Eighteenth-Century Italian Public Discourse.* Toronto: University of Toronto Press, 2002.

Miller, Nancy K. *The Heroine's Text: Readings in the French and English Novel, 1722–1782.* New York: Columbia University Press, 1980.

Miller, Naomi J. *Changing the Subject: Mary Wroth and Figurations of Gender in Early Modern England.* Lexington: University Press of Kentucky, 1996.

————, and Gary Waller, eds. *Reading Mary Wroth: Representing Alternatives in Early Modern England.* Knoxville: University of Tennessee Press, 1991.

Monson, Craig A., ed. *The Crannied Wall: Women, Religion, and the Arts in Early Modern Europe.* Ann Arbor: University of Michigan Press, 1992.

Musacchio, Jacqueline Marie. *The Art and Ritual of Childbirth in Renaissance Italy.* New Haven, CT: Yale University Press, 1999.

Newman, Barbara. *God and the Goddesses: Vision, Poetry, and Belief in the Middle Ages.* Philadelphia: University of Pennsylvania Press, 2003.

Newman, Karen. *Fashioning Femininity and English Renaissance Drama.* Chicago and London: University of Chicago Press, 1991.

Okin, Susan Moller. *Women in Western Political Thought.* Princeton, NJ: Princeton University Press, 1979.

Ozment, Steven. *The Bürgermeister's Daughter: Scandal in a Sixteenth-Century German Town.* New York: St. Martin's Press, 1995.

Pacheco, Anita, ed. *Early [English] Women Writers: 1600–1720.* New York and London: Longman, 1998.

Pagels, Elaine. *Adam, Eve, and the Serpent.* New York: Harper Collins, 1988.

Panizza, Letizia, ed. *Women in Italian Renaissance Culture and Society.* Oxford: European Humanities Research Centre, 2000.

————, and Sharon Wood, eds. *A History of Women's Writing in Italy.* Cambridge: Cambridge University Press, 2000.

Parker, Patricia. *Literary Fat Ladies: Rhetoric, Gender, and Property.* London and New York: Methuen, 1987.

Pernoud, Regine, and Marie-Veronique Clin. *Joan of Arc: Her Story.* Rev. and trans. Jeremy DuQuesnay Adams. New York: St. Martin's Press, 1998. (First published in French, 1986).

Perry, Mary Elizabeth. *Crime and Society in Early Modern Seville.* Hanover, NH: University Press of New England, 1980.

————. *Gender and Disorder in Early Modern Seville.* Princeton, NJ: Princeton University Press, 1990.

Petroff, Elizabeth Alvilda, ed. *Medieval Women's Visionary Literature.* New York: Oxford University Press, 1986.

Perry, Ruth. *The Celebrated Mary Astell: An Early English Feminist.* Chicago: University of Chicago Press, 1986.

Rabil, Albert. *Laura Cereta: Quattrocento Humanist.* Binghamton, NY: MRTS, 1981.

Rapley, Elizabeth. *A Social History of the Cloister: Daily Life in the Teaching Monasteries of the Old Regime.* Montreal: McGill-Queen's University Press, 2001.

Raven, James, Helen Small, and Naomi Tadmor, eds. *The Practice and Representation of Reading in England.* Cambridge: University Press, 1996.

Reardon, Colleen. *Holy Concord within Sacred Walls: Nuns and Music in Siena, 1575–1700.* Oxford: Oxford University Press, 2001.

Reiss, Sheryl E., and David G. Wilkins, ed. *Beyond Isabella: Secular Women Patrons of Art in Renaissance Italy.* Kirksville, MO: Truman State University Press, 2001.

Rheubottom, David. *Age, Marriage, and Politics in Fifteenth-Century Ragusa.* Oxford: Oxford University Press, 2000.

Richardson, Brian. *Printing, Writers, and Readers in Renaissance Italy.* Cambridge: University Press, 1999.

Riddle, John M. *Contraception and Abortion from the Ancient World to the Renaissance*. Cambridge, MA: Harvard University Press, 1992.

————. *Eve's Herbs: A History of Contraception and Abortion in the West*. Cambridge, MA: Harvard University Press, 1997.

Rose, Mary Beth. *The Expense of Spirit: Love and Sexuality in English Renaissance Drama*. Ithaca, NY: Cornell University Press, 1988.

————. *Gender and Heroism in Early Modern English Literature*. Chicago: University of Chicago Press, 2002.

————, ed. *Women in the Middle Ages and the Renaissance: Literary and Historical Perspectives*. Syracuse, NY: Syracuse University Press, 1986.

Rosenthal, Margaret F. *The Honest Courtesan: Veronica Franco, Citizen and Writer in Sixteenth-Century Venice*. Foreword by Catharine R. Stimpson. Chicago: University of Chicago Press, 1992.

Sackville-West, Vita. *Daughter of France: The Life of La Grande Mademoiselle*. Garden City, NY: Doubleday, 1959.

Sánchez, Magdalena S. *The Empress, the Queen, and the Nun: Women and Power at the Court of Philip III of Spain*. Baltimore, MD: Johns Hopkins University Press, 1998.

Schiebinger, Londa. *The Mind Has No Sex? Women in the Origins of Modern Science*. Cambridge, MA: Harvard University Press, 1991.

————. *Nature's Body: Gender in the Making of Modern Science*. Boston: Beacon Press, 1993.

Schutte, Anne Jacobson, Thomas Kuehn, and Silvana Seidel Menchi, eds. *Time, Space, and Women's Lives in Early Modern Europe*. Kirksville, MO: Truman State University Press, 2001.

Shannon, Laurie. *Sovereign Amity: Figures of Friendship in Shakespearean Contexts*. Chicago: University of Chicago Press, 2002.

Shemek, Deanna. *Ladies Errant: Wayward Women and Social Order in Early Modern Italy*. Durham, NC: Duke University Press, 1998.

Smith, Hilda L. *Reason's Disciples: Seventeenth-Century English Feminists*. Urbana: University of Illinois Press, 1982.

————. *Women Writers and the Early Modern British Political Tradition*. Cambridge: Cambridge University Press, 1998.

Sobel, Dava. *Galileo's Daughter: A Historical Memoir of Science, Faith, and Love*. New York: Penguin Books, 2000.

Sommerville, Margaret R. *Sex and Subjection: Attitudes to Women in Early-Modern Society*. London: Arnold, 1995.

Soufas, Teresa Scott. *Dramas of Distinction: A Study of Plays by Golden Age Women*. Lexington: University Press of Kentucky, 1997.

Spencer, Jane. *The Rise of the Woman Novelist: From Aphra Behn to Jane Austen*. Oxford: Basil Blackwell, 1986.

Spender, Dale. *Mothers of the Novel: One Hundred Good Women Writers before Jane Austen*. London and New York: Routledge, 1986.

Sperling, Jutta Gisela. *Convents and the Body Politic in Late Renaissance Venice*. Foreword by Catharine R. Stimpson. Chicago: University of Chicago Press, 1999.

Steinbrügge, Lieselotte. *The Moral Sex: Woman's Nature in the French Enlightenment*. Trans. Pamela E. Selwyn. New York: Oxford University Press, 1995.

Stephens, Sonya, ed. *A History of Women's Writing in France*. Cambridge: Cambridge University Press, 2000.

Stocker, Margarita. *Judith, Sexual Warrior: Women and Power in Western Culture.* New Haven, CT: Yale University Press, 1998.

Stretton, Timothy. *Women Waging Law in Elizabethan England.* Cambridge: Cambridge University Press, 1998.

Stuard, Susan M. "The Dominion of Gender: Women's Fortunes in the High Middle Ages." In *Becoming Visible: Women in European History,* ed. Renate Bridenthal, Claudia Koonz, and Susan M. Stuard. 3d ed. Boston: Houghton Mifflin, 1998.

Summit, Jennifer. *Lost Property: The Woman Writer and English Literary History, 1380–1589.* Chicago: University of Chicago Press, 2000.

Surtz, Ronald E. *The Guitar of God: Gender, Power, and Authority in the Visionary World of Mother Juana de la Cruz (1481–1534).* Philadelphia: University of Pennsylvania Press, 1991.

———. *Writing Women in Late Medieval and Early Modern Spain: The Mothers of Saint Teresa of Avila.* Philadelphia: University of Pennsylvania Press, 1995.

Teague, Frances. *Bathsua Makin, Woman of Learning.* Lewisburg, PA: Bucknell University Press, 1999.

Todd, Janet. *The Secret Life of Aphra Behn.* London, New York, and Sydney: Pandora, 2000.

———. *The Sign of Angelica: Women, Writing, and Fiction, 1660–1800.* New York: Columbia University Press, 1989.

Valenze, Deborah. *The First Industrial Woman.* New York: Oxford University Press, 1995.

Van Dijk, Susan, Lia van Gemert, and Sheila Ottway, eds. *Writing the History of Women's Writing: Toward an International Approach.* Proceedings of the Colloquium, Amsterdam, 9–11 September. Amsterdam: Royal Netherlands Academy of Arts and Sciences, 2001.

Vickery, Amanda. *The Gentleman's Daughter: Women's Lives in Georgian England.* New Haven, CT: Yale University Press, 1998.

Vollendorf, Lisa, ed. *Recovering Spain's Feminist Tradition.* New York: MLA, 2001.

Waithe, Mary Ellen, ed. *A History of Women Philosophers.* 3 vols. Dordrecht, Holland: Martinus Nijhoff, 1987.

Wall, Wendy. *The Imprint of Gender: Authorship and Publication in the English Renaissance.* Ithaca, NY: Cornell University Press, 1993.

Walsh, William T. *St. Teresa of Avila: A Biography.* Rockford, IL: TAN Books, 1987.

Warner, Marina. *Alone of All Her Sex: The Myth and Cult of the Virgin Mary.* New York: Knopf, 1976.

Warnicke, Retha M. *The Marrying of Anne of Cleves: Royal Protocol in Tudor England.* Cambridge: Cambridge University Press, 2000.

Watt, Diane. *Secretaries of God: Women Prophets in Late Medieval and Early Modern England.* Cambridge: D. S. Brewer, 1997.

Weber, Alison. *Teresa of Avila and the Rhetoric of Femininity.* Princeton, NJ: Princeton University Press, 1990.

Welles, Marcia L. *Persephone's Girdle: Narratives of Rape in Seventeenth-Century Spanish Literature.* Nashville, TN: Vanderbilt University Press, 2000.

Whitehead, Barbara J., ed. *Women's Education in Early Modern Europe: A History, 1500–1800.* New York and London: Garland, 1999.

Wiesner, Merry E. *Women and Gender in Early Modern Europe.* Cambridge: Cambridge University Press, 1993.

————. *Working Women in Renaissance Germany.* New Brunswick, NJ: Rutgers University Press, 1986.

Willard, Charity Cannon. *Christine de Pizan: Her Life and Works.* New York: Persea Books, 1984.

Wilson, Katharina, ed. *An Encyclopedia of Continental Women Writers.* New York: Garland, 1991.

Winn, Colette, and Donna Kuizenga, eds. *Women Writers in Pre-Revolutionary France.* New York: Garland, 1997.

Woodbridge, Linda. *Women and the English Renaissance: Literature and the Nature of Womankind, 1540–1620.* Urbana: University of Illinois Press, 1984.

Woods, Susanne. *Lanyer: A Renaissance Woman Poet.* New York: Oxford University Press, 1999.

————, and Margaret P. Hannay, eds. *Teaching Tudor and Stuart Women Writers.* New York: MLA, 2000.

INDEX